やさしく
ひもとく共通テスト

英語
リーディング

別冊
過去問題集

本冊と軽くのりづけされています。
ゆっくりと取り外して使いましょう。

Gakken

やさしくひもとく共通テスト

英語
リーディング

令和3年度(2021年度)
第1日程 試験問題

配点 ——— 100点
試験時間 —— 80分

▶ 第1問 A　　　　　　　　　　　　　　　　　　　　　　　　（配点 4 ）

A　Your dormitory roommate Julie has sent a text message to your mobile phone with a request.

Help!!!
Last night I saved my history homework on a USB memory stick. I was going to print it in the university library this afternoon, but I forgot to bring the USB with me. I need to give a copy to my teacher by 4 p.m. today. Can you bring my USB to the library? I think it's on top of my history book on my desk. I don't need the book, just the USB.♡

Sorry Julie, I couldn't find it. The history book was there, but there was no USB memory stick. I looked for it everywhere, even under your desk. Are you sure you don't have it with you? I'll bring your laptop computer with me, just in case.

You were right! I did have it. It was at the bottom of my bag. What a relief!
Thanks anyway. ☺

問1 What was Julie's request? ☐ 1

① To bring her USB memory stick
② To hand in her history homework
③ To lend her a USB memory stick
④ To print out her history homework

問2 How will you reply to Julie's second text message? ☐ 2

① Don't worry. You'll find it.
② I'm really glad to hear that.
③ Look in your bag again.
④ You must be disappointed.

第 1 問 B　　　　　　　　　　　　　　　　　　　　（配点 6）

B Your favorite musician will have a concert tour in Japan, and you are thinking of joining the fan club. You visit the official fan club website.

TYLER QUICK FAN CLUB

Being a member of the **TYLER QUICK** (**TQ**) fan club is so much fun! You can keep up with the latest news, and take part in many exciting fan club member events. All new members will receive our New Member's Pack. It contains a membership card, a free signed poster, and a copy of **TQ**'s third album ***Speeding Up***. The New Member's Pack will be delivered to your home, and will arrive a week or so after you join the fan club.

TQ is loved all around the world. You can join from any country, and you can use the membership card for one year. The **TQ** fan club has three types of membership: Pacer, Speeder, and Zoomer.

Please choose from the membership options below.

What you get (♫)	Membership Options		
	Pacer ($20)	Speeder ($40)	Zoomer ($60)
Regular emails and online magazine password	♫	♫	♫
Early information on concert tour dates	♫	♫	♫
TQ's weekly video messages	♫	♫	♫
Monthly picture postcards		♫	♫
TQ fan club calendar		♫	♫
Invitations to special signing events			♫
20% off concert tickets			♫

◇ Join before May 10 and receive a $10 discount on your membership fee!
◇ There is a $4 delivery fee for every New Member's Pack.
◇ At the end of your 1st year, you can either renew or upgrade at a 50% discount.

Whether you are a Pacer, a Speeder, or a Zoomer, you will love being a member of the **TQ** fan club. For more information, or to join, click *here*.

問1 A New Member's Pack ☐3☐ .

① includes TQ's first album
② is delivered on May 10
③ requires a $10 delivery fee
④ takes about seven days to arrive

問2 What will you get if you become a new Pacer member? ☐4☐

① Discount concert tickets and a calendar
② Regular emails and signing event invitations
③ Tour information and postcards every month
④ Video messages and access to online magazines

問3 After being a fan club member for one year, you can ☐5☐ .

① become a Zoomer for a $50 fee
② get a New Member's Pack for $4
③ renew your membership at half price
④ upgrade your membership for free

第2問 A　　　　　　　　　　　　　　　　　　　　　　　　（配点 10）

A　As the student in charge of a UK school festival band competition, you are examining all of the scores and the comments from three judges to understand and explain the rankings.

Judges' final average scores				
Qualities Band names	Performance (5.0)	Singing (5.0)	Song originality (5.0)	Total (15.0)
Green Forest	3.9	4.6	5.0	13.5
Silent Hill	4.9	4.4	4.2	13.5
Mountain Pear	3.9	4.9	4.7	13.5
Thousand Ants	(did not perform)			

Judges' individual comments	
Mr Hobbs	Silent Hill are great performers and they really seemed connected with the audience. Mountain Pear's singing was great. I loved Green Forest's original song. It was amazing!
Ms Leigh	Silent Hill gave a great performance. It was incredible how the audience responded to their music. I really think that Silent Hill will become popular! Mountain Pear have great voices, but they were not exciting on stage. Green Forest performed a fantastic new song, but I think they need to practice more.
Ms Wells	Green Forest have a new song. I loved it! I think it could be a big hit!

Judges' shared evaluation (summarised by Hobbs)
Each band's total score is the same, but each band is very different. Ms Leigh and I agreed that performance is the most important quality for a band. Ms Wells also agreed. Therefore, first place is easily determined. 　　To decide between second and third places, Ms Wells suggested that song originality should be more important than good singing. Ms Leigh and I agreed on this opinion.

問1 Based on the judges' final average scores, which band sang the best? ⬚ 6

① Green Forest
② Mountain Pear
③ Silent Hill
④ Thousand Ants

問2 Which judge gave both positive and critical comments? ⬚ 7

① Mr Hobbs
② Ms Leigh
③ Ms Wells
④ None of them

問3 One **fact** from the judges' individual comments is that ⬚ 8 .

① all the judges praised Green Forest's song
② Green Forest need to practice more
③ Mountain Pear can sing very well
④ Silent Hill have a promising future

問4 One **opinion** from the judges' comments and shared evaluation is that ⬚ 9 .

① each evaluated band received the same total score
② Ms Wells' suggestion about originality was agreed on
③ Silent Hill really connected with the audience
④ the judges' comments determined the rankings

問5 Which of the following is the final ranking based on the judges' shared evaluation? ⬚ 10

	1st	2nd	3rd
①	Green Forest	Mountain Pear	Silent Hill
②	Green Forest	Silent Hill	Mountain Pear
③	Mountain Pear	Green Forest	Silent Hill
④	Mountain Pear	Silent Hill	Green Forest
⑤	Silent Hill	Green Forest	Mountain Pear
⑥	Silent Hill	Mountain Pear	Green Forest

第2問B (配点10)

B You've heard about a change in school policy at the school in the UK where you are now studying as an exchange student. You are reading the discussions about the policy in an online forum.

New School Policy 〈Posted on 21 September 2020〉
To: P.E. Berger
From: K. Roberts

Dear Dr Berger,

On behalf of all students, welcome to St Mark's School. We heard that you are the first Head Teacher with a business background, so we hope your experience will help our school.

I would like to express one concern about the change you are proposing to the after-school activity schedule. I realise that saving energy is important and from now it will be getting darker earlier. Is this why you have made the schedule an hour and a half shorter? Students at St Mark's School take both their studies and their after-school activities very seriously. A number of students have told me that they want to stay at school until 6.00 pm as they have always done. Therefore, I would like to ask you to think again about this sudden change in policy.

Regards,
Ken Roberts
Head Student

Re: New School Policy ⟨Posted on 22 September 2020⟩
To: K. Roberts
From: P. E. Berger

Dear Ken,

Many thanks for your kind post. You've expressed some important concerns, especially about the energy costs and student opinions on school activities.

The new policy has nothing to do with saving energy. The decision was made based on a 2019 police report. The report showed that our city has become less safe due to a 5% increase in serious crimes. I would like to protect our students, so I would like them to return home before it gets dark.

Yours,
Dr P. E. Berger
Head Teacher

問1 Ken thinks the new policy 　11　 .

    ① can make students study more
    ② may improve school safety
    ③ should be introduced immediately
    ④ will reduce after-school activity time

問2 One **fact** stated in Ken's forum post is that 　12　 .

    ① more discussion is needed about the policy
    ② the Head Teacher's experience is improving the school
    ③ the school should think about students' activities
    ④ there are students who do not welcome the new policy

問3 Who thinks the aim of the policy is to save energy? 　13　

    ① Dr Berger
    ② Ken
    ③ The city
    ④ The police

問4 Dr Berger is basing his new policy on the **fact** that 　14　 .

    ① going home early is important
    ② safety in the city has decreased
    ③ the school has to save electricity
    ④ the students need protection

問5 What would you research to help Ken oppose the new policy? 　15　

    ① The crime rate and its relation to the local area
    ② The energy budget and electricity costs of the school
    ③ The length of school activity time versus the budget
    ④ The study hours for students who do after-school activities

011

(配点6)

A You are planning to stay at a hotel in the UK. You found useful information in the Q&A section of a travel advice website.

> **I'm considering staying at the Hollytree Hotel in Castleton in March 2021. Would you recommend this hotel, and is it easy to get there from Buxton Airport?**   (Liz)
>
> **Answer**
> Yes, I strongly recommend the Hollytree. I've stayed there twice. It's inexpensive, and the service is brilliant! There's also a wonderful free breakfast. (Click <u>here</u> for access information.)
>
> Let me tell you my own experience of getting there.
>
> On my first visit, I used the underground, which is cheap and convenient. Trains run every five minutes. From the airport, I took the Red Line to Mossfield. Transferring to the Orange Line for Victoria should normally take about seven minutes, but the directions weren't clear and I needed an extra five minutes. From Victoria, it was a ten-minute bus ride to the hotel.
>
> The second time, I took the express bus to Victoria, so I didn't have to worry about transferring. At Victoria, I found a notice saying there would be roadworks until summer 2021. Now it takes three times as long as usual to get to the hotel by city bus, although buses run every ten minutes. It's possible to walk, but I took the bus as the weather was bad.
>
> Enjoy your stay!   (Alex)

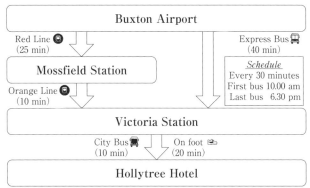

問1 From Alex's answer, you learn that Alex ⬛16⬛ .

① appreciates the convenient location of the hotel
② got lost in Victoria Station on his first visit to Castleton
③ thinks that the hotel is good value for money
④ used the same route from the airport both times

問2 You are departing on public transport from the airport at 2.00 pm on 15 March 2021. What is the fastest way to get to the hotel? ⬛17⬛

① By express bus and city bus
② By express bus and on foot
③ By underground and city bus
④ By underground and on foot

第3問 B

(配点 9)

B Your classmate showed you the following message in your school's newsletter, written by an exchange student from the UK.

Volunteers Wanted!

Hello, everyone. I'm Sarah King, an exchange student from London. I'd like to share something important with you today.

You may have heard of the Sakura International Centre. It provides valuable opportunities for Japanese and foreign residents to get to know each other. Popular events such as cooking classes and karaoke contests are held every month. However, there is a serious problem. The building is getting old, and requires expensive repairs. To help raise funds to maintain the centre, many volunteers are needed.

I learnt about the problem a few months ago. While shopping in town, I saw some people taking part in a fund-raising campaign. I spoke to the leader of the campaign, Katy, who explained the situation. She thanked me when I donated some money. She told me that they had asked the town mayor for financial assistance, but their request had been rejected. They had no choice but to start fund-raising.

Last month, I attended a lecture on art at the centre. Again, I saw people trying to raise money, and I decided to help. They were happy when I joined them in asking passers-by for donations. We tried hard, but there were too few of us to collect much money. With a tearful face, Katy told me that they wouldn't be able to use the building much longer. I felt the need to do something more. Then, the idea came to me that other students might be willing to help. Katy was delighted to hear this.

Now, I'm asking you to join me in the fund-raising campaign to help the Sakura International Centre. Please email me today! As an exchange student, my time in Japan is limited, but I want to make the most of it. By working together, we can really make a difference.

Class 3 A
Sarah King (sarahk@sakura-h.ed.jp)
セーラ・キング

問1 Put the following events (①〜④) into the order in which they happened.

| 18 | → | 19 | → | 20 | → | 21 |

① Sarah attended a centre event.
② Sarah donated money to the centre.
③ Sarah made a suggestion to Katy.
④ The campaigners asked the mayor for help.

問2 From Sarah's message, you learn that the Sakura International Centre 22 .

① gives financial aid to international residents
② offers opportunities to develop friendships
③ publishes newsletters for the community
④ sends exchange students to the UK

問3 You have decided to help with the campaign after reading Sarah's message. What should you do first? 23

① Advertise the events at the centre.
② Contact Sarah for further information.
③ Organise volunteer activities at school.
④ Start a new fund-raising campaign.

015

第4問　　　　　　　　　　　　　　　　　　　　　　　　　　（配点 16）

Your English teacher, Emma, has asked you and your classmate, Natsuki, to help her plan the day's schedule for hosting students from your sister school. You're reading the email exchanges between Natsuki and Emma so that you can draft the schedule.

Hi Emma,

We have some ideas and questions about the schedule for the day out with our 12 guests next month. As you told us, the students from both schools are supposed to give presentations in our assembly hall from 10:00 a.m. So, I've been looking at the attached timetable. Will they arrive at Azuma Station at 9:39 a.m. and then take a taxi to the school?

We have also been discussing the afternoon activities. How about seeing something related to science? We have two ideas, but if you need a third, please let me know.

Have you heard about the special exhibition that is on at Westside Aquarium next month? It's about a new food supplement made from sea plankton. We think it would be a good choice. Since it's popular, the best time to visit will be when it is least busy. I'm attaching the graph I found on the aquarium's homepage.

Eastside Botanical Garden, together with our local university, has been developing an interesting way of producing electricity from plants. Luckily, the professor in charge will give a short talk about it on that day in the early afternoon! Why don't we go?

Everyone will want to get some souvenirs, won't they? I think West Mall, next to Hibari Station, would be best, but we don't want to carry them around with us all day.

Finally, every visitor to Azuma should see the town's symbol, the statue in Azuma Memorial Park next to our school, but we can't work out a good schedule. Also, could you tell us what the plan is for lunch?

Yours,
Natsuki

Hi Natsuki,

Thank you for your email! You've been working hard. In answer to your question, they'll arrive at the station at 9:20 a.m. and then catch the school bus.

The two main afternoon locations, the aquarium and botanical garden, are good ideas because both schools place emphasis on science education, and the purpose of this program is to improve the scientific knowledge of the students. However, it would be wise to have a third suggestion just in case.

Let's get souvenirs at the end of the day. We can take the bus to the mall arriving there at 5:00 p.m. This will allow almost an hour for shopping and our guests can still be back at the hotel by 6:30 p.m. for dinner, as the hotel is only a few minutes' walk from Kaede Station.

About lunch, the school cafeteria will provide boxed lunches. We can eat under the statue you mentioned. If it rains, let's eat inside.

Thank you so much for your suggestions. Could you two make a draft for the schedule?

Best,
Emma

Attached timetable:

Train Timetable
Kaede — Hibari — Azuma

Stations	Train No.			
	108	109	110	111
Kaede	8:28	8:43	9:02	9:16
Hibari	8:50	9:05	9:24	9:38
Azuma	9:05	9:20	9:39	9:53

Stations	Train No.			
	238	239	240	241
Azuma	17:25	17:45	18:00	18:15
Hibari	17:40	18:00	18:15	18:30
Kaede	18:02	18:22	18:37	18:52

Attached graph:

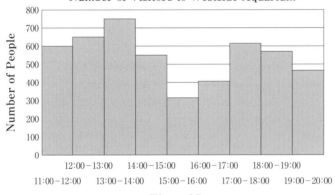

問1 The guests from the sister school will arrive on the number ⎡24⎦ train and catch the number ⎡25⎦ train back to their hotel.

① 109 ② 110 ③ 111
④ 238 ⑤ 239 ⑥ 240

問2 Which best completes the draft schedule? 26

　　A：The aquarium　　　　B：The botanical garden
　　C：The mall　　　　　　D：The school

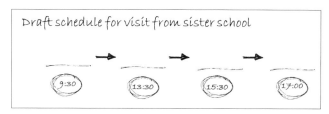

　　① D → A → B → C
　　② D → B → A → C
　　③ D → B → C → A
　　④ D → C → A → B

問3 Unless it rains, the guests will eat lunch in the 27 .

　　① botanical garden
　　② park next to the school
　　③ park next to the station
　　④ school garden

問4 The guests will **not** get around 28 on that day.

　　① by bus
　　② by taxi
　　③ by train
　　④ on foot

問5 As a third option, which would be the most suitable for your program? 29

　　① Hibari Amusement Park
　　② Hibari Art Museum
　　③ Hibari Castle
　　④ Hibari Space Center

第 5 問　　　　　　　　　　　　　　　　　　　　（配点 15）

Using an international news report, you are going to take part in an English oral presentation contest. Read the following news story from France in preparation for your talk.

Five years ago, Mrs. Sabine Rouas lost her horse. She had spent 20 years with the horse before he died of old age. At that time, she felt that she could never own another horse. Out of loneliness, she spent hours watching cows on a nearby milk farm. Then, one day, she asked the farmer if she could help look after them.

The farmer agreed, and Sabine started work. She quickly developed a friendship with one of the cows. As the cow was pregnant, she spent more time with it than with the others. After the cow's baby was born, the baby started following Sabine around. Unfortunately, the farmer wasn't interested in keeping a bull—a male cow—on a milk farm. The farmer planned to sell the baby bull, which he called Three-oh-nine (309), to a meat market. Sabine decided she wasn't going to let that happen, so she asked the farmer if she could buy him and his mother. The farmer agreed, and she bought them. Sabine then started taking 309 for walks to town. About nine months later, when at last she had permission to move the animals, they moved to Sabine's farm.

Soon after, Sabine was offered a pony. At first, she wasn't sure if she wanted to have him, but the memory of her horse was no longer painful, so she accepted the pony and named him Leon. She then decided to return to her old hobby and started training him for show jumping. Three-oh-nine, who she had renamed Aston, spent most of his time with Leon, and the two became really close friends. However, Sabine had not expected Aston to pay close attention to her training routine with Leon, nor had she expected Aston to pick up some tricks. The young bull quickly mastered walking, galloping, stopping, going backwards, and turning around on command. He responded to Sabine's voice just like a horse. And despite weighing 1,300 kg, it took him just 18 months to learn how to leap over one-meter-high horse jumps with Sabine on his back. Aston might never have learned those things without having watched Leon. Moreover, Aston understood distance and could adjust his steps before a jump. He also noticed his faults and corrected them without any help from Sabine.

That's something only the very best Olympic-standard horses can do.

Now Sabine and Aston go to weekend fairs and horse shows around Europe to show off his skills. Sabine says, "We get a good reaction. Mostly, people are really surprised, and at first, they can be a bit scared because he's big—much bigger than a horse. Most people don't like to get too close to bulls with horns. But once they see his real nature, and see him performing, they often say, 'Oh he's really quite beautiful.' "

"Look!" And Sabine shows a photo of Aston on her smartphone. She then continues, "When Aston was very young, I used to take him out for walks on a lead, like a dog, so that he would get used to humans. Maybe that's why he doesn't mind people. Because he is so calm, children, in particular, really like watching him and getting a chance to be close to him."

Over the last few years, news of the massive show-jumping bull has spread rapidly; now, Aston is a major attraction with a growing number of online followers. Aston and Sabine sometimes need to travel 200 or 300 kilometers away from home, which means they have to stay overnight. Aston has to sleep in a horse box, which isn't really big enough for him.

"He doesn't like it. I have to sleep with him in the box," says Sabine. "But you know, when he wakes up and changes position, he is very careful not to crush me. He really is very gentle. He sometimes gets lonely, and he doesn't like being away from Leon for too long; but other than that, he's very happy."

Your Presentation Slides

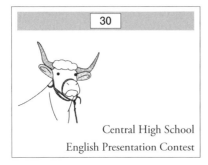

```
     30
Central High School
English Presentation Contest
```

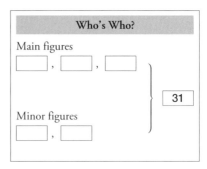

```
Who's Who?
Main figures
[   ] , [   ] , [   ]
                        } 31
Minor figures
[   ] , [   ]
```

Pre-fame Storyline

Sabine's horse dies.
↓
32
↓
33
↓
34
↓
35
↓
Aston and Sabine start going to shows.

Aston's Abilities

Aston can:
- learn by simply watching Leon's training.
- walk, gallop, and stop when Sabine tells him to.
- understand distance and adjust his steps.
- 36 .
- 37 .

Aston Now

Aston today:
- is a show-jumping bull.
- travels to fairs and events with Sabine.
- 38 .

問1 Which is the best title for your presentation? | 30 |

① Animal-lover Saves the Life of a Pony
② Aston's Summer Show-jumping Tour
③ Meet Aston, the Bull who Behaves Like a Horse
④ The Relationship Between a Farmer and a Cow

問2 Which is the best combination for the **Who's Who?** slide? | 31 |

	Main figures	Minor figures
①	309, Aston, the farmer	Sabine, the pony
②	Aston, Aston's mother, Sabine	309, the farmer
③	Aston, Leon, the farmer	Aston's mother, Sabine
④	Aston, Sabine, the pony	Aston's mother, the farmer

問3 Choose the four events in the order they happened to complete the **Pre-fame Storyline** slide. | 32 | ~ | 35 |

① Aston learns to jump.
② Sabine and Aston travel hundreds of kilometers together.
③ Sabine buys 309 and his mother.
④ Sabine goes to work on her neighbor's farm.
⑤ Sabine takes 309 for walks.

問4 Choose the two best items for the **Aston's Abilities** slide. (The order does not matter.) | 36 | · | 37 |

① correct his mistakes by himself
② jump side-by-side with the pony
③ jump with a rider on his back
④ pick up tricks faster than a horse
⑤ pose for photographs

問5 Complete the **Aston Now** slide with the most appropriate item. | 38 |

① has an increasing number of fans
② has made Sabine very wealthy
③ is so famous that he no longer frightens people
④ spends most nights of the year in a horse trailer

023

第6問 A （配点 12）

A You are working on a class project about safety in sports and found the following article. You are reading it and making a poster to present your findings to your classmates.

Making Ice Hockey Safer

Ice hockey is a team sport enjoyed by a wide variety of people around the world. The object of the sport is to move a hard rubber disk called a "puck" into the other team's net with a hockey stick. Two teams with six players on each team engage in this fast-paced sport on a hard and slippery ice rink. Players may reach a speed of 30 kilometers per hour sending the puck into the air. At this pace, both the players and the puck can be a cause of serious danger.

The speed of the sport and the slippery surface of the ice rink make it easy for players to fall down or bump into each other resulting in a variety of injuries. In an attempt to protect players, equipment such as helmets, gloves, and pads for the shoulders, elbows, and legs, has been introduced over the years. Despite these efforts, ice hockey has a high rate of concussions.

A concussion is an injury to the brain that affects the way it functions; it is caused by either direct or indirect impact to the head, face, neck, or elsewhere and can sometimes cause temporary loss of consciousness. In less serious cases, for a short time, players may be unable to walk straight or see clearly, or they may experience ringing in the ears. Some believe they just have a slight headache and do not realize they have injured their brains.

In addition to not realizing the seriousness of the injury, players tend to worry about what their coach will think. In the past, coaches preferred tough players who played in spite of the pain. In other words, while it would seem logical for an injured player to stop playing after getting hurt, many did not. Recently, however, it has been found that concussions can have serious effects that last a lifetime. People with a history of concussion may have trouble concentrating or sleeping. Moreover, they may suffer from psychological problems such as depression and mood changes. In some cases, players may develop smell and taste disorders.

The National Hockey League (NHL), consisting of teams in Canada and the United States, has been making stricter rules and guidelines to deal with concussions. For example, in 2001, the NHL introduced the wearing of visors—pieces of clear plastic attached to the helmet that protect the face. At first, it was optional and many players chose not to wear them. Since 2013, however, it has been required. In addition, in 2004, the NHL began to give more severe penalties, such as suspensions and fines, to players who hit another player in the head deliberately.

The NHL also introduced a concussion spotters system in 2015. In this system, NHL officials with access to live streaming and video replay watch for visible indications of concussion during each game. At first, two concussion spotters, who had no medical training, monitored the game in the arena. The following year, one to four concussion spotters with medical training were added. They monitored each game from the League's head office in New York. If a spotter thinks that a player has suffered a concussion, the player is removed from the game and is taken to a "quiet room" for an examination by a medical doctor. The player is not allowed to return to the game until the doctor gives permission.

The NHL has made much progress in making ice hockey a safer sport. As more is learned about the causes and effects of concussions, the NHL will surely take further measures to ensure player safety. Better safety might lead to an increase in the number of ice hockey players and fans.

Making Ice Hockey Safer

What is ice hockey?
- Players score by putting a "puck" in the other team's net
- Six players on each team
- Sport played on ice at a high speed

Main Problem: A High Rate of Concussions

Definition of a concussion
An injury to the brain that affects the way it functions

Effects

Short-term	Long-term
· Loss of consciousness	· Problems with concentration
· Difficulty walking straight	· 40
· 39	· Psychological problems
· Ringing in the ears	· Smell and taste disorders

Solutions

National Hockey League (NHL)
- Requires helmets with visors
- Gives severe penalties to dangerous players
- Has introduced concussion spotters to 41

Summary
Ice hockey players have a high risk of suffering from concussions. Therefore, the NHL has 42 .

問1 Choose the best option for [39] on your poster.

① Aggressive behavior
② Difficulty thinking
③ Personality changes
④ Unclear vision

問2 Choose the best option for [40] on your poster.

① Loss of eyesight
② Memory problems
③ Sleep disorders
④ Unsteady walking

問3 Choose the best option for [41] on your poster.

① allow players to return to the game
② examine players who have a concussion
③ fine players who cause concussions
④ identify players showing signs of a concussion

問4 Choose the best option for [42] on your poster.

① been expecting the players to become tougher
② been implementing new rules and guidelines
③ given medical training to coaches
④ made wearing of visors optional

第6問 B (配点 12)

B You are studying nutrition in health class. You are going to read the following passage from a textbook to learn more about various sweeteners.

Cake, candy, soft drinks—most of us love sweet things. In fact, young people say "Sweet!" to mean something is "good" in English. When we think of sweetness, we imagine ordinary white sugar from sugar cane or sugar beet plants. Scientific discoveries, however, have changed the world of sweeteners. We can now extract sugars from many other plants. The most obvious example is corn. Corn is abundant, inexpensive, and easy to process. High fructose corn syrup (HFCS) is about 1.2 times sweeter than regular sugar, but quite high in calories. Taking science one step further, over the past 70 years scientists have developed a wide variety of artificial sweeteners.

A recent US National Health and Nutrition Examination Survey concluded that 14.6% of the average American's energy intake is from "added sugar," which refers to sugar that is not derived from whole foods. A banana, for example, is a whole food, while a cookie contains added sugar. More than half of added sugar calories are from sweetened drinks and desserts. Lots of added sugar can have negative effects on our bodies, including excessive weight gain and other health problems. For this reason, many choose low-calorie substitutes for drinks, snacks, and desserts.

Natural alternatives to white sugar include brown sugar, honey, and maple syrup, but they also tend to be high in calories. Consequently, alternative "low-calorie sweeteners" (LCSs), mostly artificial chemical combinations, have become popular. The most common LCSs today are aspartame, Ace-K, stevia, and sucralose. Not all LCSs are artificial—stevia comes from plant leaves.

Alternative sweeteners can be hard to use in cooking because some cannot be heated and most are far sweeter than white sugar. Aspartame and Ace-K are 200 times sweeter than sugar. Stevia is 300 times sweeter, and sucralose has twice the sweetness of stevia. Some new sweeteners are even more intense. A Japanese company recently developed "Advantame," which is 20,000 times sweeter than sugar. Only a tiny amount of this substance is required to sweeten something.

When choosing sweeteners, it is important to consider health issues. Making desserts with lots of white sugar, for example, results in high-calorie dishes that could lead to weight gain. There are those who prefer LCSs for this very reason. Apart from calories, however, some research links consuming artificial LCSs with various other health concerns. Some LCSs contain strong chemicals suspected of causing cancer, while others have been shown to affect memory and brain development, so they can be dangerous, especially for young children, pregnant women, and the elderly. There are a few relatively natural alternative sweeteners, like xylitol and sorbitol, which are low in calories. Unfortunately, these move through the body extremely slowly, so consuming large amounts can cause stomach trouble.

When people want something sweet, even with all the information, it is difficult for them to decide whether to stick to common higher calorie sweeteners like sugar or to use LCSs. Many varieties of gum and candy today contain one or more artificial sweeteners; nonetheless, some people who would not put artificial sweeteners in hot drinks may still buy such items. Individuals need to weigh the options and then choose the sweeteners that best suit their needs and circumstances.

問 1 You learn that modern science has changed the world of sweeteners by ⬜ 43 ⬜ .

① discovering new, sweeter white sugar types
② measuring the energy intake of Americans
③ providing a variety of new options
④ using many newly-developed plants from the environment

問 2 You are summarizing the information you have just studied. How should the table be finished? ⬜ 44 ⬜

Sweetness	Sweetener
high	Advantame
	(A)
	(B)
	(C)
low	(D)

① (A) Stevia   (B) Sucralose
   (C) Ace-K, Aspartame   (D) HFCS
② (A) Stevia   (B) Sucralose
   (C) HFCS   (D) Ace-K, Aspartame
③ (A) Sucralose   (B) Stevia
   (C) Ace-K, Aspartame   (D) HFCS
④ (A) Sucralose   (B) Stevia
   (C) HFCS   (D) Ace-K, Aspartame

問 3 According to the article you read, which of the following are true? (Choose two options. The order does not matter.) ⬜ 45 ⬜ · ⬜ 46 ⬜

① Alternative sweeteners have been proven to cause weight gain.
② Americans get 14.6% of their energy from alternative sweeteners.
③ It is possible to get alternative sweeteners from plants.
④ Most artificial sweeteners are easy to cook with.
⑤ Sweeteners like xylitol and sorbitol are not digested quickly.

問4 To describe the author's position, which of the following is most appropriate? 47

① The author argues against the use of artificial sweeteners in drinks and desserts.
② The author believes artificial sweeteners have successfully replaced traditional ones.
③ The author states that it is important to invent much sweeter products for future use.
④ The author suggests people focus on choosing sweeteners that make sense for them.

MEMO

やさしく ひもとく 共通テスト

英語
リーディング

令和3年度（2021年度）
第2日程 試験問題

配点 ——— 100点
試験時間 —— 80分

第1問 A　　　　　　　　　　　　　　　　　　　　　（配点 4）

A　You have invited your friend Shelley to join you on your family's overnight camping trip. She has sent a text message to your mobile phone asking some questions.

> Hi! I'm packing my bag for tomorrow and I want to check some things. Will it get cold in the tent at night? Do I need to bring a blanket? I know you told me last week, but just to be sure, where and what time are we meeting?

> Shelley, I'll bring warm sleeping bags for everyone, but maybe you should bring your down jacket. Bring comfortable footwear because we'll walk up Mt. Kanayama the next day. We'll pick you up outside your house at 6 a.m. If you're not outside, I'll call you. See you in the morning!

> Thanks! I can't wait! I'll bring my jacket and hiking boots with me. I'll be ready! ☺

問1 Shelley asks you if she needs to bring [1] .

① a blanket
② a jacket
③ sleeping bags
④ walking shoes

問2 You expect Shelley to [2] tomorrow morning.

① call you as soon as she is ready
② come to see you at the campsite
③ pick you up in front of your house
④ wait for you outside her house

第1問 B

(配点6)

B You have received a flyer for an English speech contest from your teacher, and you want to apply.

The 7th Youth Leader Speech Contest

The Youth Leader Society will hold its annual speech contest. Our goal is to help young Japanese people develop communication and leadership skills.

This year's competition has three stages. Our judges will select the winners of each stage. To take part in the Grand Final, you must successfully pass all three stages.

The Grand Final

Place: Centennial Hall
Date: January 8, 2022
Topic: *Today's Youth, Tomorrow's Leaders*

GRAND PRIZE
The winner can attend
The Leadership Workshop
in Wellington, New Zealand
in March 2022.

Contest information:

Stages	Things to Upload	Details	2021 Deadlines & Dates
Stage 1	A brief outline	Number of words: 150-200	Upload by 5 p.m. on August 12
Stage 2	Video of you giving your speech	Time: 7-8 minutes	Upload by 5 p.m. on September 19
Stage 3		Local Contests: Winners will be announced and go on to the Grand Final.	Held on November 21

Grand Final Grading Information

Content	Gestures & Performance	Voice & Eye Contact	Slides	Answering Questions from Judges
50%	5%	5%	10%	30%

▷ You must upload your materials online. All dates and times are Japan Standard Time (JST).

▷ You can check the results of Stage 1 and 2 on the website five days after the deadline for each stage.

For more details and an application form, click *here*.

問1 To take part in the first stage, you should upload a ☐ 3 ☐ .

① completed speech script
② set of slides for the speech
③ summary of your speech
④ video of yourself speaking

問2 From which date can you check the result of the second stage? ☐ 4 ☐

① September 14
② September 19
③ September 24
④ September 29

問3 To get a high score in the Grand Final, you should pay most attention to your content and ☐ 5 ☐ .

① expressions and gestures
② responses to the judges
③ visual materials
④ voice control

第 2 問 A （配点 10）

A You are reading the results of a survey about single-use and reusable bottles that your classmates answered as part of an environmental campaign in the UK.

Question 1: How many single-use bottled drinks do you purchase per week?

Number of bottles	Number of students	Weekly subtotal
0	2	0
1	2	2
2	2	4
3	3	9
4	4	16
5	9	45
6	0	0
7	7	49
Total	29	125

Question 2: Do you have your own reusable bottle?

Summary of responses	Number of students	Percent of students
Yes, I do.	3	10.3
Yes, but I don't use it.	14	48.3
No, I don't.	12	41.4
Total	29	100.0

Question 3: If you don't use a reusable bottle, what are your reasons?

Summary of responses	Number of students
It takes too much time to wash reusable bottles.	24
I think single-use bottles are more convenient.	17
Many flavoured drinks are available in single-use bottles.	14
Buying a single-use bottle doesn't cost much.	10
I can buy drinks from vending machines at school.	7
I feel reusable bottles are too heavy.	4
My home has dozens of single-use bottles.	3
Single-use bottled water can be stored unopened for a long time.	2
(Other reasons)	4

問1 The results of Question 1 show that ⬚6⬚ .

① each student buys fewer than four single-use bottles a week on average
② many students buy fewer than two bottles a week
③ more than half the students buy at least five bottles a week
④ the students buy more than 125 bottles a week

問2 The results of Question 2 show that more than half the students ⬚7⬚ .

① don't have their own reusable bottle
② have their own reusable bottle
③ have their own reusable bottle but don't use it
④ use their own reusable bottle

問3 One **opinion** expressed by your classmates in Question 3 is that ⬚8⬚ .

① some students have a stock of single-use bottles at home
② there are vending machines for buying drinks at school
③ washing reusable bottles takes a lot of time
④ water in unopened single-use bottles lasts a long time

問4 One **fact** stated by your classmates in Question 3 is that single-use bottles are ⬚9⬚ .

① available to buy at school
② convenient to use
③ light enough to carry around
④ not too expensive to buy

問5 What is the most likely reason why your classmates do not use reusable bottles? ⬚10⬚

① There are many single-use bottled drinks stored at home.
② There is less variety of drinks available.
③ They are expensive for your classmates.
④ They are troublesome to deal with.

039

第2問 B (配点 10)

B You need to decide what classes to take in a summer programme in the UK, so you are reading course information and a former student's comment about the course.

COMMUNICATION AND INTERCULTURAL STUDIES

Dr Christopher Bennet   3-31 August 2021
bennet.christopher@ire-u.ac.uk   Tuesday & Friday
Call: 020–9876–1234   1.00 pm—2.30 pm
Office Hours: by appointment only   9 classes – 1 credit

Course description: We will be studying different cultures and learning how to communicate with people from different cultures. In this course, students will need to present their ideas for dealing with intercultural issues.

Goals: After this course you should be able to:
– understand human relations among different cultures
– present solutions for different intercultural problems
– express your opinions through discussion and presentations

Textbook: Smith, S. (2019). *Intercultural studies*. New York: DNC Inc.

Evaluation: 60% overall required to pass
– two presentations: 90% (45% each)
– participation: 10%

Course-takers' evaluations (87 reviewers) ★★★★★ (Average: 4.89)

Comment
☺ Take this class! Chris is a great teacher. He is very smart and kind. The course is a little challenging but easy enough to pass. You will learn a lot about differences in culture. My advice would be to participate in every class. It really helped me make good presentations.

問1 What will you do in this course? 　11

① Discuss various topics about culture
② Visit many different countries
③ Watch a film about human relations
④ Write a final report about culture

問2 This class is aimed at students who 　12　 .

① are interested in intercultural issues
② can give good presentations
③ like sightseeing in the UK
④ need to learn to speak English

問3 One **fact** about Dr Bennet is that 　13　 .

① he has good teaching skills
② he is a nice instructor
③ he is in charge of this course
④ he makes the course challenging

問4 One **opinion** expressed about the class is that 　14　 .

① it is not so difficult to get a credit
② most students are satisfied with the course
③ participation is part of the final grade
④ students have classes twice a week

問5 What do you have to do to pass this course? 　15

① Come to every class and join the discussions
② Find an intercultural issue and discuss a solution
③ Give good presentations about intercultural issues
④ Make an office appointment with Dr Bennet

041

第3問 A　　　　　　　　　　　　　　　　　　　　　（配点6）

A　Your British friend, Jan, visited a new amusement park and posted a blog about her experience.

Sunny Mountain Park: A Great Place to Visit
Posted by Jan at 9.37 pm on 15 September 2020

　　Sunny Mountain Park finally opened last month! It's a big amusement park with many exciting attractions, including a huge roller coaster (see the map). I had a fantastic time there with my friends last week.

　　We couldn't wait to try the roller coaster, but first we took the train round the park to get an idea of its layout. From the train, we saw the Picnic Zone and thought it would be a good place to have lunch. However, it was already very crowded, so we decided to go to the Food Court instead. Before lunch, we went to the Discovery Zone. It was well worth the wait to experience the scientific attractions there. In the afternoon, we enjoyed several rides near Mountain Station. Of course, we tried the roller coaster, and we weren't disappointed. On our way back to the Discovery Zone to enjoy more attractions, we took a short break at a rest stop. There, we got a lovely view over the lake to the castle. We ended up at the Shopping Zone, where we bought souvenirs for our friends and family.

　　Sunny Mountain Park is amazing! Our first visit certainly won't be our last.

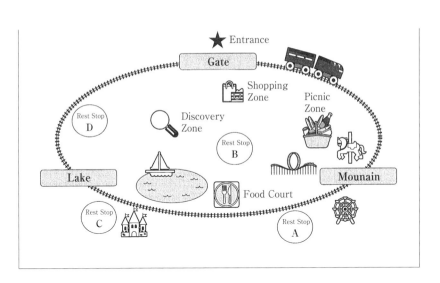

問 1 From Jan's post, you learn that 16 .

① Jan skipped going to the Shopping Zone for gifts
② Jan waited for a while to enjoy the scientific attractions
③ the Food Court was more crowded than the Picnic Zone
④ the roller coaster did not meet Jan's expectations

問 2 At which rest stop did Jan and her friends take a break in the afternoon? 17

① Rest Stop A
② Rest Stop B
③ Rest Stop C
④ Rest Stop D

 第3問 B (配点 9)

B　Your friend in the UK introduced her favourite musician to you. Wanting to learn more, you found the following article in a music magazine.

Dave Starr, a Living Legend

At one time, Black Swan were the biggest rock band in the UK, and their dynamic leader Dave Starr played a large part in that achievement. Still performing as a solo singer, Dave's incredible talent has inspired generations of young musicians.

When he was a little boy, Dave was always singing and playing with toy instruments. He was never happier than when he was playing his toy drum. At age seven, he was given his first real drum set, and by 10, he could play well. By 14, he had also mastered the guitar. When he was still a high school student, he became a member of The Bluebirds, playing rhythm guitar. To get experience, The Bluebirds played for free at school events and in community centres. The band built up a small circle of passionate fans.

Dave's big break came when, on his 18th birthday, he was asked to become the drummer for Black Swan. In just two years, the band's shows were selling out at large concert halls. It came as a shock, therefore, when the lead vocalist quit to spend more time with his family. However, Dave jumped at the chance to take over as lead singer even though it meant he could no longer play his favourite instrument.

In the following years, Black Swan became increasingly successful, topping the music charts and gaining even more fans. Dave became the principal song writer, and was proud of his contribution to the band. However, with the addition of a keyboard player, the music gradually changed direction. Dave became frustrated, and he and the lead guitarist decided to leave and start a new group. Unfortunately, Dave's new band failed to reach Black Swan's level of success, and stayed together for only 18 months.

問1 Put the following events (①～④) into the order in which they happened.

| 18 | → | 19 | → | 20 | → | 21 |

① Dave became a solo artist.
② Dave gave up playing the drums.
③ Dave joined a band as the guitarist.
④ Dave reached the peak of his career.

問2 Dave became the lead singer of Black Swan because [22] .

① he preferred singing to playing the drums
② he wanted to change the band's musical direction
③ the other band members wanted more success
④ the previous singer left for personal reasons

問3 From this story, you learn that [23] .

① Black Swan contributed to changing the direction of rock music
② Black Swan's goods sold very well at concert halls
③ Dave displayed a talent for music from an early age
④ Dave went solo as he was frustrated with the lead guitarist

第4問 (配点 16)

You are preparing a presentation on tourism in Japan. You emailed data about visitors to Japan in 2018 to your classmates, Hannah and Rick. Based on their responses, you draft a presentation outline.

The data:

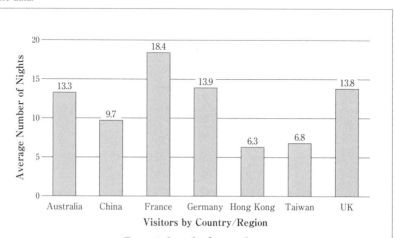

Figure 1. Length of stay in Japan.
(国土交通省観光庁による平成 30 年の統計資料の一部を参考に作成)

Table1

Average Amount of Money Spent While Visiting Japan

Visitors by country / region	Food	Entertainment	Shopping
Australia	58,878	16,171	32,688
China	39,984	7,998	112,104
France	56,933	7,358	32,472
Germany	47,536	5,974	25,250
Hong Kong	36,887	5,063	50,287
Taiwan	28,190	5,059	45,441
UK	56,050	8,341	22,641

(yen per person)
(国土交通省観光庁による平成 30 年の統計資料の一部を参考に作成)

The responses to your email:

Hi,

Thanks for your email! That's interesting data. I know that the number of international visitors to Japan increased previously, but I never paid attention to their length of stay. I assume that visitors from Asia come for shorter stays since they can go back and forth easily.

Also, the table shows that Asian visitors, overall, tend to spend more on shopping compared to visitors from Europe and Australia. I guess this is probably because gift-giving in Asian cultures is really important, and they want to buy gifts for friends and family. For example, I have seen many Asian tourists shopping around Ginza, Harajuku, and Akihabara. Perhaps they don't have to spend so much money on accommodations, so they can spend more on shopping. I'd like to talk about this.

However, I've heard that visitors from Asia are now becoming interested in doing some other things instead of shopping. We may see some changes in this kind of data in the near future!

Best,
Hannah
P.S. This message is going to Rick, too.

Hi,

Thanks for sending your data! This will help us prepare for our presentation!

I notice from the data that Australians spend the most on entertainment. I'll present on this.

Also, the other day, on Japanese TV, I saw a program about Australian people enjoying winter sports in Hokkaido. I wonder how much they spend. I'll look for more information. If you find any, please let me know. This could be good for a future project.

In addition, I agree with Hannah that there seems to be a big difference in the length of stay depending on the country or region the visitor is from.

What about you? Do you want to talk about what Hannah found in relation to the spending habits? I think this is very interesting.

All the best,
Rick
P.S. This message is going to Hannah, too.

The presentation draft:

Presentation Title: _____ 24 _____

Presenter   Topic

Hannah: _____ 25 _____

Rick: _____ 26 _____

me: Relation to the length of stay
       Example comparison:
       People from 27 stay just over half the time in
       Japan compared to people from 28 , but spend
       slightly more money on entertainment.

Themes for Future Research: _____ 29 _____

問1 Which is the best for 24 ?

① Money Spent on Winter Holidays in Hokkaido
② Shopping Budgets of International Tourists in Tokyo
③ Spending Habits of International Visitors in Japan
④ The Increase of Spending on Entertainment in Japan

問2 Which is the best for [25] ?

① Activities of Australian visitors in Japan
② Asian visitors' food costs in Japan
③ Gift-giving habits in European cultures
④ Patterns in spending by visitors from Asia

問3 Which is the best for [26] ?

① Australian tourists' interest in entertainment
② Chinese spending habits in Tokyo
③ TV programs about Hokkaido in Australia
④ Various experiences Asians enjoy in Japan

問4 You agree with Rick's suggestion and look at the data. Choose the best for [27] and [28] .

① Australia
② China
③ France
④ Taiwan

問5 Which is the best combination for [29] ?

A : Australians' budgets for winter sports in Japan
B : Future changes in the number of international visitors to Tokyo
C : Popular food for international visitors to Hokkaido
D : What Asian visitors in Japan will spend money on in the future

① A, B
② A, C
③ A, D
④ B, C
⑤ B, D
⑥ C, D

第5問　　　　　　　　　　　　　　　　　　　　　(配点 15)

You are going to give a talk on a person you would like to have interviewed if they were still alive. Read the following passage about the person you have chosen and complete your notes.

Vivian Maier

    This is the story of an American street photographer who kept her passion for taking pictures secret until her death. She lived her life as a caregiver, and if it had not been for the sale of her belongings at an auction house, her incredible work might never have been discovered.

    It was 2007. A Chicago auction house was selling off the belongings of an old woman named Vivian Maier. She had stopped paying storage fees, and so the company decided to sell her things. Her belongings—mainly old photographs and negatives—were sold to three buyers: Maloof, Slattery, and Prow.

    Slattery thought Vivian's work was interesting so he published her photographs on a photo-sharing website in July 2008. The photographs received little attention. Then, in October, Maloof linked his blog to his selection of Vivian's photographs, and right away, thousands of people were viewing them. Maloof had found Vivian Maier's name with the prints, but he was unable to discover anything about her. Then an Internet search led him to a 2009 newspaper article about her death. Maloof used this information to discover more about Vivian's life, and it was the combination of Vivian's mysterious life story and her photographs that grabbed everyone's attention.

    Details of Vivian's life are limited for two reasons. First, since no one had interviewed her while she was alive, no one knew why she took so many photographs. Second, it is clear from interviews with the family she worked for that Vivian was a very private person. She had few friends. Besides, she had kept her hobby a secret.

    Vivian was born in 1926 in the United States to an Austrian father and a French mother. The marriage was not a happy one, and it seems her mother and father lived apart for several years. During her childhood Vivian frequently moved between the US and France, sometimes living in France, and sometimes in the US. For a while, Vivian and her mother lived in New York with Jeanne Bertrand, a successful photographer. It is believed that Vivian

"film negative"　　　　　　　　　　　"printed image"

became interested in photography as a young adult, as her first photos were taken in France in the late 1940s using a very simple camera. She returned to New York in 1951, and in 1956 she moved to Chicago to work as a caregiver for the Gensburg family. This job gave her more free time for taking photographs.

In 1952, at the age of 26, she purchased her first 6 × 6 camera, and it was with this that most of her photographs of life on the streets of Chicago were taken. For over 30 years she took photos of children, the elderly, the rich, and the poor. Some people were not even aware that their picture was being taken. She also took a number of self-portraits. Some were reflections of herself in a shop window. Others were of her own shadow. Vivian continued to document Chicago life until the early 1970s, when she changed to a new style of photography.

An international award-winning documentary film called *Finding Vivian Maier* brought interest in her work to a wider audience. The film led to exhibitions in Europe and the US. To choose the photographs that best represent her style, those in charge of the exhibitions have tried to answer the question, "What would Vivian Maier have printed?" In order to answer this question, they used her notes, the photos she actually did print, and information about her preferences as reported by the Gensburgs. Vivian was much more interested in capturing moments rather than the outcome. So, one could say the mystery behind Vivian's work remains largely "undeveloped."

Presentation notes:

Vivian Maier

Vivian the photographer
☆ She took many pictures while she was working as a caregiver.
☆ Nobody interviewed her while she was alive, so we do not know much about her.
☆ ☐ 30

Vivian's work
☆ Her photographs mainly concentrated on:
  · the young and old, and the rich and poor
  · ☐ 31
  · ☐ 32

How her work gained recognition
☆ Vivian's storage fees were not paid.
☆ ☐ 33
☆ ☐ 34
☆ ☐ 35
☆ ☐ 36
☆ The combining of information on her life and work increased people's interest.

How her work became known worldwide
☆ An award-winning documentary film about her life and work helped capture a new audience.
☆ ☐ 37

The 'BIG' unanswered question: ☐ 38

問1 Choose the best statement for ☐30☐ .

① Her work remained undiscovered until it was sold at auction.
② She is thought to have become attracted to photography in her thirties.
③ She took her camera wherever she went and showed her pictures to others.
④ The majority of her photos were taken in New York.

問2 Choose the two best items for ☐31☐ and ☐32☐ . (The order does not matter.)

① documentary-style pictures
② industrial landscapes
③ natural landscapes
④ pictures of herself
⑤ shop windows

問3 Put the following events into the order in which they happened.
☐33☐ ~ ☐36☐

① A buyer linked his blog to some of her pictures.
② A report on Vivian's death was published in a newspaper.
③ An auction company started selling her old photographs and negatives.
④ Her work was published on the Internet.

問4 Choose the best statement for ☐37☐ .

① Exhibitions of her work have been held in different parts of the world.
② Her photography book featuring street scenes won an award.
③ She left detailed instructions on how her photographs should be treated.
④ The children of Vivian's employers provided their photographs.

問5 Choose the best question for ☐38☐ .

① "What type of camera did she use for taking photos?"
② "Where did she keep all her negatives and prints?"
③ "Why did she leave New York to become a caregiver?"
④ "Why did she take so many photos without showing them to anyone?"

053

第6問 A   (配点 12)

A You are an exchange student in the United States and you have joined the school's drama club. You are reading an American online arts magazine article to get some ideas to help improve the club.

Recent Changes at the Royal Shakespeare Company

By John Smith
Feb. 20, 2020

We are all different. While most people recognize that the world is made up of a wide variety of people, diversity—showing and accepting our differences—is often not reflected in performing arts organizations. For this reason, there is an increasing demand for movies and plays to better represent people from various backgrounds as well as those with disabilities. Arts Council England, in response to this demand, is encouraging all publicly funded arts organizations to make improvements in this area. One theater company responding positively is the Royal Shakespeare Company (RSC), which is one of the most influential theater companies in the world.

Based in Stratford-upon-Avon in the UK, the RSC produces plays by William Shakespeare and a number of other famous authors. These days, the RSC is focused on diversity in an attempt to represent all of UK society accurately. It works hard to balance the ethnic and social backgrounds, the genders, and the physical abilities of both performers and staff when hiring.

During the summer 2019 season, the RSC put on three of Shakespeare's comedies: *As You Like It*, *The Taming of the Shrew*, and *Measure for Measure*. Actors from all over the country were employed, forming a 27-member cast, reflecting the diverse ethnic, geographical, and cultural population of the UK today. To achieve gender balance for the entire season, half of all roles were given to male actors and half to female actors. The cast included three actors with disabilities (currently referred to as "differently-abled" actors)—one visually-impaired, one hearing-impaired, and one in a wheelchair.

Changes went beyond the hiring policy. The RSC actually rewrote parts of the plays to encourage the audience to reflect on male/female power relationships. For example, female and male roles were reversed. In *The*

Taming of the Shrew, the role of "the daughter" in the original was transformed into "the son" and played by a male actor. In the same play, a male servant character was rewritten as a female servant. That role was played by Amy Trigg, a female actor who uses a wheelchair. Trigg said that she was excited to play the role and believed that the RSC's changes would have a large impact on other performing arts organizations. Excited by all the diversity, other members of the RSC expressed the same hope—that more arts organizations would be encouraged to follow in the RSC's footsteps.

The RSC's decision to reflect diversity in the summer 2019 season can be seen as a new model for arts organizations hoping to make their organizations inclusive. While there are some who are reluctant to accept diversity in classic plays, others welcome it with open arms. Although certain challenges remain, the RSC has earned its reputation as the face of progress.

問1 According to the article, the RSC ⬚39⬚ in the summer 2019 season.

① gave job opportunities to famous actors
② hired three differently-abled performers
③ looked for plays that included 27 characters
④ put on plays by Shakespeare and other authors

問2 The author of this article most likely mentions Amy Trigg because she ⬚40⬚ .

① performed well in one of the plays presented by the RSC
② struggled to be selected as a member of the RSC
③ was a good example of the RSC's efforts to be inclusive
④ was a role model for the members of the RSC

問3 You are summarizing this article for other club members. Which of the following options best completes your summary?

[Summary]
The Royal Shakespeare Company (RSC) in the UK is making efforts to reflect the population of UK society in its productions. In order to achieve this, it has started to employ a balance of female and male actors and staff with a variety of backgrounds and abilities. It has also made changes to its plays. Consequently, the RSC has　41　.

① attracted many talented actors from all over the world
② completed the 2019 season without any objections
③ contributed to matching social expectations with actions
④ earned its reputation as a conservative theater company

問4 Your drama club agrees with the RSC's ideas. Based on these ideas, your drama club might　42　.

① perform plays written by new international authors
② present classic plays with the original story
③ raise funds to buy wheelchairs for local people
④ remove gender stereotypes from its performances

056

057

第 6 問 B　　　　　　　　　　　　　　　　　　　　　　　(配点 12)

B　You are one of a group of students making a poster presentation for a wellness fair at City Hall. Your group's title is *Promoting Better Oral Health in the Community*. You have been using the following passage to create the poster.

Oral Health: Looking into the Mirror

　　In recent years, governments around the world have been working to raise awareness about oral health. While many people have heard that brushing their teeth multiple times per day is a good habit, they most likely have not considered all the reasons why this is crucial. Simply stated, teeth are important. Teeth are required to pronounce words accurately. In fact, poor oral health can actually make it difficult to speak. An even more basic necessity is being able to chew well. Chewing breaks food down and makes it easier for the body to digest it. Proper chewing is also linked to the enjoyment of food. The average person has experienced the frustration of not being able to chew on one side after a dental procedure. A person with weak teeth may experience this disappointment all the time. In other words, oral health impacts people's quality of life.

　　While the basic functions of teeth are clear, many people do not realize that the mouth provides a mirror for the body. Research shows that good oral health is a clear sign of good general health. People with poor oral health are more likely to develop serious physical diseases. Ignoring recommended daily oral health routines can have negative effects on those already suffering from diseases. Conversely, practicing good oral health may even prevent disease. A strong, healthy body is often a reflection of a clean, well-maintained mouth.

　　Maintaining good oral health is a lifelong mission. The Finnish and US governments recommend that parents take their infants to the dentist before the baby turns one year old. Finland actually sends parents notices. New Zealand offers free dental treatment to everyone up to age 18. The Japanese government promotes an 8020 (Eighty-Twenty) Campaign. As people age, they can lose teeth for various reasons. The goal of the campaign is still to have at least 20 teeth in the mouth on one's 80th birthday.

　　Taking a closer look at Japan, the Ministry of Health, Labour and Welfare has been analyzing survey data on the number of remaining teeth in seniors for many years. One researcher divided the oldest participants into four age groups: A (70-74), B (75-79), C (80-84), D (85+). In each survey, with the exception of 1993, the percentages of people with at least 20 teeth were in A-B-C-D order from high to low. Between 1993 and 1999, however, Group A improved only about six percentage points, while the increase for B was slightly higher. In 1993, 25.5% in Group A had at least 20 teeth, but by 2016 the Group D percentage was actually 0.2 percentage points higher than Group A's initial figure. Group B increased steadily at first, but went up dramatically between 2005 and 2011. Thanks to better awareness, every group has improved significantly over the years.

Dentists have long recommended brushing after meals. People actively seeking excellent oral health may brush several times per day. Most brush their teeth before they go to sleep and then again at some time the following morning. Dentists also believe it is important to floss daily, using a special type of string to remove substances from between teeth. Another prevention method is for a dentist to seal the teeth using a plastic gel (sealant) that hardens around the tooth surface and prevents damage. Sealant is gaining popularity especially for use with children. This only takes one coating and prevents an amazing 80% of common dental problems.

Visiting the dentist annually or more frequently is key. As dental treatment sometimes causes pain, there are those who actively avoid seeing a dentist. However, it is important that people start viewing their dentist as an important ally who can, literally, make them smile throughout their lives.

Your presentation poster:

Promoting Better Oral Health in the Community

1. Importance of Teeth

A. Crucial to speak properly
B. Necessary to break down food
C. Helpful to enjoy food
D. Needed to make a good impression
E. Essential for good quality of life

2. [44]

Finland & the US: Recommendations for treatment before age 1
New Zealand: Free treatment for youth
Japan: 8020 (Eighty-Twenty) Campaign (see Figure 1)

Figure 1. The percentage of people with at least 20 teeth.

3. Helpful Advice

[46]
[47]

問1 Under the first poster heading, your group wants to express the importance of teeth as explained in the passage. Everyone agrees that one suggestion does not fit well. Which of the following should you **not** include? ☐ **43**

① A
② B
③ C
④ D
⑤ E

問2 You have been asked to write the second heading for the poster. Which of the following is the most appropriate? ☐ **44**

① National 8020 Programs Targeting Youth
② National Advertisements for Better Dental Treatment
③ National Efforts to Encourage Oral Care
④ National Systems Inviting Infants to the Dentist

問3 You want to show the results of the researcher's survey in Japan. Which of the following graphs is the most appropriate one for your poster? 45

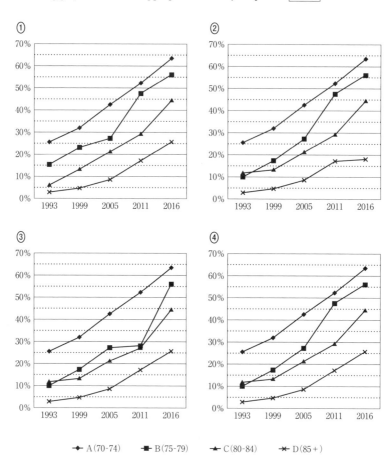

問4 Under the last poster heading, you want to add specific advice based on the passage. Which two of the following statements should you use? (The order does not matter.) 46 · 47

① Brush your teeth before you eat breakfast.
② Check your teeth in the mirror every day.
③ Make at least one visit to the dentist a year.
④ Put plastic gel on your teeth frequently.
⑤ Use dental floss between your teeth daily.

MEMO

YASASHIKU HIMOTOKU
English Reading

過去問　 解説　 実況動画

やさしくひもとく共通テスト
英語 リーディング

東進ハイスクール　武藤一也　　河合塾　高山のぞみ

YASASHIKU HIMOTOKU
English Reading

Gakken

本書の使い方

STEP 1 まずは試験時間どおりに過去問を解く

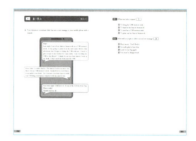
▲別冊過去問

- 本書の別冊には，令和3年度（2021年度）に実施された大学入学共通テスト（以下，共通テスト）の過去問が2回分収録されています。
- まずは第1日程の問題を解いてみましょう。
- 過去問を解くときには時間を意識して，本番と同じ想定で解きましょう。
- 試験時間を確認し，必ず時間を計りながら取り組みましょう。それにより，現在の自分の実力を知ることができます。
- 英語リーディングの場合，試験時間は80分です。

STEP 2 間違えた問題を中心に，実況動画でしっかり復習する

▲解答一覧

- 過去問を解き終わったら，まずは本冊の解答一覧で答え合わせをします。
- 答え合わせの際には，間違えた問題だけでなく，自信はなかったけれど正解していた問題や，たまたま正解した問題も必ずチェックしましょう。
- つづいて，解説ページのQRコードから動画を視聴します。
- 先生が問題を解くときの着眼点や考え方を確認することで，正解を導き出すためのプロセスを体験することができます。

問題や設問，選択肢のどの部分に注目すれば問題が解けるか，先生の実況動画で体験してみよう！

STEP 3 書籍の解説も併用しながら復習し，試験本番に備える

》 問題と解説を照らし合わせながらしっかり復習するために，問題を解くときの着眼点や解き方のプロセスがまとめられている本冊を参考にしてください。

》 本冊の巻末には，問題の和訳に加えて，英文中に登場した語句のうち注意すべきものをピックアップした語注がついています。

》 第1日程の復習が終わったら，第2日程の過去問に進みます。第1日程と同様に時間を計り，動画と書籍の解説を活用してしっかり復習し，試験本番に備えましょう。

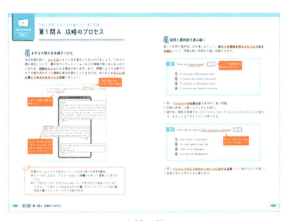

▲解　説

📹 動画の視聴方法

》 解説ページのQRコードをタブレット端末などで読み取ることで，問題を解くときの手元を映した実況動画を視聴することができます。

》 また，タブレット端末などから右下のQRコードを読み取るか，パソコンから下記のURLにアクセスして表紙画像を選択後，ユーザー名とパスワードを入力すると，一覧ページから見たい動画に進むことができます。

https://gakken-ep.jp/extra/himotoku2021/

ユーザー名：yshmer ／ パスワード：a4fieti8

＊お客様のネット環境および端末により動画を利用できない場合，当社は責任を負いかねます。
＊動画の公開は予告なく終了することがございます。

共通テストの心得

高山先生の解説動画はコチラ

① 時間配分を意識する

- 共通テストの英語リーディングは問題数が多く，センター試験より読むべき英文の量も増えています。
- また，メッセージやメールのやり取り，論説文や物語，表やグラフに加えてプレゼンテーション用資料の読解など，様々な問題形式が出題されます。
- 最初から最後までやみくもに解いてしまうと時間が足りなくなってしまうので，時間配分を意識して英文を読み，問題を解いていくことが求められます。

② 効率的に読み解く

- 「問題数が多いので，時間配分を意識するように」と言われると，「とにかく急いで読まなきゃ！」と焦ってしまう人もいるかもしれません。
- ところが，急いで読めば問題を時間内に解き終わるかというと，そうではありませんよね。
- 大切なのは，正しく，速く，効率的に本文中の正解箇所にたどり着くことです。
- たとえば，設問や選択肢に含まれるキーワードを探しながら本文を読むことで，効率よく問題を解くことができるようになります。
- 具体的な問題の解き方については，本冊でくわしく解説します。

③ 言い換えに注意

- 本文中の正解箇所にたどり着いた後で注意が必要なのは，本文で書かれている内容が選択肢にも同じ言い方で登場するとは限らないということです。
- むしろ，本文の内容が選択肢では別の表現で言い換えられている場合が多いのです。
- たとえば本文中では a week「1週間」と書かれていたものが，選択肢では seven days「7日間」と言い換えられていることがよくあります。
- このような言い換えを見抜くことが，共通テスト攻略のカギになります。

共通テスト 英語リーディング 概要

- 試験時間……80分
- 配点………100点
- 問題数……47問
- 総語数……約5,500語

やさしくひもとく共通テスト
英語リーディング ｜ もくじ

本書の使い方 ……………002
共通テストの心得 ………004

令和3年度 第1日程
（2021年度）

解答一覧 ……………007

第1問A ……………008
第1問B ……………012

第2問A ……………018
第2問B ……………026

第3問A ……………034
第3問B ……………040

第4問 ……………046

第5問 ……………058

第6問A ……………072
第6問B ……………082

全訳・語注 ……………182

令和3年度 第2日程
（2021年度）

解答一覧 ……………093

第1問A ……………094
第1問B ……………098

第2問A ……………104
第2問B ……………114

第3問A ……………122
第3問B ……………128

第4問 ……………134

第5問 ……………146

第6問A ……………160
第6問B ……………170

全訳・語注 ……………217

MEMO

令和3年度（2021年度）大学入学共通テスト
英語リーディング　第1日程

解答一覧

問題番号（配点）	設問		解答番号	正解	配点	チェック
第1問（10）	A	問1	1	①	2	
		問2	2	②	2	
	B	問1	3	④	2	
		問2	4	④	2	
		問3	5	③	2	
第2問（20）	A	問1	6	②	2	
		問2	7	②	2	
		問3	8	①	2	
		問4	9	③	2	
		問5	10	⑤	2	
	B	問1	11	④	2	
		問2	12	④	2	
		問3	13	②	2	
		問4	14	②	2	
		問5	15	①	2	
第3問（15）	A	問1	16	③	3	
		問2	17	②	3	
	B	問1	18	④	3*	
			19	②		
			20	①		
			21	③		
		問2	22	②	3	
		問3	23	②	3	

問題番号（配点）	設問	解答番号	正解	配点	チェック
第4問（16）	問1	24	①	2	
		25	⑤	2	
	問2	26	②	3	
	問3	27	②	3	
	問4	28	②	3	
	問5	29	④	3	
第5問（15）	問1	30	③	3	
	問2	31	④	3	
	問3	32	④	3*	
		33	③		
		34	⑤		
		35	①		
	問4	36－37	①－③	3	
	問5	38	①	3	
第6問（24）	A	問1	39	④	3	
		問2	40	③	3	
		問3	41	④	3	
		問4	42	②	3	
	B	問1	43	③	3	
		問2	44	③	3	
		問3	45－46	③－⑤	3*	
		問4	47	④	3	

＊は，全問正解の場合のみ点を与える
ハイフンでつながれた正解は，順序を問わない

令和３年度 大学入学共通テスト 第１日程

第１問Ａ 攻略のプロセス

 まずは大問の全体像をつかむ

本文を読む前に，リード文にさっと目を通すことを心がけましょう。これから読む英文について，書き手やシチュエーションなどの情報が短くまとめられているため，読解のヒントになる場合があります。また，問題によっては表やグラフが組み合わさった複雑な英文を読むことになるため，あらかじめどこに何が書いてあるかをざっくり把握しましょう。

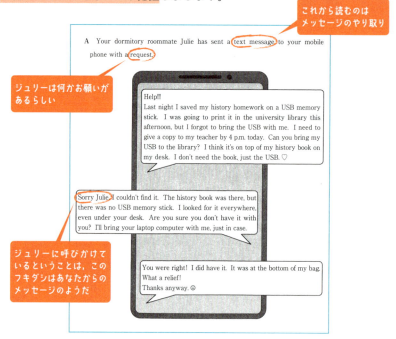

これから読むのはメッセージのやり取り

ジュリーは何かお願いがあるらしい

ジュリーに呼びかけているということは，このフキダシはあなたからのメッセージのようだ

- 寮のルームメイトであるジュリーとの**メッセージのやり取り**。
- リード文によると，ジュリーはなにか**お願い**があって連絡してきたようだ。
- ２つめのメッセージが Sorry Julie, という呼びかけで始まっていることから，１つめと３つめは**ジュリー**が書いたメッセージ，２つめが**あなた**が書いたメッセージだと判断できる。

STEP 2 設問と選択肢を読み解く

続いて設問や選択肢に目を通しましょう。探すべき情報を押さえたうえで英文を読むことで，問題を解く時間を大幅に短縮できます。

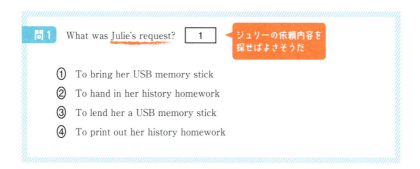

» 問1はジュリーの依頼内容を具体的に選ぶ問題。
» 依頼の表現に注意しながら本文を読む。
» 選択肢に複数回登場する USB memory stick や history homework などの語句は，本文にも出てきそうだと予想できる。

» 問2はジュリーの2つめのメッセージに対する返事として適切なものを選ぶ。
» 会話の流れを押さえる必要がある。

STEP 3 必要な情報を本文から探しながら小問を解く　難易度 やさしい

問1 What was Julie's request?　1

① To bring her USB memory stick
② To hand in her history homework
③ To lend her a USB memory stick
④ To print out her history homework

MOVIE 01

着眼点
» 設問の Julie's request「ジュリーのお願い」に注目。
» Will you ～? / Can you ～?「～していただけますか？」などの依頼を表す表現を探しながら，ジュリーからのメッセージを読む。

解き方
» 上から2つめのメッセージに Sorry Julie,「ごめん，ジュリー」という呼びかけがあるので，1つめのメッセージはジュリーが書いたものだとわかる。

> Help!!!
> Last night I saved my history homework on a USB memory stick. I was going to print it in the university library this afternoon, but I forgot to bring the USB with me. I need to give a copy to my teacher by 4 p.m. today. Can you bring my USB to the library? I think it's on top of my history book on my desk. I don't need the book, just the USB. ♡

» この中から依頼の表現を探すと，Can you bring my USB to the library?「図書館まで私の USB を持ってきてくれない？」が見つかる。この1文を書き換えた①が正解。

本文中の語句や表現は，選択肢では言い換えられていることが多いんだ

問2 How will you reply to Julie's second text message? [2]

① Don't worry. You'll find it.
② I'm really glad to hear that.
③ Look in your bag again.
④ You must be disappointed.

MOVIE 02

着眼点
» 「ジュリーの２つめのメッセージにどう返事をするか」という設問。
» 話の流れを押さえるために，すべてのメッセージに目を通す。

解き方
» ジュリーから依頼を受けて USB を探したが見つけられなかったという状況。

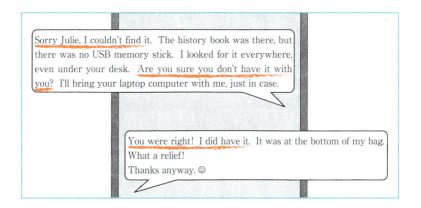

» Are you sure you don't have it with you?「手元に持っていないのは確かなの？」という発言を受けて，ジュリーは次のメッセージで You were right! I did have it.「あなたの言うとおりだったわ！　確かに私が持ってた」と言っている。it は USB を指す。
» このジュリーの発言に対する返事として適切なのは，②の I'm really glad to hear that.「それを聞いて本当によかった」である。

» ジュリーは USB を見つけているので，①の「きっと見つかるよ」や③の「もう一度カバンを探したら」という返事は不自然。
» 探しものを見つけて安心しているジュリーに「がっかりしてるだろう」と伝える④も不自然。

令和3年度 大学入学共通テスト 第1日程

第1問B 攻略のプロセス

STEP 1 まずは大問の全体像をつかむ

あらかじめ<u>リード文</u>に目を通したうえで，<u>本文のどこに何が書いてあるかを</u>
<u>ざっくり把握</u>しましょう。

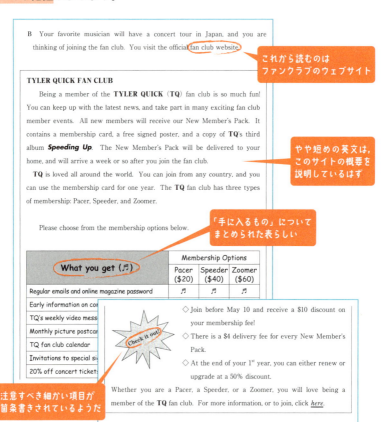

- 好きなバンドの公式ファンクラブの**ウェブサイト**。
- 英文の下には**表**がついており，さらに**注意事項**が箇条書きされている。
- どこに何が書いてあるかを**推測**しながら英文を読む。

STEP 2 設問と選択肢を読み解く

続いて設問や選択肢に目を通しましょう。探すべき情報を押さえたうえで英文を読むことで、問題を解く時間を大幅に短縮できます。ここではまず、問 1 と問 2 に注目します。

≫ 問 1 は New Member's Pack「新規会員パック」について書かれている箇所を探す。

≫ 問 2 は新しく Pacer member になると入手できるものを探す。
≫ What you get「手に入るもの」という表のタイトルから、この部分に手がかりがありそうだ。

設問からキーワードを拾う→本文のどこを読めばいいかがわかる→時間が短縮できる！

STEP 3 必要な情報を本文から探しながら小問を解く

問1 A New Member's Pack [3].

① includes TQ's first album
② is delivered on May 10
③ requires a $10 delivery fee
④ takes about seven days to arrive

MOVIE 03

着眼点
» 設問の New Member's Pack「新規会員パック」に注目。この語句を本文中から探し出し，その前後を詳しく見ていこう。

解き方
» ウェブサイトの第1段落・第3文で New Member's Pack がはじめて登場し，第4〜5文に詳しい説明が続いている。

> **TYLER QUICK FAN CLUB**
>
> Being a member of the **TYLER QUICK** (**TQ**) fan club is so much fun! You can keep up with the latest news, and take part in many exciting fan club member events. All new members will receive our New Member's Pack. It contains a membership card, a free signed poster, and a copy of **TQ**'s third album **Speeding Up**. The New Member's Pack will be delivered to your home, and will arrive a week or so after you join the fan club.

» 第5文の The New Member's Pack will be delivered to your home, and will arrive a week or so after you join the fan club.「新規会員パックはご自宅に郵送され，ファンクラブ入会後，約1週間でお届けできる見込みです」という記述から，正解は④。

» 本文の a week or so「約1週間」が，選択肢では about seven days「約7日」と言い換えられている。

» New Member's Pack については，第4文に It contains a membership card, a free signed poster, and a copy of TQ's third album Speeding Up.「それに

は会員カードと無料のサイン入りポスター，そして TQ の 3 枚目のアルバム Speeding Up が含まれます」という記述がある。パックに含まれているのは 1 枚目ではなく 3 枚目のアルバムだとわかるので，①は不適切。

》②の選択肢に含まれる May 10 という日付を本文から探すと，Check it out! の 1 つ目の項目に Join before May 10 and receive a $10 discount on your membership fee!「5 月 10 日までに入会すると，会費が 10 ドル割引になります！」という記述が見つかる。5 月 10 日は配達される日ではなく割引の期限だとわかるので，②は不適切。

》③の選択肢に含まれる $10 delivery fee「10 ドルの配送料」に該当する記述を本文から探すと，Check it out! の 2 つ目の項目に There is a $4 delivery fee for every New Member's Pack.「新規会員パックには 4 ドルの配送料がかかります」という記述がある。配送料は 10 ドルではなく 4 ドルだとわかるので，③は不適切。

自分の答えに自信がもてないときは，このように他の選択肢からキーワードを拾って本文と照らし合わせ，消去法で確認しよう

問2 What will you get if you become a new Pacer member? ☐ 4

① Discount concert tickets and a calendar
② Regular emails and signing event invitations
③ Tour information and postcards every month
④ Video messages and access to online magazines

MOVIE 04

着眼点
» 「Pacer メンバーになったら何が手に入るか？」という設問に答えるには、ウェブサイトの What you get「手に入るもの」という表を見ればよい。

解き方
» What you get「手に入るもの」の表のうち、Pacer の列に注目する。

Please choose from the membership options below.

What you get (♪)	Membership Options		
	Pacer ($20)	Speeder ($40)	Zoomer ($60)
Regular emails and online magazine password	♪	♪	♪
Early information on concert tour dates	♪	♪	♪
TQ's weekly video messages	♪	♪	♪
Monthly picture postcards		♪	♪
TQ fan club calendar		♪	♪
Invitations to special signing events			♪
20% off concert tickets			♪

» ①の Discount concert tickets と calendar は Pacer の特典に含まれない。
» ②の Regular emails は 1 段目にあるが、singing event invitations は含まれない。
» ③の Tour information は 2 段目にあるが、postcards は含まれない。
» ④の Video messages は表の 3 段目に、online magazines は 1 段目にあるので、正解は④。本文の password が、選択肢では access を使って言い換えられている。

問3 After being a fan club member for one year, you can 　5　.

① become a Zoomer for a $50 fee
② get a New Member's Pack for $4
③ renew your membership at half price
④ upgrade your membership for free

MOVIE 05

着眼点

≫ 設問に含まれている for one year「1 年間」という条件に注目。
≫ 入会 1 年後にできることは，これまで読んできた部分に出てきていないので，残る Check it out! の部分に手がかりがありそうだ。

解き方

◇ Join before May 10 and receive a $10 discount on your membership fee!
◇ There is a $4 delivery fee for every New Member's Pack.
◇ At the end of your 1st year, you can either renew or upgrade at a 50% discount.

Whether you are a Pacer, a Speeder, or a Zoomer, you will love being a member of the **TQ** fan club. For more information, or to join, click *here*.

≫ At the end of your 1st year「初年度の終わりに」で始まる 3 つ目の項目を読み進めると，you can either renew or upgrade at a 50% discount「50 パーセント割引で更新またはアップグレードできます」とあるので，正解は③。
≫ 本文の at a 50% discount「50 パーセント割引で」が，選択肢では at half price「半額で」と言い換えられている。

017

令和3年度 大学入学共通テスト 第1日程
第2問A 攻略のプロセス

STEP 1 まずは大問の全体像をつかむ

あらかじめリード文に目を通したうえで，本文のどこに何が書いてあるかをざっくり把握しましょう。

A　As the student in charge of a UK school festival band competition, you are examining all of the scores and the comments from three judges to understand and explain the rankings.

→ 審査員の点数やコメントを精査して，バンドコンテストの順位を理解する

Judges' final average scores

Band names \ Qualities	Performance (5.0)	Singing (5.0)	Song originality (5.0)	Total (15.0)
Green Forest	3.9	4.6	5.0	13.5
Silent Hill	4.9	4.4	4.2	13.5
Mountain Pear	3.9	4.9	4.7	13.5
Thousand Ants	(did not perform)			

→ 審査員がつけた点数が表になっているようだ

Judges' individual comments

Mr Hobbs	Silent Hill are great performers and they really seemed connected with the audience. Mountain Pear's singing was great. I loved Green Forest's original song. It was amazing!
Ms Leigh	Silent Hill gave a great performance. It was incredible how the audience responded to their music. I really think that Silent Hill will become popular! Mountain Pear have great voices, but they were not exciting on stage. Green Forest performed a fantastic
Ms Wells	Green Fo... big hit!

→ 審査員それぞれのコメントがまとめられているようだ

Judges' shared evaluation (summarised by Hobbs)

　Each band's total score is the same, but each band is very different. Ms Leigh and I agreed that performance is the most important quality for a band. Ms Wells also agreed. Therefore, first place is easily determined.
　To decide between second and third places, Ms Wells suggested that song originality should be more important than good singing. Ms Leigh and I agreed on this opinion.

→ 審査員の共同評価が書かれているらしい

- 学園祭のバンドコンテストの担当者として順位を説明する。
- 審査員によるスコア表や個別コメントに加えて，共同評価が載っている。
- 複数の資料を照らし合わせながら英文を読む。

STEP 2 設問と選択肢を読み解く

続いて設問や選択肢に目を通しましょう。探すべき情報を押さえたうえで英文を読むことで，問題を解く時間を大幅に短縮できます。ここでは問3の fact と opinion を分別するタイプの問題に注目します。

» それぞれの選択肢が fact「事実」なのか opinion「意見」なのか，そして本文の内容と合致しているかを確認する必要がある。

» opinion と考えられる選択肢をあらかじめ除外した上で，残った選択肢が本文の内容と合致するかを確かめると効率がよい。

» 次の例のとおり，fact は数値などの客観的な事実を，opinion は感想などの主観的な意見を指す。

FOR YOUR INFORMATION

✓ **fact と opinion の違い**

» **Ms. Takayama is 152 centimeters tall.** （高山先生は身長152センチだ）
　→数値を用いた客観的事実＝fact

» **Ms. Takayama is short.** （高山先生は背が低い）
　→この文を書いた人の主観的な意見＝opinion

» また，設問から the judges' individual comments「審査員による個別コメント」に手がかりがあることがわかる。

STEP 3 必要な情報を本文から探しながら小問を解く

 難しい

問1 Based on the judges' final average scores, which band sang the best?
6

① Green Forest
② Mountain Pear
③ Silent Hill
④ Thousand Ants

MOVIE 06

着眼点

≫ Based on the judge's final average scores...「審査員による最終得点の平均にもとづくと…」という設問から，1つめの表に注目。

解き方

≫ which band sang the best?「最も上手に歌ったバンドは？」という設問なので，1つめの表のSinging「歌唱」に注目。

Judges' final average scores				
Qualities Band names	Performance (5.0)	Singing (5.0)	Song originality (5.0)	Total (15.0)
Green Forest	3.9	4.6	5.0	13.5
Silent Hill	4.9	4.4	4.2	13.5
Mountain Pear	3.9	4.9	4.7	13.5
Thousand Ants	(did not perform)			

≫ 歌唱のスコアが最も高いのはMountain Pearの4.9なので，正解は②。

問2 Which judge gave both positive and critical comments? 7

① Mr Hobbs
② Ms Leigh
③ Ms Wells
④ None of them

MOVIE 07

着眼点

》「肯定と否定の両方のコメントを出したのはどの審査員か？」という設問から，Judges' individual comments の表に注目。

解き方

	Judges' individual comments
Mr Hobbs	Silent Hill are great performers and they really seemed connected with the audience. Mountain Pear's singing was great. I loved Green Forest's original song. It was amazing!
Ms Leigh	Silent Hill gave a great performance. It was incredible how the audience responded to their music. I really think that Silent Hill will become popular! Mountain Pear have great voices, but they were not exciting on stage. Green Forest performed a fantastic new song, but I think they need to practice more.
Ms Wells	Green Forest have a new song. I loved it! I think it could be a big hit!

》 Mr Hobbs のコメントには，great performers や really seemed connected, great や loved, amazing といったプラスの表現しか見られないので不適切。

》 Ms Leigh のコメントに注目すると，great や incredible, popular や great voices, fantastic といったプラスの表現がある一方で，but の後に not exciting や need to practice more といったマイナスの表現も見られる。

プラスの内容の後に but が来ると，マイナスの内容が続く可能性が高い！

》 Ms Wells のコメントには，loved や big hit というプラスの表現しかない。
》 よって正解は②。

021

難易度 ふつう

問3 One <u>fact</u> from the judges' individual comments is that ☐8☐ .

① all the judges praised Green Forest's song
② Green Forest need to practice more
③ Mountain Pear can sing very well
④ Silent Hill have a promising future

MOVIE 08

着眼点
» 設問から，Judges' individual comments「審査員による個別コメント」の表に注目。
» 先に選択肢を確認して opinion「意見」を除外する。
» 次に残った選択肢の中から本文の内容に合致する fact「事実」を選ぶ。

> 話者の意見や考えを表す助動詞や，主観的な意見が入る形容詞・副詞は opinion「意見」を探す目印になることが多いよ

解き方
» ①の all the judges praised Green Forest's song「全審査員がグリーン・フォレストの歌を称賛した」というのは意見ではなく事実と考えられる。
» ②は need to「必要がある」の部分が主観的なので除外。
» ③は can sing very well「とても上手に歌える」が主観的なので除外。
» ④は promising「有望な」が個人的な意見なので除外。

» ①が正しいかを確認するために Judges' individual comments を見る。
» Mr Hobbs は I loved Green Forest's original song.「グリーン・フォレストのオリジナル曲がとても気に入った」と，Ms Leigh は Green Forest performed a fantastic new song「グリーン・フォレストは素晴らしい新曲を演奏してくれた」と，Ms Wells は Green Forest have a new song. I loved it!「グリーン・フォレストには新曲がある。とても気に入った！」と全員が Green Forest の曲を褒めていることがわかる。よって正解は①。

難易度 ふつう

問4 One <u>opinion</u> from the judges' comments and shared evaluation is that ⑨ .

① each evaluated band received the same total score
② Ms Wells' suggestion about originality was agreed on
③ Silent Hill really connected with the audience
④ the judges' comments determined the rankings

MOVIE 09

着眼点
» 設問から，Judges' individual comments「審査員による個別コメント」や Judges' shared evaluation「審査員による共同評価」に注目する。
» 先に選択肢を確認して fact「事実」を除外する。
» 次に残った選択肢の中から本文の内容に合致する opinion「意見」を選ぶ。

解き方
» ①の score は数値の話であり，事実に該当するので除外。
» ②の was agreed on「同意された」というのは事実なので除外。
» ③の really connected with the audience「実に聴衆と一体感があった」というのは主観的な意見だと考えられる。
» ④の determined「決定した」というのは事実なので除外。

» connected に注目して本文を確認すると，Judges' individual comments の中で Mr Hobbs が Silent Hill について，they really seemed connected with the audience「実に聴衆との一体感が生まれているように感じられた」とコメントしている。
» これは Mr Hobbs による主観的な意見なので，正解は③。

023

問5 Which of the following is the final ranking based on the judges' shared evaluation? 10

	1st	2nd	3rd
①	Green Forest	Mountain Pear	Silent Hill
②	Green Forest	Silent Hill	Mountain Pear
③	Mountain Pear	Green Forest	Silent Hill
④	Mountain Pear	Silent Hill	Green Forest
⑤	Silent Hill	Green Forest	Mountain Pear
⑥	Silent Hill	Mountain Pear	Green Forest

MOVIE 10

着眼点

» 設問から，Judges' shared evaluation「審査員の共同評価」に final ranking「最終順位」を決めるヒントがあるとわかる。

解き方

Judges' shared evaluation (summarised by Hobbs)

Each band's total score is the same, but each band is very different. Ms Leigh and I agreed that performance is the most important quality for a band. Ms Wells also agreed. Therefore, first place is easily determined.

To decide between second and third places, Ms Wells suggested that song originality should be more important than good singing. Ms Leigh and I agreed on this opinion.

» 第1段落・第2文に performance is the most important quality for a band「演奏がバンドの最も重要な資質だ」とあり，第3文から全員がこれに賛成したことがわかる。

» よって，演奏がいちばん優れていたバンドが1位になったと判断できる。

Judges' final average scores					
Band names \ Qualities	Performance (5.0)	Singing (5.0)	Song originality (5.0)	Total (15.0)
Green Forest	3.9	4.6	5.0	13.5
Silent Hill	4.9	4.4	4.2	13.5
Mountain Pear	3.9	4.9	4.7	13.5
Thousand Ants	(did not perform)			

≫ Performance「演奏」がいちばん優れていたバンドを知るために最終得点の平均をまとめた１つめの表に戻ると，Silent Hill が 4.9 と最も高いスコアを獲得している。よって１位は Silent Hill だと判断できる。

≫ さらに共同評価の第２段落・第１文では，Ms Wells が song originality should be more important than good singing「曲のオリジナリティーのほうが歌唱のうまさよりも重要であるべきだ」と述べ，第２文から他の審査員２人も同意している。

≫ １つめの表に戻って Song originality に注目すると，最も高い 5.0 を獲得している Green Forest が２位だと判断できる。

≫ １位は Silent Hill，２位は Green Forest，残った Mountain Pear が３位だと判断できるので，正解は⑤。

複雑そうに見える問題も，英文や表から手がかりを探し出せば必ず正解にたどり着けるんだね

令和3年度 大学入学共通テスト 第1日程

第2問B 攻略のプロセス

STEP 1 まずは大問の全体像をつかむ

あらかじめリード文に目を通したうえで、**本文のどこに何が書いてあるかをざっくり把握**しましょう。

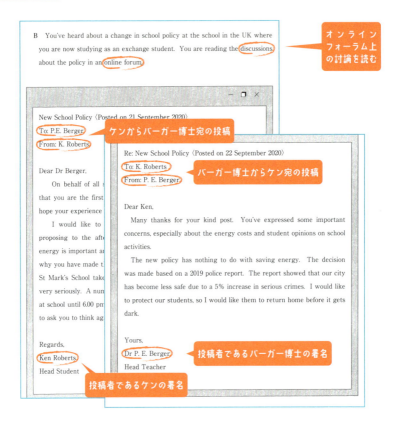

- 学校の方針に関するオンラインフォーラム上の**討論**。
- 1つめの英文は宛先と署名を見ると**ケンからバーガー博士に宛てた投稿**。
- 2つめの英文は**バーガー博士からケンへの返事**。
- **複数の資料**を照らし合わせながら英文を読む。

STEP 2 設問と選択肢を読み解く

続いて設問や選択肢に目を通しましょう。探すべき情報を押さえたうえで英文を読むことで，問題を解く時間を大幅に短縮できます。問2と問4はすでに対策を学んだ fact と opinion を分別するタイプの問題。ここでは問5に注目します。

問5 What would you research to help Ken oppose the new policy? 15

推量の助動詞が設問に含まれていることに注目

① The crime rate and its relation to the local area
② The energy budget and electricity costs of the school
③ The length of school activity time versus the budget
④ The study hours for students who do after-school activities

---

» 設問文に含まれている would に注目。この would は「〜だろう」という推量を表す助動詞。
» 本文に書かれていることから推測して正解を導くタイプの問題である。
» つまり本文に直接正解が書かれているわけではないので，全体の概要を押さえた上で最もふさわしいと考えられる選択肢を選ぶ必要がある。

設問に推量の助動詞が含まれていたら要注意！

027

STEP 3 必要な情報を本文から探しながら小問を解く　難易度 やさしい

問1 Ken thinks the new policy [11] .

① can make students study more
② may improve school safety
③ should be introduced immediately
④ will reduce after-school activity time

MOVIE 11

着眼点
≫ ケンが new policy「新しい方針」をどう考えているかを選ぶ問題。ケンの考えを知るには，ケンが送った1つめの投稿に注目すればよい。

解き方
≫ まず，ケンの投稿で何が述べられているのか確認しよう。

≫ 第1段落ではバーガー博士を歓迎する言葉が述べられている。
≫ 設問に含まれる new policy の話は第1段落にないようなので，第2段落に進もう。

> I would like to express one concern about the change you are proposing to the after-school activity schedule. I realise that saving energy is important and from now it will be getting darker earlier. Is this why you have made the schedule an hour and a half shorter? Students at St Mark's School take both their studies and their after-school activities very seriously. A number of students have told me that they want to stay at school until 6.00 pm as they have always done. Therefore, I would like to ask you to think again about this sudden change in policy.

≫ 第2段落・第1文は I would like to express one concern about...「…に関して，懸念を表明したいと思います」で始まり，the change you are proposing to the after-school activity schedule「放課後の活動スケジュールについてあなた（＝バーガー博士）が提案なさっている変更」と続く。ここから，ケンは放課後の活動スケジュールの変更に対して懸念を示していることがわかる。

>> 続く第3文の you have made the schedule an hour and a half shorter から，変更の具体的内容は「放課後のスケジュールを短くすること」だとわかる。

>> さらに第4文以降を見ていくと，多くの生徒は今までのように学校に残っていたいと話していることがわかる。

>> 最終文では総合した意見として，「方針の急な変更を考え直してほしい」と述べられている。

>> 選択肢の①は「勉強をもっとさせる」，②は「安全性を高める」，③は「直ちに導入されるべき」とどれもポジティブな意見だが，ケンは new policy に対して「考え直してほしい」とネガティブな反応を示していたので不適切。

>> 設問の new policy「新しい方針」が指すのは「放課後のスケジュールを短くすること」なので，④が正解となる。

>> 第3文の you have made the schedule an hour and a half shorter を元に，shorter を reduce「減らす」で，schedule を time「時間」で言い換えている。

029

> **問2** One <u>fact</u> stated in Ken's forum post is that 12 .
>
> ① more discussion is needed about the policy
> ② the Head Teacher's experience is improving the school
> ③ the school should think about students' activities
> ④ there are students who do not welcome the new policy

MOVIE 12

着眼点
» 設問から，ケンの投稿に注目。
» 先に選択肢を確認して opinion「意見」を除外する。
» 次に残った選択肢の中から本文の内容に合致する fact「事実」を選ぶ。

解き方
» ①の is needed「必要である」は主観的なので除外。
» ③には助動詞 should「〜すべき」が入っており，主観的だと判断できるので除外。

> I would like to express one concern about the change you are proposing to the after-school activity schedule. I realise that saving energy is important and from now it will be getting darker earlier. Is this why you have made the schedule an hour and a half shorter? Students at St Mark's School take both their studies and their after-school activities very seriously. A number of students have told me that they want to stay at school until 6.00 pm as they have always done. Therefore, I would like to ask you to think again about this sudden change in policy.

» ケンの投稿の第2段落・第5文 A number of students have told me that they want to stay at school until 6.00 pm as they have always done.「多くの生徒が私に，これまでいつもしてきたように午後6時まで学校に残りたいと言ってきました」に注目。複数の生徒が新しい方針を歓迎していないことがわかるので，正解は④。

» ②はケンが投稿の第1段落で期待していることであって，実際に校長の経験が学校をよくしているかどうかは本文から読み取れない。

問3 Who thinks the aim of the policy is to save energy? 13

① Dr Berger
② Ken
③ The city
④ The police

MOVIE 13

着眼点
≫ 設問から，方針の目的が save energy「エネルギーの節約」だと考えている人を探す。

解き方
≫ エネルギーの節約に該当する情報を探しながら本文を読む。

> I would like to express one concern about the change you are proposing to the after-school activity schedule. I realise that saving energy is important and from now it will be getting darker earlier. Is this why you have made the schedule an hour and a half shorter? Students at St Mark's School take both their studies and their after-school activities very seriously. A number of students have told me that they want to stay at school until 6.00 pm as they have always done. Therefore, I would like to ask you to think again about this sudden change in policy.

≫ ケンの投稿の第2段落・第2文に I realise that saving energy is important「エネルギーを節約することは重要だとわかっている」とあることから，ケンは方針の目的が「エネルギーの節約」にあると考えていると判断できる。よって正解は②。

≫ ①のバーガー博士は，彼の投稿の第2段落・第1文で The new policy has nothing to do with saving energy.「新しい方針はエネルギーの節約とは何の関係もありません」と述べているので不適切。

問4 Dr Berger is basing his new policy on the <u>fact</u> that 14 .

① going home early is important
② safety in the city has decreased
③ the school has to save electricity
④ the students need protection

MOVIE 14

着眼点
» 設問から，バーガー博士の投稿に注目。
» fact「事実」を探せばいいので，まずは opinion に該当する選択肢を除外する。
» 次に残った選択肢の中から本文の内容に合致する fact を選ぶ。

解き方
» ①の important「大切だ」，③の has to「〜しなければならない」，④の need「必要だ」は主観的なので除外できる。

» バーガー博士の投稿の第2段落で new policy が話題に上がっている。

> The new policy has nothing to do with saving energy. The decision was made based on a 2019 police report. The report showed that our city has become less safe due to a 5% increase in serious crimes. I would like to protect our students, so I would like them to return home before it gets dark.

» 目的が電力削減ではないことを述べたあと，第2文に The decision was made based on a 2019 police report.「この決定は2019年の警察の報告書にもとづいてなされました」とある。その報告書には our city has become less safe due to a 5% increase in serious crimes「重大犯罪が5パーセント増えたことにより，私たちの市は以前より安全ではなくなってきている」と書かれており，この報告を根拠にしてバーガー博士は生徒を守るため新しい方針を提案したと考えられる。

» つまり新しい方針が提案されたのは市の安全性が減少しているためだと判断できるので，正解は②。

問5 What would you research to help Ken oppose the new policy? 15

① The crime rate and its relation to the local area
② The energy budget and electricity costs of the school
③ The length of school activity time versus the budget
④ The study hours for students who do after-school activities

MOVIE 15

着眼点

» 設問に would「〜だろう」という推量の表現があるので，本文の情報をヒントに最もふさわしい選択肢を選ぶ必要がある。
» 新しい方針に反対するケンの手助けになることを探す。

解き方

» 「放課後のスケジュールを短くする」という新しい方針が提案された理由を，ケンはエネルギー節約のためだと考えていた。しかしバーガー博士によると地域の犯罪率が上がっており，生徒の安全を守るために新しい方針を提案したという。
» ケンが反論するためには，バーガー博士が根拠としている安全性に関する知識を得なければならない。
» よって地域の犯罪率に関する選択肢である①が正解。

» ②の energy budget は関係ないとバーガー博士が投稿の第2段落・第1文で述べているので不適切。
» ③の「活動時間と予算の関係」や，④の「放課後の勉強時間」については本文で言及されていないので不適切。

本文に直接正解が書かれていない問題も，本文の内容を踏まえて考えれば解けることが実感できたかな？

令和3年度 大学入学共通テスト 第1日程
第3問A 攻略のプロセス

STEP 1 まずは大問の全体像をつかむ

あらかじめ<u>リード文</u>に目を通したうえで，<u>本文のどこに何が書いてあるか</u>をざっくり把握しましょう。

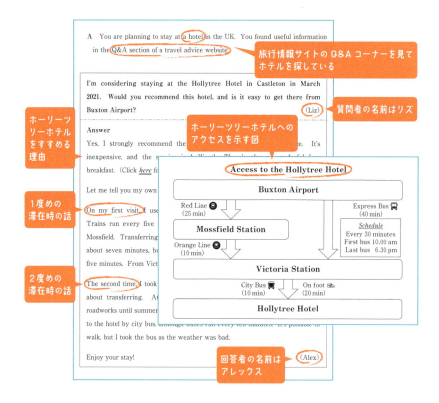

- 🎓 イギリスで滞在する**ホテルを探している**というシチュエーション。
- 旅行情報サイトの **Q&A** らしき英文の後に，**ホテルへのアクセスマップ**がついている。
- **複数の資料**を照らし合わせながら英文を読む。

STEP 2 設問と選択肢を読み解く

続いて設問や選択肢に目を通しましょう。探すべき情報を押さえたうえで英文を読むことで，問題を解く時間を大幅に短縮できます。

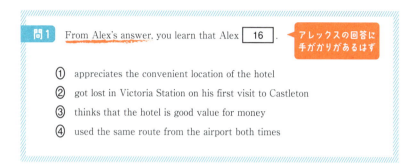

問1　From Alex's answer, you learn that Alex ⬚16⬚.
　アレックスの回答に手がかりがあるはず

① appreciates the convenient location of the hotel
② got lost in Victoria Station on his first visit to Castleton
③ thinks that the hotel is good value for money
④ used the same route from the airport both times

» ざっくりとした尋ね方になっている設問の部分からは，アレックスの回答に手がかりがあることくらいしか読み取ることができない。
» 一方，選択肢はバラバラで情報量が多いので，正誤判定を慎重に行う。

問2　You are departing on public transport from the airport at 2.00 pm on 15 March 2021. What is the fastest way to get to the hotel? ⬚17⬚
　条件らしき日時
　最速の行き方が求められているので時間の表現に注目

① By express bus and city bus
② By express bus and on foot
③ By underground and city bus
④ By underground and on foot

» ホテルまでの最速の移動手段を探す問題。
» 具体的な日時が指定されているので，この条件に関する記述が本文のどこかにあるはず。時間の表現に注意しながら本文とアクセスマップを読み解く。

設問に含まれる具体的な情報は必ずチェック！

035

STEP 3 必要な情報を本文から探しながら小問を解く

問1 From Alex's answer, you learn that Alex ⬚16⬚ .

① appreciates the convenient location of the hotel
② got lost in Victoria Station on his first visit to Castleton
③ thinks that the hotel is good value for money
④ used the same route from the airport both times

MOVIE 16

着眼点

≫ From Alex's answer「アレックスの回答から」という設問の出だしから，彼が書いた回答に注目する。

解き方

≫ アレックスの回答を見ていくと，地下鉄がconvenient「便利」だという話は第3段落・第1文にあるが，「ホテルのロケーションが便利だ」とはどこでも言っていないので①は不適切。

≫ ②に含まれるVictoria駅や最初の訪問については，アレックスの回答の第3段落で書かれている。

> On my first visit, I used the underground, which is cheap and convenient. Trains run every five minutes. From the airport, I took the Red Line to Mossfield. Transferring to the Orange Line for Victoria should normally take about seven minutes, but the directions weren't clear and I needed an extra five minutes. From Victoria, it was a ten-minute bus ride to the hotel.

≫ 第3~4文からアレックスはRed LineでMossfield駅へ行き，そこからOrange LineでVictoria駅行きの地下鉄に乗り換えるときに迷ったことがわかる。つまり迷ったのはVictoria駅ではなくMossfield駅なので，②は不適切。

≫ ③について，アレックスは第1段落でホテルのサービスに言及している。

> **Answer**
> Yes, I strongly recommend the Hollytree. I've stayed there twice. It's inexpensive, and the service is brilliant! There's also a wonderful free breakfast. (Click *here* for access information.)

» 第3文で It's inexpensive, and the service is brilliant!「高くないですし，サービスは立派です！」とホテルの価格とサービスを褒めている。

» これを the hotel is good value for money「ホテルは値段の割に価値がある」と言い換えた③が正解。

» 第3段落からアレックスは1度めは地下鉄で，第4段落から2度めは高速バスでホテルへ向かっていることがわかるので，④は不適切。

選択肢からキーワードを拾う→本文のどこに登場するかを探す→正しいかどうかをすばやく判断できる！

問2 You are departing on public transport from the airport at 2.00 pm on 15 March 2021. What is the fastest way to get to the hotel? ｜ 17 ｜

① By express bus and city bus
② By express bus and on foot
③ By underground and city bus
④ By underground and on foot

MOVIE 17

着眼点
》設問に含まれる「2021年3月15日の午後2時」という条件に注意しながら，ホテルへ行く最も速い方法を選ぶ。

解き方
》設問に含まれる2021という数字は，アレックスの回答の第4段落に登場する。

> The second time, I took the express bus to Victoria, so I didn't have to worry about transferring. At Victoria, I found a notice saying there would be roadworks until summer 2021. Now it takes three times as long as usual to get to the hotel by city bus, although buses run every ten minutes. It's possible to walk, but I took the bus as the weather was bad.
>
> Enjoy your stay! 　　　　　　　　　　　　　　　　　　　　　（Alex）

》第2文から，道路工事のため2021年の夏まではVictoria駅からホテルまでcity busを使うと通常の3倍の時間がかかることがわかる。
》アクセスマップによるとVictoria駅からホテルまではcity busで通常10分かかるので，2021年3月には3倍の30分かかることがわかる。
》20分かかる徒歩の方が速いので，city busを含む選択肢の①と③は除外できる。

≫ さらに選択肢を絞り込むためには，空港から Victoria 駅まで express bus「高速バス」と underground「地下鉄」のどちらが速いかを見極めればよい。

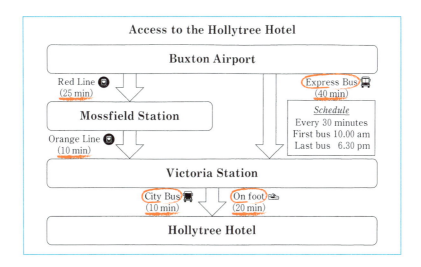

≫ 空港から Victoria 駅までは高速バスで 40 分かかる。
≫ 地下鉄を使う場合は Mossfield 駅まで 25 分，Victoria 駅まで 10 分かかることがアクセスマップからわかる。
≫ さらにアレックスの回答の第 3 段落・第 4 文 Transferring to the Orange Line for Victoria should normally take about seven minutes「ヴィクトリア行きのオレンジ線に乗り換えるには通常 7 分ほどかかるはずです」から，Red Line から Orange Line への乗り換えに about seven minutes「約 7 分」かかることがわかる。
≫ Victoria 駅まで地下鉄を使う場合の所要時間を計算すると 25 ＋ 10 ＋ 7 ＝ 42 分となるため，地下鉄より高速バスの方が速い。

≫ 以上より，express bus と on foot を組み合わせた②が正解。

令和3年度 大学入学共通テスト 第1日程
第3問 B 攻略のプロセス

STEP 1 まずは大問の全体像をつかむ

あらかじめリード文に目を通したうえで，本文のどこに何が書いてあるかをざっくり把握しましょう。

交換留学生が書いたニュースレター

B Your classmate showed you the following message in your school's newsletter, written by an exchange student from the UK.

ボランティアを募集しているらしい

Volunteers Wanted!

Hello, everyone. I'm Sarah King, an exchange student from London. I'd like to share something important with you today.

You may have heard of the Sakura International Centre. It provides valuable opportunities for Japanese and foreign residents to get to know each other. Popular events such as cooking classes and karaoke contests are held every month. However, there is a serious problem. The building is getting old, and requires expensive repairs. To help raise funds to maintain the centre, many volunteers are needed.

I learnt about the problem a few months ago. While shopping in town, I saw some people taking part in a fund-raising campaign. I spoke to the leader of the campaign, Katy, who explained the situation. She thanked me when I donated some money. She told me that they had asked the town mayor for financial assistance, but their request had been rejected. They had no choice but to start fund-raising.

Last month, I attended a lecture on art at the centre. Again, I saw people trying to raise money, and I decided to help. They were happy when I joined them in asking passers-by for donations. We tried hard, but there were too few of us to collect much money. With a tearful face, Katy told me that they wouldn't be able to use the building much longer. I felt the need to do something more. Then, the idea came to me that other students might be willing to help. Katy was delighted to hear this.

Now, I'm asking you to join me in the fund-raising campaign to help the Sakura International Centre. Please email me today! As an exchange student, my time in Japan is limited, but I want to make the most of it. By working together, we can really make a difference.

Class 3 A
Sarah King (sarahk@sakura-h.ed.jp)

筆者の署名

🎓 ● 交換留学生が書いた学校の**ニュースレター**を読む。
　● Volunteers Wanted!「ボランティア募集！」というタイトルからわかるとおり，**ボランティアを募集している**ようだ。

STEP 3 必要な情報を本文から探しながら小問を解く

問1 Put the following events (①〜④) into the order in which they happened.

18 → 19 → 20 → 21

① Sarah attended a centre event.
② Sarah donated money to the centre.
③ Sarah made a suggestion to Katy.
④ The campaigners asked the mayor for help.

MOVIE 18

着眼点
» 実際に起った順番に出来事を並べる設問。
» 先に選択肢に目を通した上で，時間を表す表現や時制に注意しながら本文を読む。

解き方
» ニュースレターの第3段落・第1文に，a few months ago「数か月前」という時間の表現が登場する。

> I learnt about the problem a few months ago. While shopping in town, I saw some people taking part in a fund-raising campaign. I spoke to the leader of the campaign, Katy, who explained the situation. She thanked me when I donated some money. She told me that they had asked the town mayor for financial assistance, but their request had been rejected. They had no choice but to start

» さらに読み進めると，第2〜3文からセーラは町で資金集めをしている人々を見かけてリーダーであるケイティと知り合ったことがわかる。
» 第4文の She thanked me when I donated some money.「私がいくらかお金を寄付すると，感謝してくれました」は，選択肢の②に該当する。

第1日程　第3問B　攻略のプロセス

STEP 2 設問と選択肢を読み解く

続いて設問や選択肢に目を通しましょう。探すべき情報を押さえたうえで英文を読むことで，問題を解く時間を大幅に短縮できます。ここでは問1に注目します。

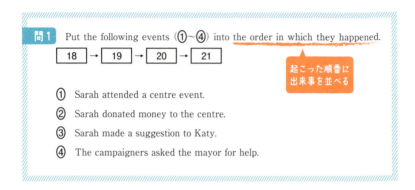

問1 Put the following events (①〜④) into the order in which they happened.

18 → 19 → 20 → 21

（起こった順番に出来事を並べる）

① Sarah attended a centre event.
② Sarah donated money to the centre.
③ Sarah made a suggestion to Katy.
④ The campaigners asked the mayor for help.

≫ 出来事を時系列順に並べるタイプの問題。
≫ 時間の表現や時制に注意しながら英文を読む。

本文に出てきた順番＝出来事が起こった順番とは限らないことに注意！

≫ 続く第5文 She told me that they had asked the town mayor for financial assistance「彼らは町長に経済的支援を求めたと私に話してくれました」は選択肢の④に該当する。時制に注目すると，had asked と過去完了形が使われているので，ケイティたちが町長に支援を求めたのは資金集め運動をする前の出来事。よって，④は②より前に起こったと判断できる。

≫ 時間の表現を探しながら読み進めると，第4段落の冒頭に目が止まるはず。

> Last month, I attended a lecture on art at the centre. Again, I saw people trying to raise money, and I decided to help. They were happy when I joined them in asking passers-by for donations. We tried hard, but there were too few of us to collect much money. With a tearful face, Katy told me that they wouldn't be able to use the building much longer. I felt the need to do something more. Then, the idea came to me that other students might be willing to help. Katy was delighted to hear this.

≫ 第1文 Last month, I attended a lecture on art at the centre.「先月，私はセンターで行われたアートについての講義に参加しました」が選択肢の①に該当する。これは先月の出来事なので，数か月前の出来事であった②よりも最近の話だと判断できる。

≫ 残った③に該当する箇所を探して本文を読み進めると，第7文が Then「それから」と時間の経過を表す表現ではじまっている。Then, the idea came to me that other students might be willing to help. Katy was delighted to hear this.「それから，他の生徒も喜んで手助けをしてくれるかもしれない，という考えを思いつきました。ケイティはこれを聞いて喜んでいました」という内容を「セーラはケイティに提案をした」とまとめた選択肢が③である。

≫ よって正解は④→②→①→③の順。

043

問2 From Sarah's message, you learn that the Sakura International Centre 22 .

① gives financial aid to international residents
② offers opportunities to develop friendships
③ publishes newsletters for the community
④ sends exchange students to the UK

MOVIE 19

着眼点
» サクラ国際センターについて説明する正しい選択肢を選ぶ問題。
» サクラ国際センターがどういう施設か詳しく書かれている箇所を探す。

解き方
» サクラ国際センターについては，第2段落で詳しく説明されている。

> You may have heard of the Sakura International Centre. <u>It provides valuable opportunities for Japanese and foreign residents to get to know each other.</u> Popular events such as cooking classes and karaoke contests are held every month. However, there is a serious problem. The building is getting old, and requires expensive repairs. To help raise funds to maintain the centre, many volunteers are needed.

» 第2文にある It provides valuable opportunities for Japanese and foreign residents to get to know each other.「センターは日本人と在留外国人がお互いを知る貴重な機会を提供しています」に注目。get to know each other を develop friendships「親交を深める」と言い換えた②が正解。
» 第5文に「建物が老朽化しつつあり，高額な修理が必要なのです」とあり，住人に援助をする余裕はなさそうだと推測できるため①は不適切。
» 地域社会向けのニュースレターに関する記述はないので③は不適切。
» イギリスに交換留学生を送っているという記述はないので④は不適切。

難易度 やさしい

問3 You have decided to help with the campaign after reading Sarah's message. What should you do first? 23

① Advertise the events at the centre.
② Contact Sarah for further information.
③ Organise volunteer activities at school.
④ Start a new fund-raising campaign.

MOVIE 20

着眼点

» 「セーラのメッセージを読んだ後で,キャンペーンを手助けするために何をすべきか」という設問。
» 第4段落まで読み進めてきてまだ書かれていない情報なので,まだ読んでいない第5段落に手がかりがあるはず。

解き方

> Now, I'm asking you to join me in the fund-raising campaign to help the Sakura International Centre. Please email me today! As an exchange student, my time in Japan is limited, but I want to make the most of it. By working together, we can really make a difference.

» 第5段落・第1文で資金集めのキャンペーンを手伝ってほしいと伝えた後の第2文に Please email me today!「今日,私にメールを送ってください!」とある。
» キャンペーンの手助けがしたい生徒は,まずセーラにメールをすればよいとわかるので,email me を contact Sarah「セーラに連絡する」と言い換えた②が正解。

» イベントの宣伝についてはどこにも書かれていないので,①は不適切。
» 自分で行動を起こすのではなく,セーラと一緒に募金活動に参加するためにメールを送ってほしいというのが第5段落の主旨なので,③や④は不適切。

令和3年度 大学入学共通テスト 第1日程
第4問 攻略のプロセス

 STEP 1 まずは大問の全体像をつかむ

あらかじめリード文に目を通したうえで，本文のどこに何が書いてあるかをざっくり把握しましょう。

> 予定を立てるためのメールのやり取り

Your English teacher, Emma, has asked you and your classmate, Natsuki, to help her plan the day's schedule for hosting students from your sister school. You're reading the email exchanges between Natsuki and Emma so that you can draft the schedule.

> 宛名はエマ

Hi Emma,

We have some ideas and questions about the schedule for the day out with our 12 guests next month. As you told us, the students from both schools are supposed to give presentations in our assembly hall from 10:00 a.m. So, I've been looking at the attached timetable. Will they arrive at Azuma Station at 9:39 a.m. and then take a taxi to the school?

We have also been discussing the afternoon activities. How about seeing something related to science? We have two ideas, but if you need a third, please let me know.

Have you heard about the special exhibition that is on at Westside Aquarium next month? It's about a new food supplement made from sea plankton. We think it would be a good choice. Since it's popular, the best time to visit will be when it is least busy. I'm attaching the graph I found on the aquarium's homepage.

Eastside Botanical Garden, together with our local university, has been developing an interesting way of producing electricity from plants. Luckily, the professor in charge will give a short talk about it on that day in the early afternoon! Why don't we go?

Everyone will want to get some souvenirs, won't they? I think West Mall, next to Hibari Station, would be best, but we don't want to carry them around with us all day.

Finally, every visitor to Azuma should see the town's symbol, the statue in Azuma Memorial Park next to our school, but we can't work out a good schedule. Also, could you tell us what the plan is for lunch?

Yours,
Natsuki

> 差出人はナツキ

Hi Natsuki,

Thank you for your email! You've been working hard. In answer to your question, they'll arrive at the station at 9:20 a.m. and then catch the school bus.

The two main afternoon locations, the aquarium and botanical garden, are good ideas because both schools place emphasis on science education, and the purpose of this program is to improve the scientific knowledge of the students. However, it would be wise to have a third suggestion just in case.

Let's get souvenirs at the end of the day. We can take the bus to the mall arriving there at 5:00 p.m. This will allow almost an hour for shopping and our guests can still be back at the hotel by 6:30 p.m. for dinner, as the hotel is only a few minutes' walk from Kaede Station.

About lunch, the school cafeteria will provide boxed lunches. We can eat under the statue you mentioned. If it rains, let's eat inside.

Thank you so much for your suggestions. Could you two make a draft for the schedule?

Best,
Emma

Attached timetable:

Train Timetable
Kaede — Hibari — Azuma

Stations	Train No.			
	108	109	110	111
Kaede	8:28	8:43	9:02	9:16
Hibari	8:50	9:05	9:24	9:38
Azuma	9:05	9:20	9:39	9:53

Stations	238
Azuma	17:25
Hibari	17:40
Kaede	18:02

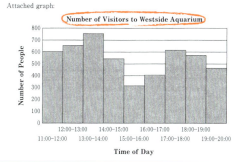

STEP 2 設問と選択肢を読み解く

続いて設問や選択肢に目を通しましょう。探すべき情報を押さえたうえで英文を読むことで、問題を解く時間を大幅に短縮できます。ここでは問5に注目します。

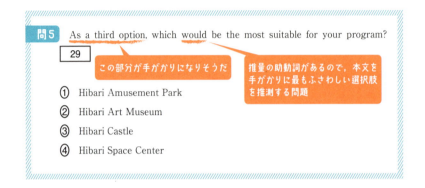

» 設問文に含まれている would は「〜だろう」という推量を表す助動詞。
» 本文に書かれていることから推測して正解を導くタイプの問題である。
» つまり本文に直接正解が書かれているわけではないので、全体の概要を押さえた上で最もふさわしいと考えられる選択肢を選ぶ必要がある。

» この設問では、As a third option「3つめの選択肢として」の部分に注目。
» 「3つめの選択肢」に言及している箇所を探したり、他の2つの選択肢を探したりすることで、効率よく正解にたどり着けるはず。

やみくもに本文を読んでいくと時間切れになってしまうから、必ず先に設問をチェックすることを心がけよう

STEP 3 必要な情報を本文から探しながら小問を解く

問1 The guests from the sister school will arrive on the number 24 train and catch the number 25 train back to their hotel.

① 109　　② 110　　③ 111
④ 238　　⑤ 239　　⑥ 240

MOVIE 21　　MOVIE 22

着眼点

» 姉妹校からの来校客が乗る**行き帰りの電車の番号**を選ぶ問題。
» 1日の予定を時系列に沿って説明する場合，行きの電車についてはメールの最初の方に，帰りの電車については最後の方に書かれていると予想できる。

解き方

» 行きの電車については，ナツキからのメールの第1段落に言及がある。

> Hi Emma,
>
> We have some ideas and questions about the schedule for the day out with our 12 guests next month. As you told us, the students from both schools are supposed to give presentations in our assembly hall from 10:00 a.m. So, I've been looking at the attached timetable. Will they arrive at Azuma Station at 9:39 a.m. and then take a taxi to the school?

» 第4文に Will they arrive at Azuma Station at 9:39 a.m. and then take a taxi to the school?「彼らはアズマ駅に午前9時39分に到着して，それから学校までタクシーに乗るのでしょうか？」という質問がある。
» この質問に対する返事を探して，エマのメールを確認する。メールの場合，最初の方で質問されたことに対しては，最初の方で返事が書かれていることが多い。

> Hi Natsuki,
>
> Thank you for your email! You've been working hard. In answer to your question, they'll arrive at the station at 9:20 a.m. and then catch the school bus.

049

≫ 第1段落・第3文に In answer to your question, they'll arrive at the station at 9:20 a.m. and then catch the school bus.「質問の答えですが，彼らは駅に午前9時20分に到着し，それからスクールバスに乗ります」とある。

≫ つまり行きの電車は**アズマ駅に午前9時20分に到着**することがわかる。

≫ 1つめの時刻表を見ると，この時間にアズマ駅につく電車は**109号**である。

Train Timetable

Kaede — Hibari — Azuma

Stations	Train No.			
	108	109	110	111
Kaede	8:28	8:43	9:02	9:16
Hibari	8:50	9:05	9:24	9:38
Azuma	9:05	9:20	9:39	9:53

≫ 帰りの電車については，エマのメールの第3段落に言及がある。

> Let's get souvenirs at the end of the day. We can take the bus to the mall arriving there at 5:00 p.m. This will allow almost an hour for shopping and our guests can still be back at the hotel by 6:30 p.m. for dinner, as the hotel is only a few minutes' walk from Kaede Station.

≫ 第3文に our guests can still be back at the hotel by 6:30 p.m. for dinner, as the hotel is only a few minutes' walk from Kaede Station.「ホテルはカエデ駅から徒歩でわずか数分のところにあるので，来校客は午後6時30分の夕食までに戻る余裕があります」とある。

≫ つまり帰りの電車は**午後6時30分の数分前にカエデ駅に着けばよい**。

Stations	Train No.			
	238	239	240	241
Azuma	17:25	17:45	18:00	18:15
Hibari	17:40	18:00	18:15	18:30
Kaede	18:02	18:22	18:37	18:52

≫ 2つめの時刻表を見ると，この条件に合致するのは18時22分にカエデ駅に到着する**239号**の電車である。

≫ よって**正解は①と⑤**。

難易度 ふつう

問2 Which best completes the draft schedule? 26

A：The aquarium　　　B：The botanical garden
C：The mall　　　　　D：The school

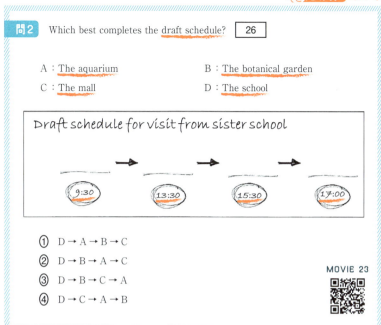

① D → A → B → C
② D → B → A → C
③ D → B → C → A
④ D → C → A → B

MOVIE 23

着眼点
» 姉妹校の生徒たちの予定表を埋める問題。
» 水族館や植物園，モールや学校といった選択肢に並ぶ施設や，予定表の空所の下にある時刻に注意しながら本文を読む。

解き方
» 選択肢はどれもDではじまっているので，出発地である9時30分の空所に入るのはDの学校だと判断できる。
» 念のため確認すると，午前中に学校で過ごすことは，ナツキのメールの第1段落・第2文の「お話いただいたように，両校の生徒は午前10時から私たちの講堂でプレゼンテーションをすることになっています」という内容や，エマのメールの第1段落・第3文の「彼らは駅に午前9時20分に到着し，それからスクールバスに乗ります」という内容によって裏づけられる。
» Aの水族館は，ナツキのメールの第3段落に登場するWestside Aquarium「ウエストサイド水族館」を指す。

> Have you heard about the special exhibition that is on at Westside Aquarium next month? It's about a new food supplement made from sea plankton. We think it would be a good choice. Since it's popular, the best time to visit will be when it is least busy. I'm attaching the graph I found on the aquarium's homepage.

≫ 第4文 Since it's popular, the best time to visit will be when it is least busy. 「人気なので, いちばん混雑していない時間に訪れるのがよいでしょう」から, 水族館の混雑具合を確かめれば正解にたどり着く。

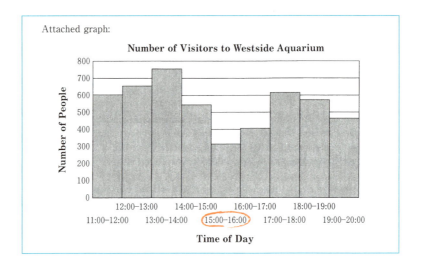

Attached graph:

Number of Visitors to Westside Aquarium

≫ 第5文で言及されているグラフを見ると, 水族館が一番忙しくないのは15時から16時の間である。よって予定表の空所のうち, この時間帯に該当する15時30分の空所にAのThe aquariumが入る。

≫ ナツキからのメールの第4段落では, Eastside Botanical Garden「イーストサイド植物園」の話をしている。

> Eastside Botanical Garden, together with our local university, has been developing an interesting way of producing electricity from plants. Luckily, the professor in charge will give a short talk about it on that day in the early afternoon! Why don't we go?

≫ 第2〜3文 Luckily, the professor in charge will give a short talk about it on

» that day in the early afternoon! Why don't we go?「運のいいことに，責任者である教授がそれについて当日の午後の早い時間に短い講演をするそうです！ 私たちも行ってみませんか？」から，ナツキは午後の早い時間に植物園を訪れることを提案している。

» エマのメールを確認すると，第2段落・第1文で水族館と植物園の訪問に賛成していることがわかる。よって予定表の空所のうち，午後の早い時間に該当する13時30分の空所にBのThe botanical gardenが入る。

» 残るThe mallは，ナツキのメールの第5段階に登場する。

> Everyone will want to get some souvenirs, won't they? I think West Mall, next to Hibari Station, would be best, but we don't want to carry them around with us all day.

» 第2文では，we don't want to carry them around with us all day「一日中それ（お土産）を持ち歩きたくはありません」とお土産を持って移動することの面倒さに言及している。

» この発言を受けて，エマはメールの第3段落・第1文でLet's get souvenirs at the end of the day.「お土産はその日の最後に買うことにしましょう」と返事をしていることから，モールを訪れるのは1日の最後になると判断できる。よって予定表の空所のうち最後の17時の空所に入るのはCのThe mallである。

» 以上から，正解は②のD→B→A→Cである。

手がかりをひとつずつ丁寧に追っていけば，どんな問題も解ける！

問3 Unless it rains, the guests will eat lunch in the 　27　 .

① botanical garden
② park next to the school
③ park next to the station
④ school garden

MOVIE 24

着眼点
» 姉妹校の生徒たちが昼食を食べる場所を選ぶ問題。
» Unless it rains「もし雨が降らなければ」という条件に注意する。

解き方
» 昼食については，ナツキからのメールの第6段落に言及がある。

> Finally, every visitor to Azuma should see the town's symbol, the statue in Azuma Memorial Park next to our school, but we can't work out a good schedule. Also, could you tell us what the plan is for lunch?
>
> Yours,
> Natsuki

» 第1文で学校の隣の公園にある町のシンボルの像に触れ，第2文で Also, could you tell us what the plan is for lunch?「それから，昼食の予定がどうなっているのか教えていただけますか？」と問いかけている。

» この質問を受けて，エマはメールの第4段落で About the lunch, the school cafeteria will provide boxed lunches. We can eat under the statue you mentioned. If it rains, let's eat inside.「昼食については，学校の食堂が昼食のお弁当を提供します。あなたが話に出していた像の下で食べられます。もし雨が降ったら，屋内で食べましょう」と答えている。

» つまり雨が降らなかった場合はナツキが言及した像の下でお弁当を食べるということ。

» ナツキのメールの第6段落・第1文 the statue in Azuma Memorial Park next to our school から，像は学校の隣の公園にあることがわかる。
» よって正解は，② の park next to the school である。

難易度 ふつう

問4 The guests will **not** get around ｜ 28 ｜ on that day.

① by bus
② by taxi
③ by train
④ on foot

MOVIE 25

着眼点

≫ 選択肢に並ぶ様々な交通手段の中から，姉妹校の生徒たちが利用しないものを選ぶ設問。

解き方

≫ エマのメールの第1段落・第3文や第3段落・第2文から，①のバスは利用すると判断できる。

≫ ②のタクシーはナツキのメールの第1段落・第4文に登場する。しかし，問1でも確認したとおり，エマのメールの第1段落・第3文によると，生徒たちは駅から学校まではタクシーではなくバスを使用するということになっていた。

≫ ③の電車を利用するのは，問1で行きと帰りの電車番号を選んだことからも明らか。

≫ エマからのメールの第3段落・第3文 the hotel is only a few minutes' walk from Kaede Station「ホテルはカエデ駅から徒歩でわずか数分のところにあるので」から，駅からホテルまでは徒歩で帰ることがわかるので，生徒たちは④の徒歩でも移動する。

≫ 以上より，利用しない交通手段は②のタクシーである。

055

> **問5** As a third option, which would be the most suitable for your program?
> 29
>
> ① Hibari Amusement Park
> ② Hibari Art Museum
> ③ Hibari Castle
> ④ Hibari Space Center

MOVIE 26

着眼点

» 設問の As a third option「3つめの選択肢として」という部分に注意しながら，ふさわしい施設の条件を探して本文を読む。
» 設問に含まれる助動詞の would から，本文に書かれていることを根拠に推測して最もふさわしい正解を選ぶ問題だとわかる。

解き方

» **third option** については，ナツキのメールの第2段落で言及がある。

> We have also been discussing the afternoon activities. How about seeing something related to science? We have two ideas, but if you need a third, please let me know.

» 第3文に We have two ideas, but if you need a third, please let me know.「2つのアイデアがありますが，もし3つめが必要でしたら教えてください」とある。
» two ideas「2つのアイデア」というのは，続く第3〜4段落で詳しく説明している水族館と植物園を指す。
» ナツキが水族館と植物園を提案した理由は，第2文 How about seeing something related to science?「科学に関するものを見学するのはどうでしょうか？」から，科学に関係した施設であるためと考えられる。
» つまり，「3つめの選択肢」も科学に関する施設のはずだと推測できる。

≫ このナツキの提案に対して，エマはメールの第2段落で賛成している。

> The two main afternoon locations, the aquarium and botanical garden, are good ideas because both schools place emphasis on science education, and the purpose of this program is to improve the scientific knowledge of the students. However, it would be wise to have a third suggestion just in case.

≫ 第1文から姉妹校がどちらも科学教育に力を入れていること，プログラムの目的が生徒の科学知識の向上であることがわかるので，やはり3つめの選択肢としてふさわしいのは科学に関連する施設だと判断できる。

≫ 選択肢のなかで最も科学に関連が深い施設は Hibari Space Center「ヒバリ宇宙センター」だと推測できるので，正解は④。

共通テストでは本文中には出てこないものが正解になることもあるんだね

ENGLISH READING
PART 5

令和3年度 大学入学共通テスト 第1日程
第5問 攻略のプロセス

STEP 1 まずは大問の全体像をつかむ

あらかじめリード文に目を通したうえで，本文のどこに何が書いてあるかをざっくり把握しましょう。

ニュース記事を読んでプレゼン資料をまとめる

Using an international news report, you are going to take part in an English oral presentation contest. Read the following news story from France in preparation for your talk.

　Five years ago, Mrs. Sabine Rouas lost her horse. She had spent 20 years with the horse before he died of old age. At that time, she felt that she could never own another horse. Out of loneliness, she spent hours watching cows on a nearby milk farm. Then, one day, she asked the farmer if she could help look after them.

　The farmer agreed, and Sabine started work. She quickly developed a friendship with one of the cows. As the cow was pregnant, she spent more time with it than with the others. After the cow's baby was born, the baby started following Sabine around. Unfortunately, the farmer wasn't interested in keeping a bull—a male cow—on a milk farm. The farmer planned to sell the baby bull, which he called Three-oh-nine (309), to a meat market. Sabine decided she wasn't going to let that happen, so she asked the farmer if she could buy him and his mother. The farmer agreed, and she bought them. Sabine then started taking 309 for walks to town. About nine months later, when at last she had permission to move the animals, they moved to Sabine's farm.

　Soon after, Sabine was offered a pony. At first, she wasn't sure if she wanted to have him, but the memory of her horse was no longer painful, so she accepted the pony and named him Leon. She then decided to return to her old hobby and started training him for show jumping. Three-oh-nine, who she had renamed Aston, spent most of his time with Leon, and the two became really close friends. However, Sabine had not expected Aston to pay close attention to her training routine with Leon, nor had she expected Aston to pick up some tricks. The young bull quickly mastered walking, galloping, stopping, going backwards, and turning around on command. He responded to Sabine's voice just like a horse. And despite weighing 1,300 kg, it took him just 18 months to learn how to leap over one-meter-high horse jumps with Sabine on his back. Aston might never have learned those things without having watched Leon. Moreover, Aston understood distance and could adjust his steps before a jump. He also noticed his faults and corrected them without any help from Sabine. That's something only the very best Olympic-standard horses can do.

　Now Sabine and Aston go to weekend fairs and horse shows around Europe to show off his skills. Sabine says, "We get a good reaction. Mostly, people are really surprised, and at first, they can be a bit scared because he's big—much bigger than a horse. Most people don't like to get too close to bulls with horns. But once they see his real nature, and see him performing, they often say, 'Oh he's really quite beautiful.'"

"Look!" And Sabine shows a photo of Aston on her smartphone. She then continues, "When Aston was very young, I used to take him out for walks on a lead, like a dog, so that he would get used to humans. Maybe that's why he doesn't mind people. Because he is so calm, children, in particular, really like watching him and getting a chance to be close to him."

Over the last few years, news of the massive show-jumping bull has spread rapidly; now, Aston is a major attraction with a growing number of online followers. Aston and Sabine sometimes need to travel 200 or 300 kilometers away from home, which means they have to stay overnight. Aston has to sleep in a horse box, which isn't really big enough for him.

"He doesn't like it. I have to sleep with him in the box," says Sabine. "But you know, when he wakes up and changes position, he is very careful not to crush me. He really is very gentle. He sometimes gets lonely, and he doesn't like being away from Leon for too long; but other than that, he's very happy."

Your Presentation Slides

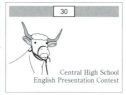

30

Central High School
English Presentation Contest

Who's Who?

Main figures

☐ · ☐ · ☐

Minor figures   31

☐ · ☐

Pre-fame Storyline

Sabine's horse dies.

32
33
34
35

Aston and Sabine start going to shows.

Aston's Abilities

Aston can:
· learn by simply watching Leon's training.
· walk, gallop, and stop when Sabine tells him to.
· understand distance and adjust his steps.
· 36
· 37

Aston Now

Aston today:
· is a show-jumping bull.
· travels to fairs and events with Sabine.
· 38

STEP 2 設問と選択肢を読み解く

続いて設問や選択肢に目を通しましょう。探すべき情報を押さえたうえで英文を読むことで、問題を解く時間を大幅に短縮できます。ここでは問2と問3に注目します。

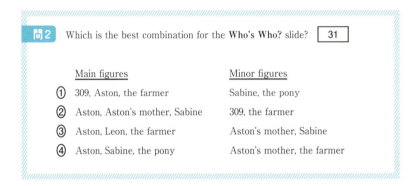

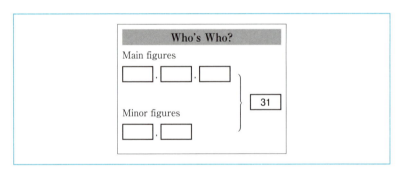

» 設問文を読むと、Who's Who?「誰が誰？」というタイトルになっている2枚めのスライドを埋めればよいことがわかる。
» スライドの中身を見ると、Main figures「主役」の下に空所が3つ、Minor figures「脇役」の下に空所が2つある。
» 以上から、選択肢に並ぶ5名の登場人物を、主役と脇役に分別する問題だと判断できる。
» 選択肢に注目すると、309という謎の数字もあれば、Aston や Aston's mother、Sabine や Leon といった固有名詞、さらに the farmer や the pony といった一般名詞が並ぶ。
» これらに該当する人物や動物を探しながら、主役と言えそうかどうかを適宜判断して物語を読み進めていく。

問3 Choose the four events in the order they happened to complete the Pre-fame Storyline slide. | 32 | ~ | 35 |

有名になるまでの出来事を起こった順番に並べる

① Aston learns to jump.
② Sabine and Aston travel hundreds of kilometers together.
③ Sabine buys 309 and his mother.
④ Sabine goes to work on her neighbor's farm.
⑤ Sabine takes 309 for walks.

最初と最後の出来事は記入済みなので，その間の出来事が書かれている箇所を本文から探す

》 出来事を時系列順に並べるタイプの問題。
》 時間の表現や時制に注意しながら英文を読む。
》 スライドにはあらかじめ最初の出来事と最後の出来事が書かれている。
》 これらの出来事が本文のどこに書かれているかを探して，その間に書かれている内容と選択肢を照らし合わせると効率がよい。

手がかりはプレゼン用のスライドの中にもあるよ！

STEP 3 必要な情報を本文から探しながら小問を解く

 難易度 難しい

問1 Which is the best title for your presentation? 30

① Animal-lover Saves the Life of a Pony
② Aston's Summer Show-jumping Tour
③ Meet Aston, the Bull who Behaves Like a Horse
④ The Relationship Between a Farmer and a Cow

MOVIE 27

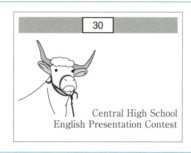

着眼点

》設問とスライドから，プレゼン全体の内容をまとめたタイトルを選ぶ。
》全体に関わる問題なので，英文をすべて読んだ後で最もふさわしい選択肢を選ぶとよい。

タイトル問題は部分的な情報しか書いていない選択肢が正解にならないことに注意

解き方

》サビーヌが救ったのはポニーではなく牛の命なので，①は不適切。
》アストンが出演するショーについては第4段落以降に書かれているが，夏期限定だとはどこにも書かれていないので②も不適切。
》農家と牛の関係性については第2段落で部分的に書かれていたが，物語の全体に関わるものではないため，④も不適切。
》以上より，牛なのに馬のような芸をして注目を集めているアストンの物語全体を端的にまとめた③が正解。

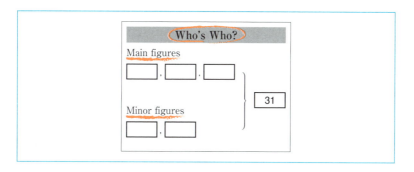

👀 着眼点

» 2枚めのスライドの Who's Who?「誰が誰か？」というタイトルから，登場人物についてまとめる問題だとわかる。

» 選択肢に並ぶ人物や動物を，主役と脇役で分別する必要がある。

物語に複数回登場したり，重要な役目を果たす人物は主役になるはず

解き方

》 選択肢に並ぶ人物や動物を探しながら，物語を読み進める。

> Five years ago, Mrs. Sabine Rouas lost her horse. She had spent 20 years with the horse before he died of old age. At that time, she felt that she could never own another horse. Out of loneliness, she spent hours watching cows on a nearby milk farm. Then, one day, she asked the farmer if she could help look after them.

》 まず，第1段落・第1文に**サビーヌ**という人物が登場する。

》 第2文からサビーヌは20年間飼っていた馬を亡くしてしまったことがわかる。

》 第4〜5文から，寂しくなった彼女は the farmer「農場主」に牛のお世話を申し出たことがわかる。

> The farmer agreed, and Sabine started work. She quickly developed a friendship with one of the cows. As the cow was pregnant, she spent more time with it than with the others. After the cow's baby was born, the baby started following Sabine around. Unfortunately, the farmer wasn't interested in keeping a bull—a male cow—on a milk farm. The farmer planned to sell the baby bull, which he called Three-oh-nine(309), to a meat market. Sabine decided she wasn't going to let that happen, so she asked the farmer if she could buy him and his mother. The farmer agreed, and she bought them. Sabine then started taking 309 for walks to town. About nine months later, when at last she had permission to move the animals, they moved to Sabine's farm.

》 第2段落を読み進めていくと，第4文で世話をしていた牛が赤ちゃんを産んだことがわかる。

》 第5〜8文から，**子牛は309と呼ばれていた**が，酪農場には不要なオスだったので食肉として売られようとしていたことがわかる。

》 これを防ぐため，サビーヌが子牛と**母親牛**を買ったことが第7〜8文に書かれている。

》 続く第9文には，309を散歩のため町に連れて行くようになったとある。

064　第1日程 第5問 攻略のプロセス

> Soon after, Sabine was offered a pony. At first, she wasn't sure if she wanted to have him, but the memory of her horse was no longer painful, so she accepted the pony and named him Leon. She then decided to return to her old hobby and started training him for show jumping. Three-oh-nine, who she had renamed Aston, spent most of his time with Leon, and the two became really close friends. However, Sabine had not expected Aston to pay close attention to her training routine with Leon, nor had she expected Aston to pick up some

》 第3段落へ進むと，第1〜2文でサビーヌはポニーをもらい受け，レオンという名前をつけた。
》 第4文の冒頭で，309 はアストンと改名されている。
》 さらに読み進めていくと，サビーヌとアストン，そしてレオンの物語が続くため，この3名は主役と言えそうだ。

》 登場人物がひと通り登場したので，選択肢を確認してみよう。
》 ①の主役には 309 とアストンが含まれているが，309 が改名した後の名前がアストンなので，並列されているのはおかしい。
》 また，the farmer「農場主」は元々アストンを飼っていた人物だが，ほとんど登場しない彼を主役としている点もおかしい。

》 ②にも 309 とアストンが登場するが主役と脇役とで分裂しており，さらに第2段落にしか登場しないアストンの母親を主役としている点もおかしい。

》 脇役のはずの農場主を主役とし，物語の最初から最後にいたるまで登場する中心人物のサビーヌを脇役としている③もおかしい。

》 残った④を確認すると，物語で重要な役割を果たすアストンとサビーヌ，そしてポニーが主役になっている。
》 そこまで重要でないアストンの母親と農場主が脇役になっているのも適切だと考えられる。よって正解は④。

選択肢の the pony = Leon のことだと見抜けたかな？

問3 Choose the four events in the order they happened to complete the Pre-fame Storyline slide. 32 〜 35

① Aston learns to jump.
② Sabine and Aston travel hundreds of kilometers together.
③ Sabine buys 309 and his mother.
④ Sabine goes to work on her neighbor's farm.
⑤ Sabine takes 309 for walks.

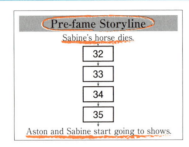

着眼点

» Pre-fame Storyline という3枚めのスライドのタイトルから，有名になる前の出来事を起きた順番に並べる問題だとわかる。
» すでにスライドに書かれている最初の出来事 Sabine's horse dies.「サビーヌの馬が死ぬ」から，最後の出来事 Aston and Sabine start going to shows.「アストンとサビーヌがショーに出始める」までの話の流れを完成させる。

選択肢は5つ，でも空所は4つしかないから，選択肢のうち1つはダミーだよ

解き方

» 最初の出来事 Sabine's horse dies. は，第1段落・第2文 She had spent 20 years with the horse before he died of old age. に該当する。
» 最後の出来事 Aston and Sabine start going to shows. は，第4段落・第1文の horse shows に該当すると考えられる。

>> よってスライドの空所を埋めるには，第1段落～第3段落の出来事を時系列に沿って並べればよい。

>> 選択肢①の「アストンがジャンプできるようになる」という出来事は，第3段落・第8文に登場する比較的最近の話。

>> ②の「何百キロも一緒に旅する」という話は，ショーに出はじめた第4段落冒頭の時点ではまだ書かれていなかったので一旦保留。

>> ③の「309と母親を買う」という話は，アストンと名づけられる前の出来事で，第2段落・第7～8文に登場する。

>> ④の「近所の農場の仕事に行く」という話は，第1段落・最終文に該当する。これはサビーヌが飼っていた馬が亡くなってすぐの出来事だったので，最初の空所に入るのは④になりそうだ。

>> ⑤の「309を散歩に連れて行く」という話は，まだアストンが309と呼ばれていた頃の出来事で第2段落・第9文に登場するが，サビーヌが親子を買い取った後の出来事なので，③→⑤の順番になる。

>> 第3段落でアストンがジャンプなどの芸ができるようになり，第4段落でショーへ行くという流れになっていたので，最後の空所には①が入る。

>> よって正解は④→③→⑤→①の順。

>> サビーヌとアストンが一緒に何百キロも一緒に旅するという②の出来事は，第6段落・第2文の Aston and Sabine sometimes need to travel 200 or 300 kilometers away from home「アストンとサビーヌは時に自宅から200～300キロメートルも離れて移動する必要がある」に該当するが，これはサビーヌとアストンがショーに出るようになった後の話なので，スライドの空所には入らない。

067

問4 Choose the two best items for the Aston's Abilities slide. (The order does not matter.) 　36　・　37　

① correct his mistakes by himself
② jump side-by-side with the pony
③ jump with a rider on his back
④ pick up tricks faster than a horse
⑤ pose for photographs

MOVIE 30

Aston's Abilities

Aston can:
・learn by simply watching Leon's training.
・walk, gallop, and stop when Sabine tells him to.
・understand distance and adjust his steps.
・　36　.
・　37　.

着眼点

》 スライドの Aston's Abilities「アストンの能力」というタイトルに注目。アストンができることとして正しい選択肢を選ぶ問題。

》 空所の上には Aston can という見出しに続いて様々なアストンの能力が並んでいる。

》 これらの項目に該当する情報がまとまっている箇所を本文から探して、まだスライドに書かれていないアストンの能力を空所に入れる。

解き方

≫ アストンの能力については，第3段落・第6文以降で詳しく説明されている。

> tricks. The young bull quickly mastered walking, galloping, stopping, going backwards, and turning around on command. He responded to Sabine's voice just like a horse. And despite weighing 1,300 kg, <u>it took him just 18 months to learn how to leap over one-meter-high horse jumps with Sabine on his back.</u> Aston might never have learned those things without having watched Leon. Moreover, Aston understood distance and could adjust his steps before a jump. <u>He also noticed his faults and corrected them without any help from Sabine.</u> That's something only the very best Olympic-standard horses can do.

≫ 第8文の it took him just 18 months to learn how to leap over one-meter-high horse jumps with Sabine on his back「サビーヌを背中に乗せたまま，1メートルの馬用の障害物の飛び越え方を習得するのにわずか18か月しかかからなかった」という能力は③の jump with a rider on his back「背中に騎手を乗せてジャンプする」に該当し，まだスライドに書かれていない。

≫ アストンに乗るサビーヌが選択肢では a rider「騎手」と言い換えられていることに注意。

≫ もう1つの能力である，第11文の He also noticed his faults and corrected them without any help from Sabine.「また自分の間違いに気づき，サビーヌからの手助けもなしに修正した」は，①の correct his mistakes by himself「自分の間違いを自分で修正する」に該当する。

≫ without any help from Sabine の部分が，選択肢では by himself「自力で」と言い換えられていることに注意。

≫ よって<u>正解は①と③</u>。

すでにスライドに書かれている能力と，まだ書かれていない能力をうまく見分けられたかな？

問5 Complete the Aston Now slide with the most appropriate item. 38

① has an increasing number of fans
② has made Sabine very wealthy
③ is so famous that he no longer frightens people
④ spends most nights of the year in a horse trailer

MOVIE 31

Aston Now

Aston today:
・is a show-jumping bull.
・travels to fairs and events with Sabine.
・ 38 .

着眼点

» 5枚めのスライドの Aston Now「アストンの現在」というタイトルに注目。
» アストンの現在について書かれている箇所を探しながら，本文を読み進めていく。

💡 解き方

>> 第4段落・第1文が Now ではじまっていることや，第3段落まではほとんど過去形の動詞が用いられているのに対して第4段落以降では主に現在形になっていることからもわかるように，アストンの現在については第4段落以降で説明されている。

> Now Sabine and Aston go to weekend fairs and horse shows around Europe to show off his skills. Sabine says, "We get a good reaction. Mostly, people are really surprised, and at first, they can be a bit scared because he's big—much bigger than a horse. Most people don't like to get too close to bulls with horns. But once they see his real nature, and see him performing, they often say, 'Oh he's really quite beautiful.'"
>
> "Look!" And Sabine shows a photo of Aston on her smartphone. She then continues, "When Aston was very young, I used to take him out for walks on a lead, like a dog, so that he would get used to humans. Maybe that's why he doesn't mind people. Because he is so calm, children, in particular, really like watching him and getting a chance to be close to him."
>
> Over the last few years, news of the massive show-jumping bull has spread rapidly; now, Aston is a major attraction with a growing number of online followers. Aston and Sabine sometimes need to travel 200 or 300 kilometers away from home, which means they have to stay overnight. Aston has to sleep in a horse box, which isn't really big enough for him.

>> 第6段落・第1文の now, Aston is a major attraction with a growing number of online followers「アストンは現在ますます多くのオンラインのフォロワーの大きな関心を集めている」に注目。現在のアストンはネット上で有名になり，人気を集め続けていることがわかる。

>> スライドにまだ書かれていないこの情報について，followers を fans「ファン」と言い換えた①が正解。

071

令和3年度 大学入学共通テスト 第1日程

第6問A 攻略のプロセス

STEP 1 まずは大問の全体像をつかむ

あらかじめリード文に目を通したうえで，本文のどこに何が書いてあるかをざっくり把握しましょう。

記事を読んで発表用ポスターをつくる

A You are working on a class project about safety in sports and found the following article. You are reading it and making a poster to present your findings to your classmates.

Making Ice Hockey Safer

「アイスホッケーをもっと安全に」

Ice hockey is a team sport enjoyed by a wide variety of people around the world. The object of the sport is to move a hard rubber disk called a "puck" into the other team's net with a hockey stick. Two teams with six players on each team engage in this fast-paced sport on a hard and slippery ice rink. Players may reach a speed of 30 kilometers per hour sending the puck into the air. At this pace, both the players and the puck can be a cause of serious danger.

The speed of the sport and the slippery surface of the ice rink make it easy for players to fall down or bump into each other resulting in a variety of injuries. In an attempt to protect players, equipment such as helmets, gloves, and pads for the shoulders, elbows, and legs, has been introduced over the years. Despite these efforts, ice hockey has a high rate of concussions.

A concussion is an injury to the brain that affects the way it functions; it is caused by either direct or indirect impact to the head, face, neck, or elsewhere and can sometimes cause temporary loss of consciousness. In less serious cases, for a short time, players may be unable to walk straight or see clearly, or they may experience ringing in the ears. Some believe they just have a slight headache and do not realize they have injured their brains.

In addition to not realizing the seriousness of the injury, players tend to worry about what their coach will think. In the past, coaches preferred tough players who played in spite of the pain. In other words, while it would seem logical for an injured player to stop playing after getting hurt, many did not. Recently, however, it has been found that concussions can have serious effects that last a lifetime. People with a history of concussion may have trouble concentrating or sleeping. Moreover, they may suffer from psychological problems such as depression and mood changes. In some cases, players may develop smell and taste disorders.

The National Hockey League (NHL), consisting of teams in Canada and the United States, has been making stricter rules and guidelines to deal with concussions. For example, in 2001, the NHL introduced the wearing of visors—pieces of clear plastic attached to the helmet that protect the face.

At first, it was optional and many players chose not to wear them. Since 2013, however, it has been required. In addition, in 2004, the NHL began to give more severe penalties, such as suspensions and fines, to players who hit another player in the head deliberately.

The NHL also introduced a concussion spotters system in 2015. In this system, NHL officials with access to live streaming and video replay watch for visible indications of concussion during each game. At first, two concussion spotters, who had no medical training, monitored the game in the arena. The following year, one to four concussion spotters with medical training were added. They monitored each game from the League's head office in New York. If a spotter thinks that a player has suffered a concussion, the player is removed from the game and is taken to a "quiet room" for an examination by a medical doctor. The player is not allowed to return to the game until the doctor gives permission.

The NHL has made much progress in making ice hockey a safer sport. As more is learned about the causes and effects of concussions, the NHL will surely take further measures to ensure player safety. Better safety might lead to an increase in the number of ice hockey players and fans.

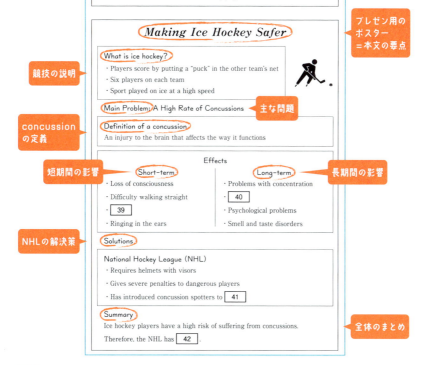

STEP 2 設問と選択肢を読み解く

続いて設問や選択肢に目を通しましょう。探すべき情報を押さえたうえで英文を読むことで、問題を解く時間を大幅に短縮できます。ここでは問1に注目します。

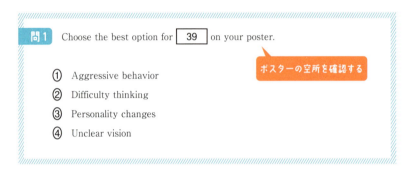

問1 Choose the best option for 39 on your poster.

① Aggressive behavior
② Difficulty thinking
③ Personality changes
④ Unclear vision

ポスターの空所を確認する

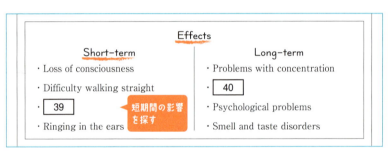

Effects

Short-term
・Loss of consciousness
・Difficulty walking straight
・ 39
・Ringing in the ears

短期間の影響を探す

Long-term
・Problems with concentration
・ 40
・Psychological problems
・Smell and taste disorders

≫ プレゼン用ポスターにすでに書かれている Effects や Short-term などの手がかりから、「短期間の影響」を本文から探せばよいことがわかる。
≫ Loss of consciousness や Difficulty walking straight などに並列される症状が空所に入ると考えられる。
≫ これらの症状について書かれている箇所を本文から探し、まだポスターには書かれていない情報を読み取る。

ポスターから「逆算」すれば、時間が短縮できるよ！

STEP 3 必要な情報を本文から探しながら小問を解く

問1 Choose the best option for ⬚39⬚ on your poster.

① Aggressive behavior
② Difficulty thinking
③ Personality changes
④ Unclear vision

MOVIE 32

Effects

Short-term	Long-term
・Loss of consciousness	・Problems with concentration
・Difficulty walking straight	・ ⬚40⬚
・ ⬚39⬚	・Psychological problems
・Ringing in the ears	・Smell and taste disorders

着眼点

» プレゼン用ポスターの空所に注目すると，concussion「脳震とう」がもたらす短期間の影響の例として Loss of consciousness や Difficulty walking straight，Ringing in the ears といった症状が挙げられている。
» これらの症状について情報がまとめられている箇所を本文から探して，まだ書かれていないものを空所に入れる。

解き方

» 第3段落・第1文に，脳震とうが引き起こす症状の例として temporary loss consciousness「一時的な意識の喪失」が挙げられている。これはポスターの Loss of consciousness「意識の喪失」に該当する。
» 続く第2文に for a short time「短期間」という語句が含まれるので，このあたりに手がかりがありそうだ。

075

> A concussion is an injury to the brain that affects the way it functions; it is caused by either direct or indirect impact to the head, face, neck, or elsewhere and can sometimes cause <u>temporary loss of consciousness</u>. In less serious cases, (for a short time,) players may be <u>unable to walk straight or see clearly</u>, or they may experience <u>ringing in the ears</u>. Some believe they just have a slight headache and do not realize they have injured their brains.

》 unable to walk straight「まっすぐ歩けない」の部分はポスターの Difficulty walking straight「まっすぐ歩くことの困難」に該当し，ringing in the ears「耳鳴り」の部分はそのままポスターに書かれている。

》 ポスターにまだ書かれていない情報は unable to ... see clearly「はっきり見えない」の部分なので，これを言い換えた④の Unclear vision「不明瞭な視界」が空所に入る。

問2 Choose the best option for [40] on your poster.

① Loss of eyesight
② Memory problems
③ Sleep disorders
④ Unsteady walking

MOVIE 33

```
┌─────────────────────────────────────────────┐
│                   Effects                   │
│   Short-term            Long-term           │
│ ・Loss of consciousness  ・Problems with     │
│ ・Difficulty walking       concentration    │
│   straight              ・[ 40 ]            │
│ ・[ 39 ]                ・Psychological     │
│ ・Ringing in the ears     problems          │
│                         ・Smell and taste   │
│                            disorders        │
└─────────────────────────────────────────────┘
```

着眼点

» ポスターの空所に注目すると，脳震とうがもたらす長期間の影響の例として Problems with concentration や Psychological problems のほか，Smell and taste disorders といった症状が挙げられている。

» これらの症状について情報がまとめられている箇所を本文から探して，まだ書かれていないものを空所に入れる。

解き方

» 第4段落・第4文に Recently, however, it has been found that concussions can have serious effects that last a long time.「しかし最近では，脳震とうは生涯にわたって続く深刻な影響を及ぼしうることがわかってきた」とある。a long time の部分がスライドでは Long-term と言い換えられていると考えられるので，このあたりに手がかりがありそうだ。

> Recently, however, it has been found that concussions can have serious effects that last a lifetime. People with a history of concussion may have trouble concentrating or sleeping. Moreover, they may suffer from psychological problems such as depression and mood changes. In some cases, players may develop smell and taste disorders.

» 第5文の trouble concentrating or sleeping「集中や睡眠の障がい」について，前半はポスターの Problems with concentration「集中力の障がい」に該当するが，睡眠の障がいについてはポスターに書かれていない。

» 第6文の psychological problems「精神的な障がい」や，第7文の smell and taste disorders「嗅覚と味覚の障がい」は，そのままポスターに書かれている。

» よって trouble ... sleeping を言い換えた③の Sleep disorders「睡眠障がい」が空所に入る。

問3 Choose the best option for ⬚41⬚ on your poster.

① allow players to return to the game
② examine players who have a concussion
③ fine players who cause concussions
④ identify players showing signs of a concussion

MOVIE 34

Solutions

National Hockey League (NHL)
・Requires helmets with visors
・Gives severe penalties to dangerous players
・Has introduced concussion spotters to ⬚41⬚

着眼点

» ポスターの空所に注目すると，脳震とうをめぐる諸問題の解決策として NHL が concussion spotters「脳震とう監視員」を導入したことがわかる。
» 空所直前の to は，「～するために」という目的を表す to 不定詞の副詞的用法だと推測できる。
» concussion spotters を本文から探し，導入の目的に注意しながら読む。

解き方

» concussion spotters という語句は，第 6 段落・第 1 文で登場する。

The NHL also introduced a concussion spotters system in 2015. In this system, NHL officials with access to live streaming and video replay watch for visible indications of concussion during each game. At first, two concussion spotters, who had no medical training, monitored the game in the arena. The following year, one to four concussion spotters with medical training were added. They monitored each game from the League's head office in New York. If a spotter thinks that a player has suffered a concussion, the player is removed from the game and is taken to a "quiet room" for an examination by a medical doctor. The player is not allowed to return to the game until the doctor gives permission.

» concussion spotters が導入された目的を探して読み進めると，第2文に In this system, NHL officials ... watch for visible indications of concussion during each game.「この制度では，NHL の職員が…各試合中の目に見える脳震とうの兆候を監視する」とあり，試合中の脳震とうの兆しを見つけるために導入されたことがわかる。

> The NHL also introduced a concussion spotters system in 2015. In this system, NHL officials with access to live streaming and video replay (watch for) (visible indications) of concussion during each game. At first, two concussion
>
> ④ (identify) players (showing signs) of a concussion

» よって watch for の部分を identify「～を特定する」で，visible indications を showing signs「兆候を示している」で言い換えている④が正解。

» 第6段落・第6文に，If a spotter thinks that a player has suffered a concussion, the player is removed from the game and is taken to a "quiet room" for an examination by a medical doctor.「選手が脳震とうを起こしていると監視員が思えば，その選手は試合から外されて医師の検査を受けるために『静かな部屋』に運ばれる」とある。監視員が導入されたのは脳震とうを起こしている選手を見つけるためであり，検査するのは医者の仕事なので②は不適切。

ポスターからキーワードを拾う→本文のどこに登場するかを探す→近くに手がかりがあるはず！

問4 Choose the best option for ⬚42⬚ on your poster.

① been expecting the players to become tougher
② been implementing new rules and guidelines
③ given medical training to coaches
④ made wearing of visors optional

MOVIE 35

Summary
Ice hockey players have a high risk of suffering from concussions. Therefore, the NHL has ⬚42⬚.

着眼点
» ポスターの空所に注目すると，記事全体の総括である Summary「まとめ」を完成させる問題だとわかる。
» 「アイスホッケー選手は脳震とうに苦しむ危険性が高い」という問題を解決するために NHL がどう対策したか，正しい選択肢を選ぶ。

解き方
» NHL が登場する第5段落以降に注目。

> The National Hockey League (NHL), consisting of teams in Canada and the United States, has been making stricter rules and guidelines to deal with concussions. For example, in 2001, the NHL introduced the wearing of visors—pieces of clear plastic attached to the helmet that protect the face. At first, it was optional and many players chose not to wear them. Since 2013, however, it has been required. In addition, in 2004, the NHL began to give more severe penalties, such as suspensions and fines, to players who hit another player in the head deliberately.

» 「選手にもっと強くなってほしい」というような期待はどこにも書かれていないので，①は不適切。

≫ ②の新しいルールやガイドラインについては，記事の第5段落・第1文で The National Hockey League (NHL), consisting of teams in Canada and the United States, has been making stricter rules and guidelines to deal with concussions.「ナショナルホッケーリーグ（NHL）は，カナダとアメリカ合衆国のチームからなり，脳震とうに対処するために，より厳しいルールとガイドラインを定めてきた」と言及されている。よって正解は②。

≫ 「監督に医療トレーニングを施している」という記述はどこにもないので，③は不適切。

≫ 第5段落・第2～3文から，visor「バイザー」の着用は導入当初こそ任意だったが現在では義務であるとわかるので，④は不適切。

令和３年度 大学入学共通テスト 第１日程
第６問 B 攻略のプロセス

 まずは大問の全体像をつかむ

あらかじめリード文に目を通したうえで，本文のどこに何が書いてあるかをざっくり把握しましょう。

甘味料のことを学ぶために教科書を読む

B　You are studying nutrition in health class. You are going to read the following passage from a textbook to learn more about various sweeteners.

　　Cake, candy, soft drinks—most of us love sweet things. In fact, young people say "Sweet!" to mean something is "good" in English. When we think of sweetness, we imagine ordinary white sugar from sugar cane or sugar beet plants. Scientific discoveries, however, have changed the world of sweeteners. We can now extract sugars from many other plants. The most obvious example is corn. Corn is abundant, inexpensive, and easy to process. High fructose corn syrup (HFCS) is about 1.2 times sweeter than regular sugar, but quite high in calories. Taking science one step further, over the past 70 years scientists have developed a wide variety of artificial sweeteners.

　　A recent US National Health and Nutrition Examination Survey concluded that 14.6% of the average American's energy intake is from "added sugar," which refers to sugar that is not derived from whole foods. A banana, for example, is a whole food, while a cookie contains added sugar. More than half of added sugar calories are from sweetened drinks and desserts. Lots of added sugar can have negative effects on our bodies, including excessive weight gain and other health problems. For this reason, many choose low-calorie substitutes for drinks, snacks, and desserts.

　　Natural alternatives to white sugar include brown sugar, honey, and maple syrup, but they also tend to be high in calories. Consequently, alternative "low-calorie sweeteners" (LCSs), mostly artificial chemical combinations, have become popular. The most common LCSs today are aspartame, Ace-K, stevia, and sucralose. Not all LCSs are artificial—stevia comes from plant leaves.

　　Alternative sweeteners can be hard to use in cooking because some cannot be heated and most are far sweeter than white sugar. Aspartame and Ace-K are 200 times sweeter than sugar. Stevia is 300 times sweeter, and sucralose has twice the sweetness of stevia. Some new sweeteners are even more intense. A Japanese company recently developed "Advantame," which is 20,000 times sweeter than sugar. Only a tiny amount of this substance is required to sweeten something.

When choosing sweeteners, it is important to consider health issues. Making desserts with lots of white sugar, for example, results in high-calorie dishes that could lead to weight gain. There are those who prefer LCSs for this very reason. Apart from calories, however, some research links consuming artificial LCSs with various other health concerns. Some LCSs contain strong chemicals suspected of causing cancer, while others have been shown to affect memory and brain development, so they can be dangerous, especially for young children, pregnant women, and the elderly. There are a few relatively natural alternative sweeteners, like xylitol and sorbitol, which are low in calories. Unfortunately, these move through the body extremely slowly, so consuming large amounts can cause stomach trouble.

When people want something sweet, even with all the information, it is difficult for them to decide whether to stick to common higher calorie sweeteners like sugar or to use LCSs. Many varieties of gum and candy today contain one or more artificial sweeteners; nonetheless, some people who would not put artificial sweeteners in hot drinks may still buy such items. Individuals need to weigh the options and then choose the sweeteners that best suit their needs and circumstances.

資料などがついていないシンプルな長文問題だからといって，いきなり読み始めるのは厳禁！ 先に必ず設問や選択肢をチェックして，探すべき情報をインプットしてから本文を読もう

- 栄養について授業で学んでいるという設定。
- 様々な甘味料に関する文章を読む。

STEP 2 設問と選択肢を読み解く

続いて設問や選択肢に目を通しましょう。探すべき情報を押さえたうえで英文を読むことで、問題を解く時間を大幅に短縮できます。ここでは問2に注目します。

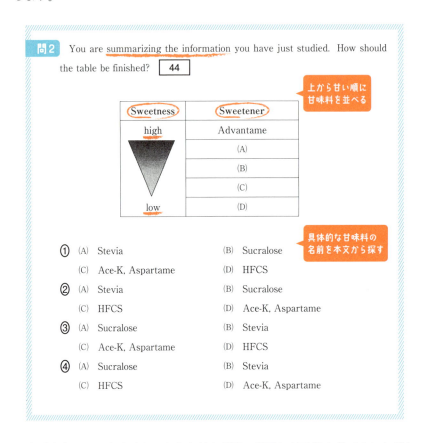

» まず表をチェックすると、上から甘さが高い順番に甘味料を並べることがわかる。
» 選択肢に並ぶ様々な甘味料の名前と、それぞれの甘さについて書かれた箇所を探しながら本文を読めばよい。

STEP 3 必要な情報を本文から探しながら小問を解く

問1 You learn that modern science has changed the world of sweeteners by 43 .

① discovering new, sweeter white sugar types
② measuring the energy intake of Americans
③ providing a variety of new options
④ using many newly-developed plants from the environment

MOVIE 36

着眼点
» 設問から，現代科学がどのように甘味料の世界を変えたかを探す。
» science や change に該当する語句を探しながら本文を読んでいく。

解き方
» 第1段落・第4文に，**Scientific discoveries, however, have changed the world of sweeteners.**「しかし，科学的な発見が甘味料の世界を変えました」という設問と似た内容の英文が登場する。このあたりに手がかりがありそうだ。

> plants. Scientific discoveries, however, have changed the world of sweeteners. We can now extract sugars from many other plants. The most obvious example is corn. Corn is abundant, inexpensive, and easy to process. High fructose corn syrup (HFCS) is about 1.2 times sweeter than regular sugar, but quite high in calories. Taking science one step further, over the past 70 years scientists have developed a wide variety of artificial sweeteners.

» 第9文に … **scientists have developed a wide variety of artificial sweeteners**「科学者たちは様々な人工甘味料を開発してきました」とある。
» 科学者が開発してきた artificial sweeteners「人工甘味料」を new options「新しい選択肢」と言い換えた③が正解。

» 新種の白砂糖や新開発の植物の話はしていないので①や④は不適切。
» アメリカ人のエネルギー摂取については第2段落で書かれているが，それを計測することで変化がもたらされたわけではないので，②は不適切。

085

問2 You are summarizing the information you have just studied. How should the table be finished? 44

Sweetness	Sweetener
high	Advantame
	(A)
	(B)
	(C)
low	(D)

① (A) Stevia　　　　　　　(B) Sucralose
　 (C) Ace-K, Aspartame　(D) HFCS

② (A) Stevia　　　　　　　(B) Sucralose
　 (C) HFCS　　　　　　　(D) Ace-K, Aspartame

③ (A) Sucralose　　　　　(B) Stevia
　 (C) Ace-K, Aspartame　(D) HFCS

④ (A) Sucralose　　　　　(B) Stevia
　 (C) HFCS　　　　　　　(D) Ace-K, Aspartame

MOVIE 37

着眼点
» 設問中の表は，上から甘さが高い順番に甘味料が並んでいる。
» 選択肢に並ぶ5つの甘味料の名前を本文から探し，それぞれの甘さに関する記述を丁寧に読み取る。

解き方
» 選択肢の甘味料を探しながら読み進めると，HFCS が第1段落・第8文に登場する。

> example is corn. Corn is abundant, inexpensive, and easy to process. High fructose corn syrup (HFCS) is about 1.2 times sweeter than regular sugar, but quite high in calories. Taking science one step further, over the past 70 years scientists have developed a wide variety of artificial sweeteners.

» ここから，HFCS の甘さは砂糖の 1.2 倍であることがわかる。

» その他の甘味料は第 3 段落の後半に登場し，第 4 段落で詳しく説明されている。

> Natural alternatives to white sugar include brown sugar, honey, and maple syrup, but they also tend to be high in calories. Consequently, alternative "low-calorie sweeteners" (LCSs), mostly artificial chemical combinations, have become popular. The most common LCSs today are aspartame, Ace-K, stevia, and sucralose. Not all LCSs are artificial—stevia comes from plant leaves.
>
> Alternative sweeteners can be hard to use in cooking because some cannot be heated and most are far sweeter than white sugar. Aspartame and Ace-K are 200 times sweeter than sugar. Stevia is 300 times sweeter, and sucralose has twice the sweetness of stevia. Some new sweeteners are even more intense. A Japanese company recently developed "Advantame," which is 20,000 times sweeter than sugar. Only a tiny amount of this substance is required to sweeten something.

» 第 4 段落・第 2 文から，Aspartame と Ace-K の甘さは砂糖の 200 倍だとわかる。

» 同じく第 3 文から Stevia の甘さは砂糖の 300 倍であり，さらに Sucralose の甘さは Stevia の 2 倍，つまり砂糖の 600 倍であるとわかる。

» 以上から選択肢を甘さが高い順番に並べると，Sucralose → Stevia → Ace-K, Aspartame → HFCS の順になる。よって正解は ③。

» ちなみに表の一番上にある Advantame は第 4 段落・第 5 文に登場し，甘さは砂糖の 20,000 倍と群を抜いている。

甘味料の名前はどれも大文字で始まるから探しやすいはず。
倍数表現を見抜けたかな？

問3 According to the article you read, which of the following are true?
(Choose two options. The order does not matter.) 45 ・ 46

① Alternative sweeteners have been proven to cause weight gain.
② Americans get 14.6% of their energy from alternative sweeteners.
③ It is possible to get alternative sweeteners from plants.
④ Most artificial sweeteners are easy to cook with.
⑤ Sweeteners like xylitol and sorbitol are not digested quickly.

MOVIE 38

着眼点
» 設問から，文章全体を読んで内容に合致する選択肢を選ぶ問題だとわかる。
» 全体の概要を把握し，1つずつ選択肢を正誤判定していく。

解き方
» ①は「代用甘味料は体重増加を引き起こすことが証明されてきた」という内容だが，代用甘味料が体重増加をもたらすというようなことは本文には書かれていないので不適切。選択肢では have been proven「証明されてきた」と強く断言しているが，このような強い言い方は本文にはっきりと書かれていない限り正解になりにくいことを覚えておこう。

» ②の「アメリカ人はエネルギーの14.6％を代用甘味料から摂取している」に含まれる14.6％という具体的な数字を探すと，第2段落・第1文 A recent US National Health and Nutrition Examination Survey concluded that **14.6% of the average American's energy intake is form "added sugar,"** which refers to sugar that is not derived from whole foods. 「最近のアメリカの国民健康栄養調査は，平均的なアメリカ人のエネルギー摂取のうち14.6パーセントが，自然食品に由来していない砂糖を指す『添加糖類』からだと結論づけました」にたどり着く。added sugar「添加糖類」と alternative sweeteners「代用甘味料」は別物なので②は不適切。

数字や人物名・地名などの具体的な情報は，それを使った引っかけの選択肢が作られやすいので注意

» ③は「植物から代用甘味料を得ることは可能だ」という内容。植物について言及されている箇所を本文から探そう。

> Natural alternatives to white sugar include brown sugar, honey, and maple syrup, but they also tend to be high in calories. Consequently, alternative "low-calorie sweeteners" (LCSs), mostly artificial chemical combinations, have become popular. The most common LCSs today are aspartame, Ace-K, stevia, and sucralose. <u>Not all LCSs are artificial—stevia comes from plant leaves.</u>

》第3段落・第4文の Not all LCSs are artificial—stevia comes from plant leaves.「すべてのLCSが人工的というわけではなく,ステビアは植物の葉に由来します」から,植物由来の代用甘味料が存在するとわかるので,③は正しい。

》第4段落・第1文 Alternative sweeteners can be hard to use in cooking because some cannot be heated and most are far sweeter than white sugar.「代用甘味料には加熱できないものもあり,大半が白砂糖よりはるかに甘いので,料理では使いづらいことがあります」から,ほとんどの人工甘味料は料理には使いづらいことがわかる。よって「大抵の人工甘味料は料理しやすい」という④は不適切。

》⑤に含まれる xylitol and sorbitol を探すと,第5段落の第5～6文に登場する。

> especially for young children, pregnant women, and the elderly. There are a few relatively natural alternative sweeteners, like <u>xylitol and sorbitol</u>, which are low in calories. Unfortunately, <u>these move through the body extremely slowly</u>, so consuming large amounts can cause stomach trouble.

》キシリトールとソルビトールはゆっくりと体内を移動するということなので,これらの甘味料を not digested quickly「直ちには消化されない」と言い換えた⑤は正しい。

》よって正解は③と⑤。

選択肢からキーワードを拾う→本文のどこに登場するかを探す→正しいかどうかをすばやく判断できる!

> **問 4** To describe the author's position, which of the following is most appropriate? 47
>
> ① The author argues against the use of artificial sweeteners in drinks and desserts.
> ② The author believes artificial sweeteners have successfully replaced traditional ones.
> ③ The author states that it is important to invent much sweeter products for future use.
> ④ The author suggests people focus on choosing sweeteners that make sense for them.
>
> MOVIE 39
>
>

着眼点
» 筆者の主張は文章全体の内容を踏まえて最後の方に書かれていることが多い。
» important のような形容詞や助動詞など，筆者の主観を表す目印を探しながら最終段落を読む。

解き方
» 文章の最終段落である第 6 段落に注目。

> When people want something sweet, even with all the information, it is difficult for them to decide whether to stick to common higher calorie sweeteners like sugar or to use LCSs. Many varieties of gum and candy today contain one or more artificial sweeteners; nonetheless, some people who would not put artificial sweeteners in hot drinks may still buy such items. Individuals need to weigh the options and then choose the sweeteners that best suit their needs and circumstances.

» 最終文に含まれる need to「〜する必要がある」という助動詞は，筆者の主張を表していると考えられる。

» Individuals need to weigh the options and then choose the sweeteners that best suit their needs and circumstance.「一人ひとりがこれらの選択肢を比較考慮し，それから自分たちの必要性と状況に最適な甘味料を選ぶ必要があるのです」という内容から，筆者は必要性や環境に合わせて適切な甘味料を選ぶべきだと考えていることがわかる。

» 筆者は人口甘味料の使用に反対しているわけではないので①は不適切。

» 人口甘味料が伝統的な甘味料に完全に取って代わったというような話はしていないので②は不適切。

» もっと甘い甘味料を作ることが重要だというような話はしていないので③は不適切。

» 最終文の best suit their needs and circumstance「自分たちの必要性と状況に最適な」を make sense for them「自分にふさわしい」と言い換えている④が正解。

この問題のように，本文では具体的に説明されていた内容が選択肢ではざっくりまとめられていることがあるんだ

MEMO

令和3年度（2021年度）大学入学共通テスト
英語リーディング　第2日程
解答一覧

問題番号（配点）	設問		解答番号	正解	配点	チェック
第1問（10）	A	問1	1	①	2	
		問2	2	④	2	
	B	問1	3	③	2	
		問2	4	③	2	
		問3	5	②	2	
第2問（20）	A	問1	6	③	2	
		問2	7	②	2	
		問3	8	③	2	
		問4	9	①	2	
		問5	10	④	2	
	B	問1	11	①	2	
		問2	12	①	2	
		問3	13	③	2	
		問4	14	①	2	
		問5	15	③	2	
第3問（15）	A	問1	16	②	3	
		問2	17	②	3	
	B	問1	18	③	3*	
			19	②		
			20	④		
			21	①		
		問2	22	④	3	
		問3	23	③	3	

問題番号（配点）	設問	解答番号	正解	配点	チェック
第4問（16）	問1	24	③	3	
		25	④	3	
	問2	26	①	3	
	問3	27	②	2	
	問4	28	③	2	
	問5	29	③	3	
第5問（15）	問1	30	①	3	
	問2	31－32	①－④	3	
	問3	33	③	3*	
		34	④		
		35	①		
		36	②		
	問4	37	①	3	
	問5	38	④	3	
第6問（24）	A	問1	39	②	3	
		問2	40	③	3	
		問3	41	③	3	
		問4	42	④	3	
	B	問1	43	④	3	
		問2	44	④	3	
		問3	45	④	3*	
		問4	46－47	③－⑤	3	

＊は，全問正解の場合のみ点を与える
ハイフンでつながれた正解は，順序を問わない

093

令和3年度 大学入学共通テスト 第2日程

第1問A 攻略のプロセス

 まずは大問の全体像をつかむ

本文を読む前に，リード文にさっと目を通すことを心がけましょう。これから読む英文について，書き手やシチュエーションなどの情報が短くまとめられているため，読解のヒントになる場合があります。また，問題によっては表やグラフが組み合わさった複雑な英文を読むことになるため，あらかじめどこに何が書いてあるかをざっくり把握しましょう。

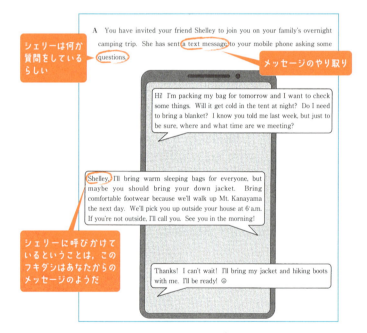

シェリーは何か質問をしているらしい

メッセージのやり取り

シェリーに呼びかけているということは、このフキダシはあなたからのメッセージのようだ

- キャンプ旅行に誘った友人のシェリーとの**メッセージのやり取り**。
- リード文によると，シェリーは何か**質問**があって連絡してきたようだ。
- 2つめのメッセージが Shelley, という呼びかけで始まっていることから，1つめと3つめは**シェリー**が書いたメッセージ，2つめが**あなた**が書いたメッセージだと判断できる。

STEP 2 設問と選択肢を読み解く

続いて設問や選択肢に目を通しましょう。探すべき情報を押さえたうえで英文を読むことで，問題を解く時間を大幅に短縮できます。

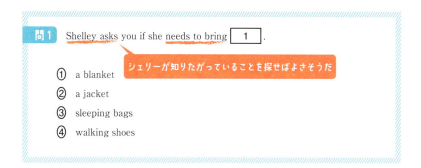

» 問1はシェリーが知りたがっていることを具体的に選ぶ問題。
» needs to「～する必要がある」を意味する表現に注意しながら本文を読む。

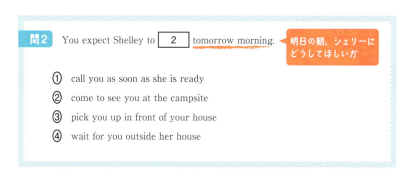

» 問2は tomorrow morning「明日の朝」という条件が設問に含まれていることに注目。
» 明日の朝，シェリーにしてもらいたいことを本文から探す。

設問に含まれるキーワードに注目！

STEP 3 必要な情報を本文から探しながら小問を解く 難易度 やさしい

問1 Shelley asks you if she needs to bring 　1　.

① a blanket
② a jacket
③ sleeping bags
④ walking shoes

MOVIE 40

着眼点
» 設問の needs to「〜する必要がある」に注目。
» Do I need to bring 〜? / Do I have to bring 〜?「〜を持っていく必要がありますか?」のような表現に注意しながら，シェリーからのメッセージを読む。

解き方
» 上から2つめのメッセージが Shelly, という呼びかけで始まっているので，1つめのメッセージはシェリーが書いたものだとわかる。

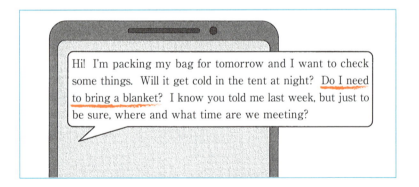

» この中から「〜する必要がある」を意味する表現を探すと，Do I need to bring a blanket?「毛布を持っていく必要があるかしら?」が見つかる。この1文に合致する①が正解。

問2 You expect Shelley to [2] tomorrow morning.

① call you as soon as she is ready
② come to see you at the campsite
③ pick you up in front of your house
④ wait for you outside her house

MOVIE 41

着眼点

» tomorrow morning「明日の朝」，あなたがシェリーにしてもらいたいことを本文から探す。
» expect 人 to do は「人が〜することを期待する」という意味の表現。

解き方

» あなたがシェリーにしてもらいたいと思っていることは，あなたが送ったメッセージに書かれているはず。

> Shelley, I'll bring warm sleeping bags for everyone, but maybe you should bring your down jacket. Bring comfortable footwear because we'll walk up Mt. Kanayama the next day. We'll pick you up outside your house at 6 a.m. If you're not outside, I'll call you. See you in the morning!

» 「明日の朝」に該当する表現を探すと，We'll pick you up outside your house at 6 a.m. If you're not outside, I'll call you.「朝6時に家の外にあなたを迎えに行くわ。もしあなたが外にいなかったら，電話するわ」が見つかる。
» 「シェリーに家の前で待っていてほしい」というのがあなたの要望なので，正解は④。

» 選択肢③に含まれる you や your はあなた自身を指し，シェリーに迎えに来てもらうことになってしまうので不適切。

令和3年度 大学入学共通テスト 第2日程
第1問B 攻略のプロセス

STEP 1 まずは大問の全体像をつかむ

あらかじめリード文に目を通したうえで、本文のどこに何が書いてあるかをざっくり把握しましょう。

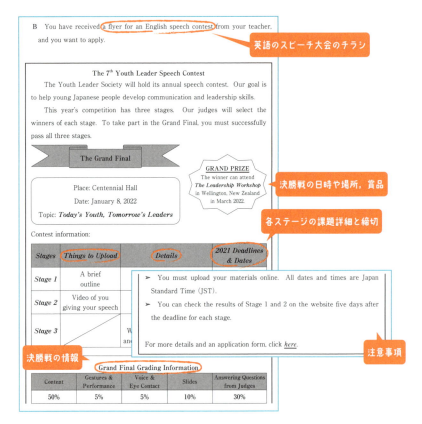

- 英語のスピーチ大会のチラシ。
- 英文の下には複数の表がついており、さらにその下には矢印で注意事項が記されている。
- どこに何が書いてあるかを推測しながら英文を読む。

STEP 2 設問と選択肢を読み解く

続いて設問や選択肢に目を通しましょう。探すべき情報を押さえたうえで英文を読むことで、問題を解く時間を大幅に短縮できます。ここでは問1と問2に注目します。

» 問1は first stage「最初のステージ」に参加するためにアップロードすべきものを探しながら本文を読む。

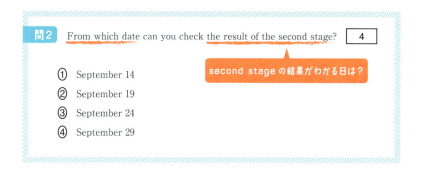

» 問2は second stage「2つめのステージ」の結果について書かれている箇所や、日時に注意して本文を読む。

STEP 3 必要な情報を本文から探しながら小問を解く　難易度 やさしい

問1 To take part in the first stage, you should upload a 3 .

① completed speech script
② set of slides for the speech
③ summary of your speech
④ video of yourself speaking

MOVIE 42

着眼点
» 設問の first stage「最初のステージ」と upload「〜をアップロードする」に注目。これらの語句を本文中から探し出そう。

解き方
» 1つめの表に注目。

Contest information:

Stages	Things to Upload	Details	2021 Deadlines & Dates
Stage 1	A brief outline	Number of words: 150-200	Upload by 5 p.m. on August 12
Stage 2	Video of you giving your speech	Time: 7-8 minutes	Upload by 5 p.m. on September 19
Stage 3		Local Contests: Winners will be announced and go on to the Grand Final.	Held on November 21

» Stage 1 の Things to Upload「アップロードするもの」に書かれているのは A brief outline「簡潔な概要」である。
» これに最も近い選択肢は③の summary of your speech「スピーチの要約」だと考えられるので、正解は③。

難易度 ふつう

問2 From which date can you check the result of the second stage? 　4

① September 14
② September 19
③ September 24
④ September 29

MOVIE 43

着眼点

≫ 設問文と選択肢から，second stage「2つめのステージ」の結果がわかる日付を本文から探せばよいとわかる。

解き方

≫ 1つめの表には課題提出の締め切り日はあるが，結果がわかる日付は書かれていない。

≫ result「結果」を探していくと，チラシの下部にある2つめの矢印にたどり着く。

> ➤ You must upload your materials online. All dates and times are Japan Standard Time (JST).
> ➤ You can check the results of Stage 1 and 2 on the website five days after the deadline for each stage.
>
> For more details and an application form, click *here*.

≫ You can check the results of Stage 1 and 2 on the website five days after the deadline for each stage.「ステージ1と2の結果は，それぞれのステージの締め切りの5日後からウェブサイトで確認できます」から，まず締め切りを確認し，それに5日を足せば結果発表の日付がわかる。

101

Stages	Things to Upload	Details	2021 Deadlines & Dates
Stage 1	A brief outline	Number of words: 150-200	Upload by 5 p.m. on August 12
Stage 2	Video of you giving your speech	Time: 7-8 minutes	Upload by 5 p.m. on September 19

≫ 1つめの表に戻って Stage 2 の締め切りを確認すると，September 19「9月19日」だとわかる。
≫ 結果発表はその5日後の September 24「9月24日」だと判断できるので，正解は③。

英文や表にヒントが散らばっていても，焦らずきちんと解けたかな？

難易度 やさしい

問3 To get a high score in the Grand Final, you should pay most attention to your content and ⬜5⬜ .

① expressions and gestures
② responses to the judges
③ visual materials
④ voice control

MOVIE 44

着眼点

» Grand Final「決勝戦」で高評価を得るために注意すべき項目を探す。
» 最も注意すべきは content「内容」ともう1つは何か,という設問になっていることに注意。

解き方

» 決勝戦の評価について書かれている箇所を探すと,Grand Final Grading Information「決勝戦の評価に関する情報」というタイトルの表が見つかるはず。

Grand Final Grading Information

Content	Gestures & Performance	Voice & Eye Contact	Slides	Answering Questions from Judges
50%	5%	5%	10%	30%

» 表によると Content「内容」が最も大きく,評価の50%を占めている。
» 「最も注意すべきは内容ともう1つは何か」という設問なので,内容の次に大きな比重を占めている項目を探すと,Answering Questions from Judges「審査員からの質問に対する回答」が30%を占めていることがわかる。
» これを responses to the judges「審査員への応答」と言い換えた②が正解。

令和3年度 大学入学共通テスト 第2日程
第2問A 攻略のプロセス

STEP 1 まずは大問の全体像をつかむ

あらかじめリード文に目を通したうえで，本文のどこに何が書いてあるかをざっくり把握しましょう。

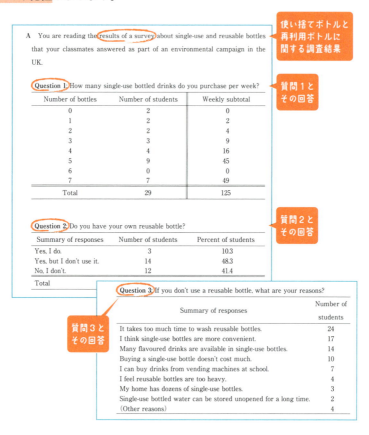

- 使い捨てのボトルと再利用できるボトルに関する**調査結果**。
- **3つの質問**と，それぞれの質問に対するクラスメイトの**回答**が表にまとめられている。
- 複数の資料を照らし合わせながら英文を読む。

STEP 2 設問と選択肢を読み解く

続いて設問や選択肢に目を通しましょう。探すべき情報を押さえたうえで英文を読むことで,問題を解く時間を大幅に短縮できます。ここでは問1と問3,問5に注目します。

問1 The results of Question 1 show that 　6　.

> Question 1 の表に手がかりがある

① each student buys fewer than four single-use bottles a week on average
② many students buy fewer than two bottles a week
③ more than half the students buy at least five bottles a week
④ the students buy more than 125 bottles a week

》問1の手がかりは Question 1「質問1」にあるようだ。
》選択肢には様々な数字に関する表現が含まれている。

> それぞれの表現の正確な意味を押さえておかなければ解けない問題になっているので注意しよう

FOR YOUR INFORMATION

● 数字に関する注意すべき表現
》**fewer than ...**　…より少ない
　fewer than four　4未満（4は含まない）
》**on average**　平均して
》**at least**　少なくとも
》**more than ...**　…より多い
　more than 125　125より多い（125は含まない）

問3 One <u>opinion</u> expressed by your classmates in Question 3 is that ⬚8⬚ .

Question 3から読み取れる意見

① some students have a stock of single-use bottles at home
② there are vending machines for buying drinks at school
③ washing reusable bottles takes a lot of time
④ water in unopened single-use bottles lasts a long time

» それぞれの選択肢が fact「事実」なのか opinion「意見」なのか，そして本文の内容と合致しているかを確認する必要がある。
» fact と考えられる選択肢をあらかじめ除外した上で，残った選択肢が Question 3 の内容と合致するかを確かめると効率がよい。
» fact は数値などの客観的な事実を指し，opinion は感想などの主観的な意見を指す。

問5 What is the most likely reason why your classmates do not use reusable bottles? ⬚10⬚

本文中の手がかりから最もありそうな理由を推測する

① There are many single-use bottled drinks stored at home.
② There is less variety of drinks available.
③ They are expensive for your classmates.
④ They are troublesome to deal with.

» 設問文を和訳すると，「クラスメイトが再利用可能なボトルを使わない理由として最もあり得るのは何か？」という意味になる。
» most likely は「最もありそうだ」という意味なので，本文に正解が直接書かれているわけではなく，本文に書かれていることを手がかりに推量して最も適切な選択肢を選ぶ問題だと判断できる。

would や might などの推量を表す助動詞や，best「最も適切な」などの語が含まれる設問も，推測して最も適切な選択肢を選ぶ必要があるよ

STEP 3 必要な情報を本文から探しながら小問を解く　難易度 ふつう

問1 The results of Question 1 show that ⑥ 　.

① each student buys fewer than four single-use bottles a week on average
② many students buy fewer than two bottles a week
③ more than half the students buy at least five bottles a week
④ the students buy more than 125 bottles a week

着眼点
» 設問文から Question 1 の表に注目。
» 設問文が漠然とした尋ね方になっているので，表と照らし合わせながら選択肢を1つずつチェックしていく。

解き方
» 「1週間に使い捨てボトル入りの飲み物を何本購入しますか？」という質問に対する回答が Question 1 の表にまとまっている。

Question 1: How many single-use bottled drinks do you purchase per week?

Number of bottles	Number of students	Weekly subtotal
0	2	0
1	2	2
2	2	4
3	3	9
4	4	16
5	9	45
6	0	0
7	7	49
Total	29	125

» 左の列は「1週間で購入するボトルの数」を，中央の列は「その数のボトルを購入する生徒数」を，右の列は両者を掛け算した「週の小計」を表しているようだ。Total「合計」は各行の数字を合計したもの。

» ①については，生徒1人あたりの1週間の使い捨てボトルの購入数の平均を計算すればよい。

≫ 1週間で購入するボトルの合計（125本）を生徒数（29人）で割ると平均がわかる。125÷29＝4.3... より平均は4本以上なので，①は不適切。

≫ ②については，1週間に2本より少ない使い捨てボトルを購入する生徒の数を計算する。0本買う2人と1本買う2人を合わせると2＋2＝4人。全29人中の4人なので，「多くの生徒」とは言えない。

≫ ③については，1週間に少なくとも5本，つまり5本以上の使い捨てボトルを購入する生徒の数を計算する。5本買う9人と7本買う7人を合わせると9＋7＝16人。これは全29人の生徒の過半数に当たるので，③は正しい。

≫ ④については，生徒が買う使い捨てボトルの総数はちょうど125本である。more than 125「125本より多い（＝126本以上）」という表現は正確でないので不適切。

≫ よって正解は③。

108　第2日程　第2問A　攻略のプロセス

問2 The results of Question 2 show that more than half the students ⑦ .

① don't have their own reusable bottle
② have their own reusable bottle
③ have their own reusable bottle but don't use it
④ use their own reusable bottle

MOVIE 46

着眼点
≫ 設問文から Question 2 の表に注目。過半数の生徒に当てはまる項目を選ぶ。

解き方
≫「自分の再利用可能なボトルを持っていますか？」という質問に対する回答が Question 2 の表にまとまっている。

Question 2: Do you have your own reusable bottle?

Summary of responses	Number of students	Percent of students
Yes, I do.	3	10.3
Yes, but I don't use it.	14	48.3
No, I don't.	12	41.4
Total	29	100.0

≫ 左の列は「回答の概要」を，中央の列は「回答した生徒数」を，右の列は「回答した生徒の割合」を表しているようだ。
≫ ①のように「再利用ボトルを持っていない」と答えた生徒の割合は，表の No, I don't. の列に注目すると 41.4％なので，過半数ではない。
≫ ②のように「再利用ボトルを持っている」と答えた生徒は，表の Yes, I do.「持っている」と答えた生徒と Yes, but I don't use it.「持っているが使っていない」と答えた生徒の合計だと考えられる。10.3％＋48.3％＝58.6％なので，過半数である。
≫ ③のように「再利用できるボトルを持っているが使っていない」と答えた生徒は 48.3％なので，過半数ではない。
≫「持っているが使っていない」という回答が別に用意されていることを踏まえると，「持っている」という回答には「持っているし使っている」という意味が含まれていると考えられる。④のように「再利用できるボトルを使っている」と答えた生徒は 10.3％ だと判断できるので，過半数ではない。
≫ よって正解は②。

問3 One opinion expressed by your classmates in Question 3 is that 　8　 .

① some students have a stock of single-use bottles at home
② there are vending machines for buying drinks at school
③ washing reusable bottles takes a lot of time
④ water in unopened single-use bottles lasts a long time

MOVIE 47

着眼点

» 設問文から Question 3 の表に注目。
» 先に選択肢を確認して fact「事実」を除外する。
» 次に本文の内容に合致する opinion「意見」を選ぶ。
» 話者の意見や考えを表す助動詞や，主観的な意見が入る形容詞・副詞は opinion を探す目印になる。

解き方

» ①の some students have a stock of single-use bottles at home「何人かの生徒は自宅に使い捨てボトルのストックがある」は，あるかないかの事実を述べているので除外。

» ②の there are vending machines for buying drinks at school「学校に飲み物を買うための自動販売機がある」は，意見ではなく事実なので除外。

» ③の washing reusable bottles takes a lot of time「再利用ボトルを洗うのはとても時間がかかる」は，人によって変わる主観的な意見と考えられる。

» ④の water in unopened single-use bottles lasts a long time「未開封の使い捨てボトルに入った水は長期間持つ」は，事実とも意見とも考えられそうだ。

» 現時点では意見だと考えられる③と④が内容的に正しいかを確認するために，Question 3 の表を見る。

Question 3: If you don't use a reusable bottle, what are your reasons?	
Summary of responses	Number of students
It takes too much time to wash reusable bottles.	24
I think single-use bottles are more convenient.	17
Many flavoured drinks are available in single-use bottles.	14
Buying a single-use bottle doesn't cost much.	10
I can buy drinks from vending machines at school.	7
I feel reusable bottles are too heavy.	4
My home has dozens of single-use bottles.	3
Single-use bottled water can be stored unopened for a long time.	2
(Other reasons)	4

≫ 「再利用可能なボトルを使用していない場合，理由は何ですか？」という質問に対する回答が Question 3 の表にまとまっている。

≫ ③に該当するのは，いちばん上の It takes too much time to wash reusable bottles. 「再利用ボトルを洗うのにとても時間がかかる」である。これはやはり too much time 「とても多くの時間」の部分が，人によって判断が異なる主観的な表現である。

≫ ④に該当するのは，表の下のほうにある Single-use bottled water can be stored unopened for a long time. 「使い捨てボトルの水は長期間未開封で保管できる」だと考えられる。
≫ 表では助動詞の can を用いて主観的な意見のように書かれているが，選択肢では lasts と現在形で断言する書き方になっている。Question 3 の表の内容とは一致しないため，④は不適切。

≫ よって正解は③。

ふだんの学習でも意見と事実を見分ける練習をしておこう

難易度 やさしい

問4 One <u>fact</u> stated by your classmates in Question 3 is that single-use bottles are ☐9☐ .

① available to buy at school
② convenient to use
③ light enough to carry around
④ not too expensive to buy

MOVIE 48

着眼点
≫ 設問文から Question 3 の表に注目。
≫ 先に選択肢を確認して opinion「意見」を除外する。
≫ 次に本文の内容に合致する fact「事実」を選ぶ。

解き方
≫ ①の available to buy at school「学校で購入可能である」は，事実と考えられる。

≫ ②の convenient to use「使うのに便利である」は，便利かどうかは人の主観による意見なので除外。

≫ ③の light enough to carry around「持ち運ぶのに十分軽い」は，軽いかどうかは人の主観による意見なので除外。

≫ ④の not too expensive to buy「購入するのに高すぎない」は，値段が高くないかどうかは人の主観による意見なので除外。

≫ ①が内容的に正しいかどうかを Question 3 の表に戻って確認すると，上から5つめの I can buy drinks from vending machines at school.「学校の自動販売機で飲み物を購入できる」という回答が見つかる。これを書き換えたのが①だと考えられるので，正解は①。

問5 What is the most likely reason why your classmates do not use reusable bottles? ☐10☐

① There are many single-use bottled drinks stored at home.
② There is less variety of drinks available.
③ They are expensive for your classmates.
④ They are troublesome to deal with.

MOVIE 49

着眼点
» 「クラスメイトが再利用ボトルを使わない最もありそうな理由」を探す。
» 再利用ボトルを使わない理由は Question 3 の表にまとめられていたので，そこに手がかりがありそうだ。

解き方
» 「最もありそうな理由」を選ぶので，表の中で上位の回答を確認する。

Question 3: If you don't use a reusable bottle, what are your reasons?	
Summary of responses	Number of students
It takes too much time to wash reusable bottles.	24
I think single-use bottles are more convenient.	17
Many flavoured drinks are available in single-use bottles.	14
Buying a single-use bottle doesn't cost much.	10
I can buy drinks from vending machines at school.	7
I feel reusable bottles are too heavy.	4
My home has dozens of single-use bottles.	3
Single-use bottled water can be stored unopened for a long time.	2
(Other reasons)	4

» It takes too much time to wash reusable bottles.「再利用ボトルを洗うのに時間がかかりすぎる」や，I think single-use bottles are more convenient.「使い捨てボトルの方が便利だと思う」といった回答に共通するのは，「再利用ボトルは扱いづらい」ということ。

» よって最もありそうな理由は④の They are troublesome to deal with.「取り扱うのがやっかいだ」だと判断できる。よって正解は④。

113

令和3年度 大学入学共通テスト 第2日程
第2問B 攻略のプロセス

STEP 1 まずは大問の全体像をつかむ

あらかじめリード文に目を通したうえで，本文のどこに何が書いてあるかをざっくり把握しましょう。

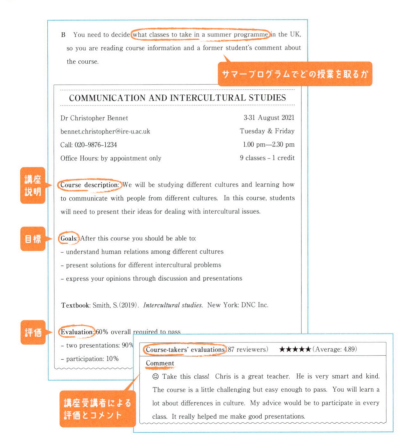

- サマープログラムの**講座**に関する情報。
- **概要**をまとめた英文に加えて，実際に講座を受講した生徒による**評価**と**コメント**がある。

STEP 2 設問と選択肢を読み解く

続いて設問や選択肢に目を通しましょう。探すべき情報を押さえたうえで英文を読むことで、問題を解く時間を大幅に短縮できます。ここでは問3と問4に注目します。

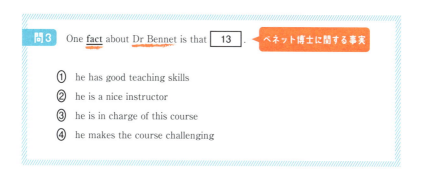

≫ それぞれの選択肢が fact「事実」なのか opinion「意見」なのか、そして本文の内容と合致しているかを確認する必要がある。
≫ opinion と考えられる選択肢をあらかじめ除外した上で、Dr Bennet という名前で本文をスキャニングして、残った選択肢が本文の内容と合致するかを確かめると効率がよい。
≫ fact は数値などの客観的な事実を指し、opinion は感想などの主観的な意見を指す。

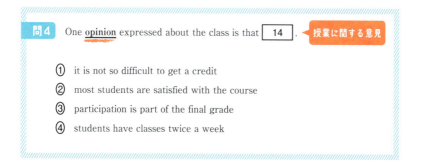

≫ 一般的に、講座説明には「事実」が書かれていると考えられる。
≫ 反対に、「意見」はコメント欄に書かれていると予測できる。
≫ 問4の場合、「意見」が書かれていそうなコメント欄に注目することで、時間を短縮できる。

STEP 3 必要な情報を本文から探しながら小問を解く　難易度 やさしい

問1 What will you do in this course?　11

① Discuss various topics about culture
② Visit many different countries
③ Watch a film about human relations
④ Write a final report about culture

MOVIE 50

着眼点
≫ この講座ですることを探して本文を読む。

解き方
≫ Course description「講座説明」のあたりに手がかりがありそうだ，と目星をつけて読む。

Course description: We will be studying different cultures and learning how to communicate with people from different cultures. In this course, students will need to present their ideas for dealing with intercultural issues.

Goals: After this course you should be able to:
- understand human relations among different cultures
- present solutions for different intercultural problems
- express your opinions through discussion and presentations

≫ 講座説明には，「異文化を研究し，異文化出身の人々とコミュニケーションをとる方法を学びます。本講座では，学生は異文化間で起こる問題に対処するための自分の考えを発表する必要があります」と概要が書かれている。
≫ Goals「目標」の部分も確認すると，3つめの項目の through discussion and presentations「議論やプレゼンテーションを通じて」から，この講座では議論を行うことがわかる。
≫ 以上より，「文化に関する様々なトピックについて話し合う」という内容の①が本文の内容に合致する。よって正解は①。

難易度 ふつう

問2 This class is aimed at students who [12].

① are interested in intercultural issues
② can give good presentations
③ like sightseeing in the UK
④ need to learn to speak English

MOVIE 51

着眼点
≫ この講座が<u>どのような学生を対象としているか</u>を本文から探す。

解き方
≫ Course description「講座説明」をもう一度確認すると，この講座では <u>different cultures「様々な文化」</u>について勉強したり，<u>how to communicate with people from different cultures「異文化出身の人々とのコミュニケーションの方法」</u>について学んだり，<u>present their ideas for dealing with intercultural issues「異文化間の問題に対処する考えを発表」</u>したりすることになっていた。

≫ つまり，この講座は<u>異文化や異文化間の問題に関心がある学生</u>を対象にしていると考えられる。これに最も近い選択肢は①の are interested in intercultural issues「異文化間で起こる問題に興味がある」なので，<u>正解は①</u>。

117

難易度 やさしい

問3 One <u>fact</u> about Dr Bennet is that ⬜13⬜ .

① he has good teaching skills
② he is a nice instructor
③ he is in charge of this course
④ he makes the course challenging

MOVIE 52

🔍 着眼点
» 設問文から，ベネット博士に当てはまる事実を選ぶ。
» 先に選択肢を確認して opinion「意見」を除外する。
» 次に本文の内容に合致する fact「事実」を選ぶ。
» 話者の意見や考えを表す助動詞や，主観的な意見が入る形容詞・副詞は opinion を探す目印になる。

💡 解き方
» ① he has good teaching skills は「教える技術が高い」という内容だが，教え方がよいか悪いかは主観によって異なる意見なので除外。
» ② he is a nice instructor は「よい教師である」という内容だが，よい先生かどうかは主観によって異なるので除外。
» ③ he is in charge of this course は「この講座の担当である」という内容で，事実と考えられる。
» ④ he makes the course challenging は「その講座を難しくやりがいのあるものにしている」という内容だが，難しくやりがいがあるかどうかは主観によって異なるので除外。

» ③について，ベネット博士がこの講座を担当しているかどうかを確認すると，講座情報のいちばん上に Dr Christopher Bennet と名前がある。

COMMUNICATION AND INTERCULTURAL STUDIES

Dr Christopher Bennet   3-31 August 2021
bennet.christopher@ire-u.ac.uk   Tuesday & Friday
Call: 020-9876-1234   1.00 pm—2.30 pm
Office Hours: by appointment only   9 classes – 1 credit

≫ さらにコメント欄に Chris is a great teacher.「クリスは素晴らしい先生です」とあるので，やはりベネット博士はこの講座の担当教師であると判断できる。よって正解は③。

> Course-takers' evaluations (87 reviewers)　★★★★★ (Average: 4.89)
>
> Comment
>
> ☺ Take this class! Chris is a great teacher. He is very smart and kind. The course is a little challenging but easy enough to pass. You will learn a lot about differences in culture. My advice would be to participate in every class. It really helped me make good presentations.

Chris は Christopher の愛称だよ

 やさしい

問4　One opinion expressed about the class is that ⬜14⬜ .

① it is not so difficult to get a credit
② most students are satisfied with the course
③ participation is part of the final grade
④ students have classes twice a week

MOVIE 53

🔍 着眼点
≫ 設問文から，この講座に当てはまる意見を選ぶ。
≫ 先に選択肢を確認して fact「事実」を除外する。
≫ 次に本文の内容に合致する opinion「意見」を選ぶ。
≫ 意見を探すので，「コメント欄に手がかりがありそうだ」と目星をつける。

💡 解き方

» ①の it is not so difficult to get a credit「単位を取るのはそれほど難しくない」は，主観的な意見なので残す。

» ②の most students are satisfied with the course「ほとんどの生徒は講座に満足している」は，satisfied の部分が主観的に見えるが，事実とも考えられる書き方になっているので保留。

» ③の participation is part of the final grade「参加が最終成績の一部である」は，断定的な言い方で事実だと判断できるので除外。

» ④の students have classes twice a week「生徒は週に 2 回授業がある」は，断定的な言い方で事実だと判断できるので除外。

» 残した①と②が内容的に正しいか，コメント欄を確認する。

Course-takers' evaluations(87 reviewers)　★★★★★(Average: 4.89)

Comment

　☺ Take this class!　Chris is a great teacher.　He is very smart and kind. The course is a little challenging but easy enough to pass.　You will learn a lot about differences in culture.　My advice would be to participate in every class.　It really helped me make good presentations.

» The course is a little challenging but easy enough to pass.「講座は少しだけ難しくやりがいがありますが，十分合格できます」という意見があるので，①は内容的にも正しいと判断できる。

» ②については，Course-takers' evaluations「コース受講者の評価」という見出しの右にある星の数に注目。この星は受講者の満足度を表しているらしく，5 段階中の 4.89 と具体的な数値の高評価を得ているので，「ほとんどの学生が講座に満足している」というのは意見ではなく事実だと判断できる。

» よって**正解は①**。

» get a credit は「単位を得る」という意味で，pass「合格する」の言い換えになっている。

問5 What do you have to do to pass this course?　15

① Come to every class and join the discussions
② Find an intercultural issue and discuss a solution
③ Give good presentations about intercultural issues
④ Make an office appointment with Dr Bennet

MOVIE 54

着眼点
» 「この講座に合格するために必要なこと」を本文から探す。

解き方
» この講座の評価については，講座情報のいちばん下に書かれている。

> Evaluation: 60% overall required to pass
> - two presentations: 90%（45% each）
> - participation: 10%

» 60% overall required to pass から，合格するには合計60％の評価が必要だとわかる。
» 評価の内訳は，1回につき45％のプレゼンテーションが2回で計90％，残る10％は出席が占めている。
» 合格に必要とされる60％以上の評価を得るには，計90％と比重が高いプレゼンテーションに力を入れるべきだと判断できる。
» この講座で学ぶことのひとつに異文化間の問題が含まれていたことを考え合わせると，正解は③。

» ①の「すべての授業に出席して議論に参加する」については，出席はたしかに評価の一部に含まれるが10％だけなので，これだけでは合格できない。

本文のどこに手がかりがあるか，すぐに判断できたかな？

令和３年度 大学入学共通テスト 第２日程
第３問Ａ 攻略のプロセス

 STEP 1 まずは大問の全体像をつかむ

あらかじめ リード文 に目を通したうえで，本文のどこに何が書いてあるかを ざっくり把握 しましょう。

> A Your British friend, Jan, visited a new amusement park and posted a blog about her experience.
>
> **Sunny Mountain Park: A Great Place to Visit**
> Posted by Jan at 9.37 pm on 15 September 2020
>
> Sunny Mountain Park finally opened last month! It's a big amusement park with many exciting attractions, including a huge roller coaster (see the map). I had a fantastic time there with my friends last week.
>
> We couldn't wait to try the roller coaster, but first we took the train round the park to get an idea of its layout. From the train, we saw the Picnic Zone and thought it would be a good place to have lunch. However, it was already very crowded, so we decided to go to the Food Court instead. Before lunch, we went to the Discovery Zone. It was well worth the wait to experience the scientific attractions there. In the afternoon, we enjoyed several rides near Mountain Station. Of course, we tried the roller coaster, and we weren't disappointed. On our way back to the Discovery Zone to enjoy more attractions, we took a short break at a rest stop. There, we got a lovely view over the lake to the castle. We ended up at the Shopping Zone, where we bought souvenirs for our
>
> Sunny Mountain Pa
> last.

- ジャンが投稿したブログ（a blog）
- ブログのタイトルや投稿者などの情報

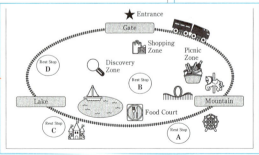

遊園地のマップ

- イギリス人の友だちが書いた遊園地についての**ブログ記事**。
- ブログの文章の後に，**遊園地のマップ**がついている。
- 記事とマップを照らし合わせながら英文を読む。

STEP 2 設問と選択肢を読み解く

続いて設問や選択肢に目を通しましょう。探すべき情報を押さえたうえで英文を読むことで、問題を解く時間を大幅に短縮できます。

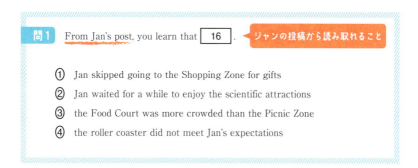

» ジャンの投稿と照らし合わせて正しい選択肢を選ぶ問題。
» ざっくりとした尋ね方になっている設問の部分からは、ジャンの投稿に手がかりがあることくらいしか読み取ることができない。
» 一方、選択肢はバラバラで情報量が多いので、それぞれの選択肢からキーワードを拾い、本文に戻って正解を見つけるとよい。

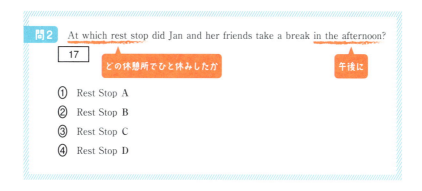

» ジャンたちが午後に休息を取った休憩所を探す問題。
» マップに描かれている施設名や休憩所の位置に注意しながら、記事とマップを照らし合わせる。

STEP 3 必要な情報を本文から探しながら小問を解く

問1 From Jan's post, you learn that ⎡ 16 ⎤ .

① Jan skipped going to the Shopping Zone for gifts
② Jan waited for a while to enjoy the scientific attractions
③ the Food Court was more crowded than the Picnic Zone
④ the roller coaster did not meet Jan's expectations

MOVIE 55

着眼点
» From Jan's post という設問の出だしから，ジャンの投稿全体に注目する。
» 漠然とした尋ね方になっているので，すべての選択肢に目を通してから，内容的に正しいかどうか本文を確認する。

解き方
» 選択肢の内容を1つずつ確認すると，①は「ジャンはお土産のためにショッピングゾーンに行くのを省いた」という内容。
» ②は「ジャンは科学的なアトラクションを楽しむためにしばらく待った」という内容。
» ③は「フードコートはピクニックゾーンよりも混んでいた」という内容。
» ④は「ジェットコースターはジャンの期待に見合わなかった」という内容。

» 選択肢に並ぶ様々な施設名や乗り物を探して本文を読む。これらが登場するのは，具体的な行動が時系列順に書かれているブログの第2段落。

> We couldn't wait to try the roller coaster, but first we took the train round the park to get an idea of its layout. From the train, we saw the Picnic Zone and thought it would be a good place to have lunch. However, it was already very crowded, so we decided to go to the Food Court instead. Before lunch, we went to the Discovery Zone. It was well worth the wait to experience the scientific attractions there. In the afternoon, we enjoyed several rides near Mountain Station. Of course, we tried the roller coaster, and we weren't disappointed. On our way back to the Discovery Zone to enjoy more attractions, we took a short break at a rest stop. There, we got a lovely view over the lake to the castle. We ended up at the Shopping Zone, where we bought souvenirs for our friends and family.

≫ 第2～3文の From the train, we saw the Picnic Zone and thought it would be a good place to have lunch. However, it was already very crowded, so we decided to go to the Food Court instead.「電車からはピクニックゾーンが見えて，昼食を取るのに良い場所だろうと思いました。しかし，そこはすでにとても混んでいたので，代わりにフードコートへ行くことに決めました」から，ピクニックゾーンが混んでいたのでフードコートに行ったことがわかる。よって，反対のことを言っている③は不適切。

≫ 第4～5文の Before lunch, we went to the Discovery Zone. **It was well worth the wait to experience the scientific attractions there.**「昼食の前に，私たちはディスカバリーゾーンに行きました。そこでの科学的なアトラクションの体験は，十分待つ価値がありました」を言い換えたのが②だと判断できる。

≫ 第7文の Of course, we tried the roller coaster, and we weren't disappointed.「もちろんジェットコースターに乗ってみましたが，がっかりすることはありませんでした」から，反対のことを言っている④は不適切。

≫ 第10文の We ended up at the Shopping Zone, where we bought souvenirs for our friends and family.「私たちは最後にショッピングゾーンに行き着き，そこで友だちや家族にお土産を買いました」から，ショッピングゾーンに行かなかったとする①は不適切。

≫ よって正解は②。

難易度 ふつう

問2 At which rest stop did Jan and her friends take a break in the afternoon?
17

① Rest Stop A
② Rest Stop B
③ Rest Stop C
④ Rest Stop D

MOVIE 56

着眼点
» 休憩所の場所と午後の行動に注意しながら本文を読む。

解き方
» In the afternoon で始まる第2段落・第6文以降に注目。

> scientific attractions there. In the afternoon, we enjoyed several rides near Mountain Station. Of course, we tried the roller coaster, and we weren't disappointed. On our way back to the Discovery Zone to enjoy more attractions, we took a short break at a rest stop. There, we got a lovely view over the lake to the castle. We ended up at the Shopping Zone, where we

» 午後はまずマウンテンステーションの近くでジェットコースターなどの乗り物に乗って楽しんだことがわかる。
» 第8文に「もっと多くのアトラクションを楽しむためにディスカバリーゾーンへ戻る途中、私たちは休憩所で短い休息を取りました」とあるので、マウンテンステーションとディスカバリーゾーンの間にあるBの休憩所で休んだと推測できる。
» さらに次の第9文から「そこで湖越しに美しい城を眺めた」ことがわかる。Bの休憩所から見える湖と城の位置関係を確認すると、やはり休息を取ったのはここで間違いないと確認できる。よって正解は②。

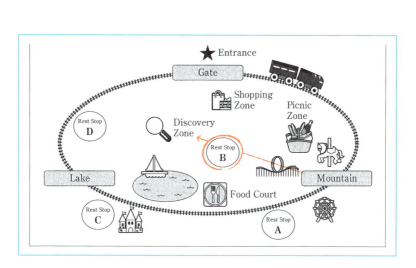

英文中の条件とマップを照らし合わせ，正解を導き出そう！

令和3年度 大学入学共通テスト 第2日程
第3問B 攻略のプロセス

 まずは大問の全体像をつかむ

あらかじめリード文に目を通したうえで，本文のどこに何が書いてあるかをざっくり把握しましょう。

> B Your friend in the UK introduced her favourite musician to you. Wanting to learn more, you found the following article in a music magazine.
>
> 音楽雑誌の記事
>
> ### Dave Starr, a Living Legend
>
> 伝説的なミュージシャンに関する伝記だと推測
>
> At one time, Black Swan were the biggest rock band in the UK, and their dynamic leader Dave Starr played a large part in that achievement. Still performing as a solo singer, Dave's incredible talent has inspired generations of young musicians.
>
> When he was a little boy, Dave was always singing and playing with toy instruments. He was never happier than when he was playing his toy drum. At age seven, he was given his first real drum set, and by 10, he could play well. By 14, he had also mastered the guitar. When he was still a high school student, he became a member of The Bluebirds, playing rhythm guitar. To get experience, The Bluebirds played for free at school events and in community centres. The band built up a small circle of passionate fans.
>
> Dave's big break came when, on his 18th birthday, he was asked to become the drummer for Black Swan. In just two years, the band's shows were selling out at large concert halls. It came as a shock, therefore, when the lead vocalist quit to spend more time with his family. However, Dave jumped at the chance to take over as lead singer even though it meant he could no longer play his favourite instrument.
>
> In the following years, Black Swan became increasingly successful, topping the music charts and gaining even more fans. Dave became the principal song writer, and was proud of his contribution to the band. However, with the addition of a keyboard player, the music gradually changed direction. Dave became frustrated, and he and the lead guitarist decided to leave and start a new group. Unfortunately, Dave's new band failed to reach Black Swan's level of success, and stayed together for only 18 months.

- イギリスの友人がすすめるミュージシャンに関する**雑誌記事**。
- 記事のタイトルから，1人の人物を取り上げた**伝記的な内容**だと推測できる。

STEP 2 設問と選択肢を読み解く

続いて設問や選択肢に目を通しましょう。探すべき情報を押さえたうえで英文を読むことで、問題を解く時間を大幅に短縮できます。ここでは問1と問3に注目します。

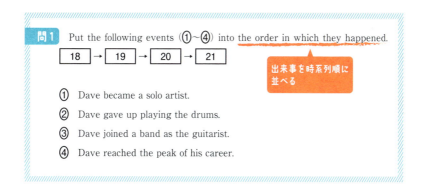

» 出来事を時系列順に並べるタイプの問題。
» 本文に出てきた順番＝出来事が起こった順番とは限らない。
» 時間の表現や時制に注意しながら英文を読む。

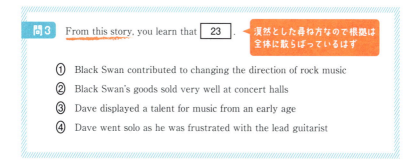

» 設問がざっくりとした尋ね方になっている一方、選択肢はバラバラで情報量が多いので、それぞれの選択肢から本文に戻って正解をみつけるとよい。
» 選択肢を先読みしてキーワードを拾ってから、本文と合致するかを確かめていく。

必要な情報を本文から探しながら小問を解く

問1 Put the following events (①〜④) into the order in which they happened.

18 → 19 → 20 → 21

① Dave became a solo artist.
② Dave gave up playing the drums.
③ Dave joined a band as the guitarist.
④ Dave reached the peak of his career.

MOVIE 57

着眼点
» 実際に起こった順番に出来事を並べる問題。時間の表現や時制に注意。
» 選択肢に目を通した後,該当する記述を探して本文を読む。

解き方
» ①は「デイヴはソロのアーティストになった」という内容。
» ②は「デイヴはドラムの演奏をあきらめた」という内容。
» ③は「デイヴはギタリストとしてバンドに加入した」という内容。
» ④は「デイヴはキャリアの頂点に達した」という内容。

> At one time, Black Swan were the biggest rock band in the UK, and their dynamic leader Dave Starr played a large part in that achievement. Still performing as a solo singer, Dave's incredible talent has inspired generations of young musicians.

» 第1段落の最終文から,現在のデイヴはソロの歌手として活動していることがわかる。これは選択肢の①に該当する。

> When he was a little boy, Dave was always singing and playing with toy instruments. He was never happier than when he was playing his toy drum. At age seven, he was given his first real drum set, and by 10, he could play well. By 14, he had also mastered the guitar. When he was still a high school student, he became a member of The Bluebirds, playing rhythm guitar. To get experience, The Bluebirds played for free at school events and in community centres. The band built up a small circle of passionate fans.

≫ 第2段落・第5文の「まだ高校生だったとき，**彼はザ・ブルーバーズのメンバーになり，リズムギターを弾いた**」に該当する選択肢が③である。

≫ これは高校生の頃の話なので，①より前の出来事だと推測できる。

> Dave's big break came when, on his 18th birthday, he was asked to become the drummer for Black Swan. In just two years, the band's shows were selling out at large concert halls. It came as a shock, therefore, when the lead vocalist quit to spend more time with his family. However, Dave jumped at the chance to take over as lead singer even though it meant he could no longer play his favourite instrument.

≫ 第3段落の最終文「**それは彼がもはやお気に入りの楽器を演奏できないことを意味していた**」から，デイヴは幼少期から慣れ親しんだドラムを辞めてリードシンガーになったことがわかる。これは選択肢の②に該当し，第1〜2文の時間の表現に注目すると20歳頃の話だとわかる。

> In the following years, Black Swan became increasingly successful, topping the music charts and gaining even more fans. Dave became the principal song writer, and was proud of his contribution to the band. However, with the addition of a keyboard player, the music gradually changed direction. Dave became frustrated, and he and the lead guitarist decided to leave and start a new group. Unfortunately, Dave's new band failed to reach Black Swan's level of success, and stayed together for only 18 months.

≫ 残った④に該当する箇所を探して本文を読み進めると，第4段落・第1文の「それから数年で**ブラック・スワンはますます成功をおさめ，音楽チャートのトップに載り**，さらに多くのファンを獲得した」が該当しそうだと推測できる。

≫ 最終文「残念ながら，**デイヴの新しいバンドはブラック・スワンほどの成功に達することはできず**，結成されていたのはわずか18か月であった」から，デイヴのキャリアの頂点はブラック・スワンでボーカルになった数年後のことだと判断できる。よって④は②より後の出来事。

≫ ③→②→④は時系列順に過去の話をしていたが，①は現在の話だったので，**正解は③→②→④→①**の順。

131

難易度 やさしい

問2 Dave became the lead singer of Black Swan because 22 .

① he preferred singing to playing the drums

② he wanted to change the band's musical direction

③ the other band members wanted more success

④ the previous singer left for personal reasons

MOVIE 58

着眼点

≫ デイヴがブラック・スワンのリードシンガーになった理由を読み取る。

解き方

≫ デイヴがブラック・スワンのリードシンガーになった経緯は，第3段落に詳しく書かれていた。

> Dave's big break came when, on his 18th birthday, he was asked to become the drummer for Black Swan. In just two years, the band's shows were selling out at large concert halls. It came as a shock, therefore, when the lead vocalist quit to spend more time with his family. However, Dave jumped at the chance to take over as lead singer even though it meant he could no longer play his favourite instrument.

≫ 第3文の It came as a shock, therefore, when the lead vocalist quit to spend more time with his family. However, Dave jumped at the chance to take over as lead singer 「だからこそ，リードボーカルがもっと多くの時間を家族と過ごすために辞めたときは衝撃的だった。しかし，デイヴはリードシンガーを引き継ぐチャンスに飛びついた」という記述から，デイヴがリードシンガーになった理由は，元のボーカルが家族との時間を優先すべくバンドを辞めたためだと判断できる。

≫ この理由を for personal reasons 「個人的な理由のため」と言い換えた④が正解。

132 第2日程 第3問B 攻略のプロセス

難易度 ふつう

問3 From this story, you learn that ☐23☐ .

① Black Swan contributed to changing the direction of rock music
② Black Swan's goods sold very well at concert halls
③ Dave displayed a talent for music from an early age
④ Dave went solo as he was frustrated with the lead guitarist

MOVIE 59

着眼点

» From this story という設問の出だしから，記事全体に注目する。
» 漠然とした尋ね方になっているので，すべての選択肢に目を通してから，内容的に正しいかどうか本文の該当箇所を確認する。

解き方

» ①は「ブラック・スワンはロックミュージックの方向性を変えることに貢献した」という内容だが，第4段落・第3文から変わったのはバンドの音楽性であり，ロックミュージックの方向性ではないので不適切。

» ②は「ブラック・スワンのグッズはコンサートホールでとてもよく売れた」という内容。コンサートのチケットが売り切れたという話は第3段落・第2文にあったが，グッズの話はなかったので不適切。

» ③は「デイヴは幼い頃から音楽の才能を発揮した」という内容。デイヴは幼少期からドラムに親しみ，By 14, he had also mastered the guitar.「14歳になるまでに，ギターも習得した」と第2段落に書かれていた。

» ④は「デイヴはリードギタリストに不満を抱いたのでソロになった」という内容。ブラック・スワンに加入したキーボードとの不和は第4段落・第4文に書かれていたが，リードギタリストに対する不満はどこにも書かれていないので不適切。

» よって正解は③。

選択肢中のキーワードを本文から探して時間短縮！

令和３年度 大学入学共通テスト 第２日程
第４問 攻略のプロセス

STEP 1 まずは大問の全体像をつかむ

あらかじめリード文に目を通したうえで，本文のどこに何が書いてあるかをざっくり把握しましょう。

Hi,

Thanks for sending your data! This will help us prepare for our presentation!

I notice from the data that Australians spend the most on entertainment. I'll present on this.

Also, the other day, on Japanese TV, I saw a program about Australian people enjoying winter sports in Hokkaido. I wonder how much they spend. I'll look for more information. If you find any, please let me know. This could be good for a future project.

In addition, I agree with Hannah that there seems to be a big difference in the length of stay depending on the country or region the visitor is from.

What about you? Do you want to talk about what Hannah found in relation to the spending habits? I think this is very interesting.

All the best,
Rick
P.S. This message is going to Hannah, too.

リックの署名
＝リックからのメール

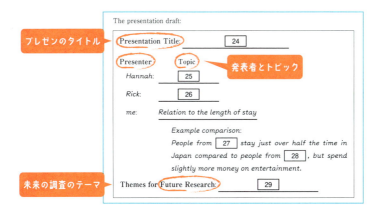

プレゼンのタイトル

Presenter／Topic
発表者とトピック

未来の調査のテーマ

The presentation draft:

Presentation Title: ___24___

Presenter   Topic
Hannah: 25
Rick: 26
me: Relation to the length of stay

Example comparison:
People from ___27___ stay just over half the time in Japan compared to people from ___28___, but spend slightly more money on entertainment.

Themes for Future Research: ___29___

- クラスメイトと一緒に，**日本の観光に関するプレゼンの準備をしている**という設定。
- クラスメイトのハンナとリックにあなたが送った**資料**に加えて，**ハンナとリックのメール**，さらにプレゼンテーション用の**下書き**がついている。
- 様々な資料を照らし合わせて，プレゼン用の下書きを完成させる。

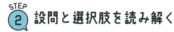
設問と選択肢を読み解く

続いて設問や選択肢に目を通しましょう。探すべき情報を押さえたうえで英文を読むことで、問題を解く時間を大幅に短縮できます。ここでは問1と問4に注目します。

» プレゼン用の資料やポスター内の空所を埋めるタイプの問題は、まず設問を見て資料内の空所の位置を確認する。
» 資料内の空所の前後から、どのような情報を探せばよいかが推測できる場合がある。
» 問1の場合、プレゼン全体のタイトルとして最も適切なものを選ぶ。
» 全体に関わる設問なので全体の概要を押さえてから解くこと、一部だけを取り上げた選択肢は正解にならないことに注意。

一部だけを切り取った選択肢は、内容的に正しくても全体をまとめるタイトルとしては不正解になるので要注意!

問4 You agree with Rick's suggestion and look at the data. Choose the best for 　27　 and 　28　 .

① Australia

② China

③ France

④ Taiwan

> リックの提案の内容と
> データを確認する

---

me:　　　*Relation to the length of stay*

Example comparison:
People from 　27　 *stay just over half the time in Japan compared to people from* 　28　 *, but spend slightly more money on entertainment.*

≫ 問４の場合，まずは設問中の Rick's suggestion「リックの提案」が具体的に何を指すかを読み取る必要がある。

≫ また，the date「データ」を見るように指示されているので，冒頭の棒グラフと表に手がかりがあることがわかる。

≫ さらにプレゼン用の下書き内の空所を確認すると，空所以外の部分から訪日客の滞在期間や消費傾向を比較して，条件に合う国・地域を選ぶ問題であると判断できる。日本での滞在時間と娯楽に使った金額に手がかりがありそうだと推測できる。

STEP 3 必要な情報を本文から探しながら小問を解く

問1 Which is the best for 24 ?

① Money Spent on Winter Holidays in Hokkaido
② Shopping Budgets of International Tourists in Tokyo
③ Spending Habits of International Visitors in Japan
④ The Increase of Spending on Entertainment in Japan

着眼点

》下書きを確認すると，プレゼンテーション全体のタイトルが空所になっている。
》タイトル問題は原則，全体に目を通してから最後に解く。
》一部分だけを切り取った選択肢ではなく，全体を過不足なくまとめた選択肢を選ぶ。

解き方

》①は「北海道での冬季休暇に使われるお金」という内容だが，これはリックのメールの第3段落だけに登場する一部分だけを切り取った話。

》②は「東京における海外からの観光客の買い物にかける予算」という内容だが，ハンナのメールの第2段落だけに登場する一部分だけを切り取った話。

》③は「海外からの訪日客の消費傾向」という内容で，ハンナとリック双方のメールや資料の内容を端的にまとめたタイトルだと判断できる。

》④は「日本における娯楽への支出の増加」という内容だが，娯楽の話はリックのメールの第2段落だけに登場する一部分だけを切り取った話。

》よって正解は③。

難易度 ふつう

問2 Which is the best for ⬚25⬚ ?

① Activities of Australian visitors in Japan
② Asian visitors' food costs in Japan
③ Gift-giving habits in European cultures
④ Patterns in spending by visitors from Asia

MOVIE 61

The presentation draft:

Presentation Title: _____⬚24⬚_____

Presenter	Topic
Hannah:	⬚25⬚
Rick:	⬚26⬚
me:	*Relation to the length of stay*

Example comparison:
People from ⬚27⬚ *stay just over half the time in Japan compared to people from* ⬚28⬚ *, but spend slightly more money on entertainment.*

Themes for Future Research: _____⬚29⬚_____

着眼点
» プレゼン用の下書きを確認すると，ハンナのトピックが空所になっている。
» ハンナのメールから，彼女が何について話そうとしているかを読み取る。

解き方

» ハンナが話したいと思っているトピックを探して，彼女のメールを読み進めていく。

> Also, the table shows that Asian visitors, overall, tend to spend more on shopping compared to visitors from Europe and Australia. I guess this is probably because gift-giving in Asian cultures is really important, and they want to buy gifts for friends and family. For example, I have seen many Asian tourists shopping around Ginza, Harajuku, and Akihabara. Perhaps they don't have to spend so much money on accommodations, so they can spend more on shopping. I'd like to talk about this.

» ハンナは第2段落・第1文で Also, the table shows that **Asian visitors, overall, tend to spend more on shopping compared to visitors from Europe and Australia.**「ヨーロッパやオーストラリアからの訪日客と比べて，アジアからの訪日客は全体として，より買い物にお金を費やす傾向があることも，その表は示しているわね」と書いている。

» この「アジアからの訪日客が買い物にお金を費やす傾向」について，ハンナは続く第2〜4文で理由を推測し，第5文で **I'd like to talk about this.**「私はこれについて話したいと思っているの」と締めくくっている。この this は，ハンナが第2段落全体で言及している「アジアからの訪日客の消費傾向」を指すと考えられる。

» よって，アジアからの訪日客の消費傾向を Patterns in spending by visitors from Asia「アジアからの訪日客の支出パターン」と書き換えた ④ が正解。

代名詞が指す内容を正しくとらえることができたかな？

問3 Which is the best for 26 ?

① Australian tourists' interest in entertainment
② Chinese spending habits in Tokyo
③ TV programs about Hokkaido in Australia
④ Various experiences Asians enjoy in Japan

MOVIE 62

着眼点
» プレゼン用の下書きを確認すると，**リックのトピック**が空所になっている。
» リックのメールから，彼が何について話そうとしているかを読み取る。

解き方
» リックが話したいと思っているトピックを探して，彼のメールを読み進めていく。

> I notice from the data that Australians spend the most on entertainment. I'll present on this.

» リックは第2段落・第1文で I notice from the data that **Australians spend the most on entertainment**.「データから，**オーストラリア人はいちばん娯楽にお金を費やしている**ことに気づいたんだ」と述べている。
» これを受けて，第2文に **I'll present on this.**「僕はこれについて発表するよ」とあるので，この this が指す第1文の**「オーストラリア人と娯楽」**がリックのトピックだと判断できる。
» 第1文の内容を Australian tourists' interest in entertainment「オーストラリアからの観光客の娯楽への関心」と書き換えた**①が正解**。

問 4 You agree with Rick's suggestion and look at the data. Choose the best for ⬚27⬚ and ⬚28⬚.

① Australia
② China
③ France
④ Taiwan

MOVIE 63

---

me: Relation to the length of stay

Example comparison:
People from ⬚27⬚ stay just over half the time in Japan compared to people from ⬚28⬚, but spend slightly more money on entertainment.

Themes for Future Research: ⬚29⬚

着眼点

≫ プレゼン用の下書きを確認すると自分のトピックの一部が空所になっている。
≫ 設問中の Rick's suggestion「リックの提案」や data「資料」に手がかりがありそうだ。

解き方

≫ プレゼン用の下書きの空所に注目すると，⬚27⬚ から来た人は ⬚28⬚ から来た人の半分より少し長く日本に滞在することがわかる。
≫ さらに，⬚27⬚ から来た人は ⬚28⬚ から来た人よりも娯楽にかけるお金が少し多いことがわかる。
≫ これら2つの手がかりをもとに，資料に含まれる Length of stay in Japan「日本での滞在期間」というタイトルの棒グラフと，Average Amount of Money Spent While Visiting Japan「訪日中に使った平均金額」というタイトルの表を確認する。
≫ グラフや表には様々な国や地域が並ぶが，選択肢にあるオーストラリア，中国，フランス，台湾のうち，条件に当てはまる組み合わせを探せばよい。

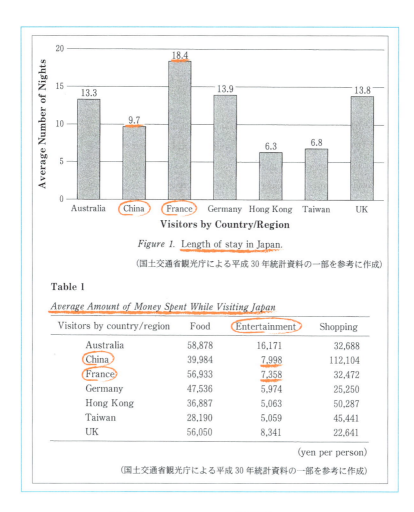

» 棒グラフから，「 27 」から来た人々は，「 28 」から来た人々と比べると半分よりわずかに長い期間だけ日本に滞在する」という条件に当てはまるのは 13.3 日滞在のオーストラリアと 6.8 日滞在の台湾の組み合わせと，18.4 日滞在のフランスと 9.7 日滞在の中国の組み合わせである。

» この組み合わせのうち，「 27 」から来た人々は，「 28 」から来た人々よりも娯楽に少しだけ多くお金を使っている」という条件に当てはまるのは，表から 7,998 円の中国と 7,358 円のフランスだけである。

» よって 27 には②の中国が，28 には③のフランスが入る。

» ちなみに設問中の「リックの提案」はリックのメールの第 5 段落にあり，「お金の使い道に関してハンナが発見したことについて話す」という提案を指している。

143

問5 Which is the best combination for 29 ?

A：Australians' budgets for winter sports in Japan
B：Future changes in the number of international visitors to Tokyo
C：Popular food for international visitors to Hokkaido
D：What Asian visitors in Japan will spend money on in the future

① A，B
② A，C
③ A，D
④ B，C
⑤ B，D
⑥ C，D

MOVIE 64

着眼点
» プレゼン用の下書きを確認すると，Themes for Future Research「将来の調査テーマ」に入る項目として正しい組み合わせを選べばよい。
» ハンナとリックのメールから，将来のことについて話している箇所を探す。

解き方
» ハンナが将来のことについて話している箇所を探して，彼女のメールを読み進めていく。

> However, I've heard that visitors from Asia are now becoming interested in doing some other things instead of shopping. We may see some changes in this kind of data in the near future!

» ハンナは第3段落・第1文で However, I've heard that visitors from Asia are now becoming interested in doing some other things instead of shopping.「でもアジアからの訪日客は今，買い物の代わりに何か他のことをするのに興味を持ち始めていると聞いたわ」と述べている。
» 第2文で We may see some changes in this kind of data in the near future!「近い将来，この種のデータに変化が見られるかもしれないわね！」と将来の話をしているので，第1文の内容に合致する D：What Asian visitors in

Japan will spend money on in the future「アジアからの訪日客が，将来お金を使うであろうもの」が将来の調査テーマの1つだと判断できる。

≫ 続いてリックが将来のことについて話している箇所を探して，彼のメールを読み進めていく。

> Also, the other day, on Japanese TV, I saw a program about Australian people enjoying winter sports in Hokkaido. I wonder how much they spend. I'll look for more information. If you find any, please let me know. This could be good for a future project.

≫ リックは第3段落・第1〜2文で Also, the other day, on Japanese TV, I saw a program about Australian people enjoying winter sports in Hokkaido. I wonder how much they spend.「それに先日，日本のテレビで，北海道でウィンタースポーツを楽しんでいるオーストラリア人に関する番組を見たんだ。彼らはいくらお金を使うのかな」と述べている。

≫ これについて第3〜4文で情報を求めた後，第5文で This could be good for a future project.「これは将来のプロジェクトにふさわしいかもね」と将来の話をしているので，第1〜2文の内容に合致する A：Australians' budgets for winter sports in Japan「オーストラリアの人々が日本でのウィンタースポーツにかける予算」がもう1つの将来の調査テーマだと判断できる。

≫ よって，AとDの組み合わせになっている ③ が正解。

一見フクザツそうな問題も，ひとつずつ手がかりを追っていけば必ず解けるように問題は作られているんだ

145

令和3年度 大学入学共通テスト 第2日程
第5問 攻略のプロセス

 まずは大問の全体像をつかむ

あらかじめリード文に目を通した上で，本文のどこに何が書いてあるかを，ざっくり把握しましょう。

> 【インタビューしてみたい人について話すため，ノートをまとめる】
>
> You are going to give a talk on a person you would like to have interviewed if they were still alive. Read the following passage about the person you have chosen and complete your notes.
>
> Vivian Maier 【この人に関する文章を読むようだ】
>
> This is the story of an American street photographer who kept her passion for taking pictures secret until her death. She lived her life as a caregiver, and if it had not been for the sale of her belongings at an auction house, her incredible work might never have been discovered.
>
> It was 2007. A Chicago auction house was selling off the belongings of an old woman named Vivian Maier. She had stopped paying storage fees, and so the company decided to sell her things. Her belongings—mainly old photographs and negatives—were sold to three buyers: Maloof, Slattery, and Prow.
>
> Slattery thought Vivian's work was interesting so he published her photographs on a photo-sharing website in July 2008. The photographs received little attention. Then, in October, Maloof linked his blog to his selection of Vivian's photographs, and right away, thousands of people were viewing them. Maloof had found Vivian Maier's name with the prints, but he was unable to discover anything about her. Then an Internet search led him to a 2009 newspaper article about her death. Maloof used this information to discover more about Vivian's life, and it was the combination of Vivian's mysterious life story and her photographs that grabbed everyone's attention.
>
> Details of Vivian's life are limited for two reasons. First, since no one had interviewed her while she was alive, no one knew why she took so many photographs. Second, it is clear from interviews with the family she worked

"film negative"   "printed image"

for that Vivian was a very private person. She had few friends. Besides, she had kept her hobby a secret.

Vivian was born in 1926 in the United States to an Austrian father and a French mother. The marriage was not a happy one, and it seems her mother and father lived apart for several years. During her childhood Vivian frequently moved between the US and France, sometimes living in France, and sometimes in the US. For a while, Vivian and her mother lived in New York with Jeanne Bertrand, a successful photographer. It is believed that Vivian became interested in photography as a young adult, as her first photos were taken in France in the late 1940s using a very simple camera. She returned to New York in 1951, and in 1956 she moved to Chicago to work as a caregiver for the Gensburg family. This job gave her more free time for taking photographs.

In 1952, at the age of 26, she purchased her first 6 × 6 camera, and it was with this that most of her photographs of life on the streets of Chicago were taken. For over 30 years she took photos of children, the elderly, the rich, and the poor. Some people were not even aware that their picture was being taken. She also took a number of self-portraits. Some were reflections of herself in a shop window. Others were of her own shadow. Vivian continued to document Chicago life until the early 1970s, when she changed to a new style of photography.

An international award-winning documentary film called *Finding Vivian Maier* brought interest in her work to a wider audience. The film led to exhibitions in Europe and the US. To choose the photographs that best represent her style, those in charge of the exhibitions have tried to answer the question, "What would Vivian Maier have printed?" In order to answer this question, they used her notes, the photos she actually did print, and information about her preferences as reported by the Gensburgs. Vivian was much more interested in capturing moments rather than the outcome. So, one could say the mystery behind Vivian's work remains largely "undeveloped."

長文とその情報をまとめたノートを照らし合わせながら問題を解いていくよ

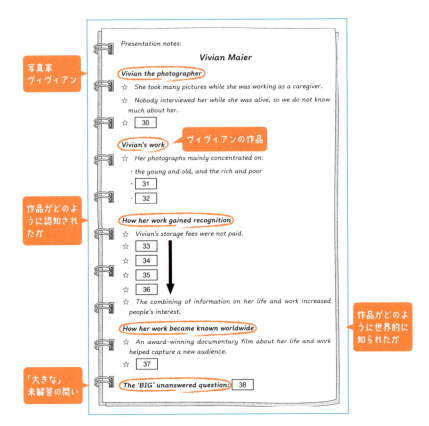

- 存命であればインタビューしてみたい人について**話をする**という設定。
- 英文に続いて，プレゼン用に情報をまとめた**ノート**がついている。
- まずはノートの内容と設問を確認してから本文を読む。

設問と選択肢を読み解く

続いて設問や選択肢に目を通しましょう。==探すべき情報を押さえたうえで英文を読む==ことで，問題を解く時間を大幅に短縮できます。ここでは問 3 に注目します。

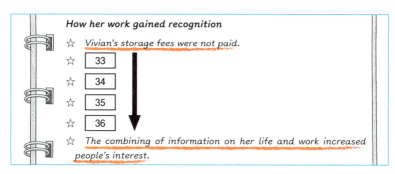

» 出来事を時系列順に並べるタイプの問題。
» 時間の表現や時制に注意しながら英文を読む。
» ノートにはあらかじめ最初の出来事と最後の出来事が書かれている。これらの出来事が本文のどこに書かれているかを探して，その間に書かれている内容と選択肢を照らし合わせると効率がよい。

STEP 3 必要な情報を本文から探しながら小問を解く

問1 Choose the best statement for ｜ 30 ｜．

① Her work remained undiscovered until it was sold at auction.
② She is thought to have become attracted to photography in her thirties.
③ She took her camera wherever she went and showed her pictures to others.
④ The majority of her photos were taken in New York.

MOVIE 65

Vivian the photographer
☆ She took many pictures while she was working as a caregiver.
☆ Nobody interviewed her while she was alive, so we do not know much about her.
☆ ｜ 30 ｜

着眼点
» ノートの小見出し Vivian the photographer「写真家ヴィヴィアン」から，彼女に関する正しい情報を選ぶ。
» ノートの内容を先に確認しておくと，彼女は介護士として働いていた間にたくさんの写真を撮った人物であり，生きている間に誰もインタビューしなかったので，あまり知られていないことがわかる。

解き方
» ①は「オークションで販売されるまで彼女の作品は未発見のままだった」という内容。
» ②は「彼女は30代で写真に魅了されたと考えられている」という内容。
» ③は「彼女はどこへ行くにもカメラを持って行き，写真を他の人に見せた」という内容。
» ④は「彼女の写真の大半がニューヨークで撮影された」という内容。

» それぞれの選択肢に散りばめられたキーワードを探して本文を読んでいく。
» ①のキーワードである「オークション」は，第1段落に登場する。

> This is the story of an American street photographer who kept her passion for taking pictures secret until her death. She lived her life as a caregiver, and if it had not been for the sale of her belongings at an auction house, her incredible work might never have been discovered.

» 第1段落・第2文に注目。if it had not been for ～は仮定法過去完了の文で用いられる表現で，「～がなかったら（…だったかもしれない）」という意味になる。

» したがって，She lived her life as a caregiver, and if it had not been for the sale of her belongings at an auction house, her incredible work might never have been discovered. は「彼女は介護士として人生を送り，もしオークション会場で所持品が売りに出されていなかったら，彼女の素晴らしい作品が発見されることは決してなかったかもしれない」という訳になる。

» つまり「オークションで販売されるまで未発見のままだった」ということになるので，①は本文の内容に合致すると考えられる。

» また，オークションにかけられるまでずっと未発見だったことを考慮すると，「写真を他の人に見せていた」とする③は不適切だと判断できる。

» ②のキーワードである「30代」や「ヴィヴィアンが写真に興味をもった時期」を探していくと，彼女の来歴を語る第5段落にたどり着く。

> Vivian was born in 1926 in the United States to an Austrian father and a French mother. The marriage was not a happy one, and it seems her mother and father lived apart for several years. During her childhood Vivian frequently moved between the US and France, sometimes living in France, and sometimes in the US. For a while, Vivian and her mother lived in New York with Jeanne Bertrand, a successful photographer. It is believed that Vivian became interested in photography as a young adult, as her first photos were taken in France in the late 1940s using a very simple camera. She returned to New York in 1951, and in 1956 she moved to Chicago to work as a caregiver for the Gensburg family. This job gave her more free time for taking photographs.

» 第5文から彼女は young adult「成人初期」に写真に興味をもち，初めて写真を撮ったのは1940年代後半だとわかる。

» このときヴィヴィアンが何歳だったかを知るためには，彼女が生まれた年を確認すればよい。第1文に **1926生まれ** とあるので，ヴィヴィアンが写真に

興味をもつようになったのは **20代**のことだと判断できる。
≫ よって「30 代で写真に魅了された」とする②は不適切。

≫ ④のキーワードである「ヴィヴィアンの写真の大半」や「ニューヨーク」に関する言及を探していくと，第 6 段落・第 1 文に In 1952, at the age of 26, she purchased her first 6 × 6 camera, and it was with this that most of her photographs of life on the streets of Chicago were taken. 「1952 年，26 歳で彼女は最初の 6 × 6 判カメラを購入したが，シカゴの街の暮らしの写真の大半を撮影したのはこのカメラであった」という記述はあるが，「写真の大半がニューヨークで撮影された」というようなことはどこにも書かれていない。ヴィヴィアンはフランスやシカゴでも写真を撮っているので，「大半がニューヨークで撮影された」とする④は不適切だと判断できる。

≫ よって<u>正解は①</u>。

難易度 **難しい**

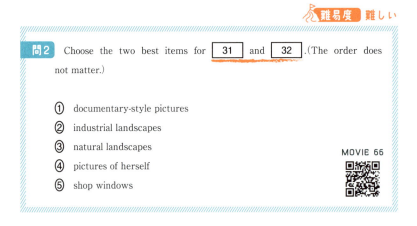

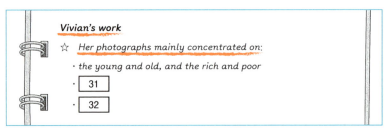

≫ ノートの小見出し **Vivian's work**「ヴィヴィアンの作品」から，彼女の作品に関する正しい情報を選ぶ。

💡 解き方

≫ Her photographs mainly concentrated on「彼女の写真が主に対象としているのは」という空所の前の手がかりをもとに，すでに書かれている the young and old, and the rich and poor「若者や老人，お金持ちや貧しい人々」に該当する箇所を探して本文を読み進める。

In 1952, at the age of 26, she purchased her first 6 × 6 camera, and it was with this that most of her photographs of life on the streets of Chicago were taken. For over 30 years she took photos of children, the elderly, the rich, and the poor. Some people were not even aware that their picture was being taken. She also took a number of self-portraits. Some were reflections of herself in a shop window. Others were of her own shadow. Vivian continued to document Chicago life until the early 1970s, when she changed to a new style of photography.

≫ 第6段落・第2文の For over 30 years she took photos of children, the elderly, the rich, and the poor.「30年以上の間，彼女は子どもやお年寄り，お金持ちや貧しい人々の写真を撮った」という内容が，ノートでは the young and old, and the rich and poor とまとめられていると判断できるので，このあたりに手がかりがありそうだ。

≫ 第4文 She also took a number of self-portraits.「彼女はまた，数多くの自画像を撮影した」は，選択肢の④ pictures of herself「彼女自身の写真」に該当すると考えられる。

≫ もう1つの空所に入る情報を探していくと，第7文 Vivian continued to document Chicago life until the early 1970s, when she changed to a new style of photography.「ヴィヴィアンは1970年代前半までシカゴの生活を写真で記録し続け，それから新しい写真のスタイルに移行した」は，選択肢の① documentary-style pictures「ドキュメンタリー風の写真」に該当すると考えられる。

≫ よって正解は①と④。

153

問3 Put the following events into the order in which they happened.
33 ~ 36

① A buyer linked his blog to some of her pictures.
② A report on Vivian's death was published in a newspaper.
③ An auction company started selling her old photographs and negatives.
④ Her work was published on the Internet.

MOVIE 67

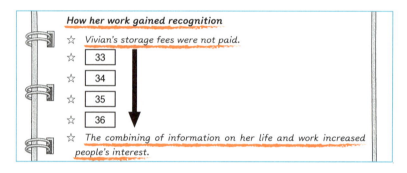

着眼点

» ノートの小見出し How her work gained recognition「彼女の作品はどのように認知されたか」に注目。
» すでにノートに書かれている最初の出来事 Vivian's storage fees were not paid. から，最後の出来事 The combining of information on her life and work increased people's interest. までの過程を完成させればよい。
» 先に選択肢の内容を確認し，**時間の表現**に注意しながら，それぞれの選択肢に該当する内容を探して本文を読む。

💡 解き方

≫ ①は「ある買い手がブログに彼女の写真の一部へのリンクを貼った」という内容。

≫ ②は「ヴィヴィアンの死に関する記事が新聞で公表された」という内容。

≫ ③は「あるオークション会社が彼女の古い写真とネガを販売し始めた」という内容。

≫ ④は「彼女の作品がインターネットで公表された」という内容。

≫ ノートに書かれた最初の出来事 Vivian's storage fees were not paid.「ヴィヴィアンの倉庫料が支払われなかった」に該当する内容を探して本文を読み進める。第2段落に注目。

It was 2007. A Chicago auction house was selling off the belongings of an old woman named Vivian Maier. She had stopped paying storage fees, and so the company decided to sell her things. Her belongings—mainly old photographs and negatives—were sold to three buyers: Maloof, Slattery, and Prow.

≫ 最初の出来事は, 本文の第2段落・第3文 She had stopped paying storage fees, and so the company decided to sell her things.「彼女が倉庫料の支払いをやめたので, 会社は彼女の物を売ることに決めた」の前半に該当する。

≫ 第3文の後半でオークション会社が売ることに決めた「彼女の物」が何かというと, 第4文で old photographs and negatives「古い写真やネガ」だと具体的に説明されている。これは, 選択肢の③に該当する。

≫ 第3文の前半は had stopped と過去完了形, 後半は decided と過去形になっていることからも,「ヴィヴィアンが倉庫料の支払いをやめた」のが先で,「オークション会社が彼女の物を売ることにした」のが後だということになる。よって, 最初の出来事の次の空所に入るのは③だと判断できる。第1文から, これは2007年の出来事だとわかる。

≫ 続いて第３段落を読み進めていく。

> Slattery thought Vivian's work was interesting so he published her photographs on a photo-sharing website in July 2008. The photographs received little attention. Then, in October, Maloof linked his blog to his selection of Vivian's photographs, and right away, thousands of people were viewing them. Maloof had found Vivian Maier's name with the prints, but he was unable to discover anything about her. Then an Internet search led him to a 2009 newspaper article about her death. Maloof used this information to discover more about Vivian's life, and it was the combination of Vivian's mysterious life story and her photographs that grabbed everyone's attention.

≫ 第１文 Slattery thought Vivian's work was interesting so he published her photographs on a photo-sharing website in July 2008.「スラッタリーはヴィヴィアンの作品を面白いと思い，彼は 2008 年７月に写真共有ウェブサイトで彼女の写真を公表した」から，これに該当する④が次の空所に入る。これは 2008 年の７月の出来事。

≫ 第３文 Then, in October, Maloof linked his blog to his selection of Vivian's photographs「それから 10 月に，マルーフがブログに自分で選んだヴィヴィアンの写真へのリンクを貼りつけた」から，ブログに言及している①が次の空所に入る。これは 2008 年 10 月の話。

≫ 続いて第５文 Then an Internet search led him to a 2009 newspaper article about her death.「その後，インターネットでの検索によって，彼は彼女の死を報じる 2009 年の新聞記事にたどり着いた」に該当する②が最後の空所に入る。これは 2009 年の出来事。

≫ よって正解は③→④→①→②の順番。

≫ ちなみに，ノートの最後の出来事 The combining of information on her life and work increased people's interest.「彼女の人生と作品に関する情報の結びつきが人々の興味を増大させた」は，第３段落・最終文の後半 it was the combination of Vivian's mysterious life story and her photographs that grabbed everyone's attention. に該当する。

本文中の具体的な年月は，選択肢を時系列に並べるヒントになっているよ

156 第2日程 第5問 攻略のプロセス

問4 Choose the best statement for ⬚37⬚.

① Exhibitions of her work have been held in different parts of the world.
② Her photography book featuring street scenes won an award.
③ She left detailed instructions on how her photographs should be treated.
④ The children of Vivian's employers provided their photographs.

MOVIE 68

How her work became known worldwide
☆ *An award-winning documentary film about her life and work helped capture a new audience.*
☆ ⬚37⬚

着眼点

≫ ノートの小見出し How her work became known worldwide「彼女の作品はどのように世界的に知られたのか」から，ヴィヴィアンの作品が世界的に知られるようになったきっかけを選ぶ。

解き方

≫ すでにノートに書かれている award-winning documentary film「賞を受賞したドキュメンタリー映画」は，第7段落・第1文に登場する。このあたりに手がかりがありそうだ。

An international award-winning documentary film called *Finding Vivian Maier* brought interest in her work to a wider audience. The film led to exhibitions in Europe and the US. To choose the photographs that best represent her style, those in charge of the exhibitions have tried to answer the question, "What would Vivian Maier have printed?" In order to answer this question, they used her notes, the photos she actually did print, and information about her preferences as reported by the Gensburgs. Vivian was much more interested in capturing moments rather than the outcome. So, one could say the mystery behind Vivian's work remains largely "undeveloped."

157

>> 第2文 The film led to exhibitions in Europe and the US.「その映画はヨーロッパとアメリカでの展覧会につながった」から，この映画がきっかけとなってヨーロッパやアメリカで展覧会が催され，その結果世界的に知られるようになったと考えられる。

>> ヨーロッパやアメリカという開催地を in different parts of the world「世界の様々な場所」とまとめて言い換えた①が正解。

この問題のように，本文の具体的な情報が選択肢では抽象的に言い換えられる場合があるんだ

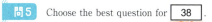

問5 Choose the best question for ☐ 38 ☐.

① "What type of camera did she use for taking photos?"
② "Where did she keep all her negatives and prints?"
③ "Why did she leave New York to become a caregiver?"
④ "Why did she take so many photos without showing them to anyone?"

MOVIE 69

The 'BIG' unanswered question: ☐ 38 ☐

着眼点

» ノートの小見出し The 'BIG' unanswered question「『大きな』未解答の問い」に注目。
» 'BIG' と引用符と大文字で強調されていることから，部分的ではなく全体に関わる「まだ答えられていない問い」を選ぶ。

解き方

» ①は「写真を撮るのにどんな種類のカメラを使ったのか？」という問いだが，使用していたカメラは第6段落・第1文で言及があったので「まだ答えられていない問い」ではない。
» ②は「ネガや写真のすべてをどこに保管していたのか？」という問いだが，第1～2段落の写真が発見された経緯を思い出すと，倉庫に保管されていたと考えられる。
» ③は「なぜ介護士になるためにニューヨークを離れたのか？」という問いだが，本文の話題の中心は写真家としてのヴィヴィアンなので，部分的な問いだと判断できる。
» ④は「なぜ誰にも見せることなくそれほど多くの写真を撮ったのか？」という問いで，謎めいた写真家をめぐる本文の全体に関わる質問であり，かつ答えはどこにも書かれていない。

» よって正解は④。

令和3年度 大学入学共通テスト 第2日程
第6問A 攻略のプロセス

 まずは大問の全体像をつかむ

あらかじめリード文に目を通したうえで，本文のどこに何が書いてあるかをざっくり把握しましょう。

演劇に関する雑誌記事を読む

A You are an exchange student in the United States and you have joined the school's drama club. You are reading an American online arts magazine article to get some ideas to help improve the club.

Recent Changes at the Royal Shakespeare Company

記事の筆者などの情報

By John Smith
Feb. 20, 2020

「ロイヤル・シェイクスピア・カンパニーの最近の変化」

　　We are all different. While most people recognize that the world is made up of a wide variety of people, diversity—showing and accepting our differences—is often not reflected in performing arts organizations. For this reason, there is an increasing demand for movies and plays to better represent people from various backgrounds as well as those with disabilities. Arts Council England, in response to this demand, is encouraging all publicly funded arts organizations to make improvements in this area. One theater company responding positively is the Royal Shakespeare Company (RSC), which is one of the most influential theater companies in the world.

　　Based in Stratford-upon-Avon in the UK, the RSC produces plays by William Shakespeare and a number of other famous authors. These days, the RSC is focused on diversity in an attempt to represent all of UK society accurately. It works hard to balance the ethnic and social backgrounds, the genders, and the physical abilities of both performers and staff when hiring.

　　During the summer 2019 season, the RSC put on three of Shakespeare's comedies: *As You Like It*, *The Taming of the Shrew*, and *Measure for Measure*. Actors from all over the country were employed, forming a 27-member cast, reflecting the diverse ethnic, geographical, and cultural population of the UK today. To achieve gender balance for the entire season, half of all roles were given to male actors and half to female actors. The cast included three actors with disabilities (currently referred to as "differently-abled" actors)—one visually-impaired, one hearing-impaired, and one in a wheelchair.

Changes went beyond the hiring policy. The RSC actually rewrote parts of the plays to encourage the audience to reflect on male/female power relationships. For example, female and male roles were reversed. In *The Taming of the Shrew*, the role of "the daughter" in the original was transformed into "the son" and played by a male actor. In the same play, a male servant character was rewritten as a female servant. That role was played by Amy Trigg, a female actor who uses a wheelchair. Trigg said that she was excited to play the role and believed that the RSC's changes would have a large impact on other performing arts organizations. Excited by all the diversity, other members of the RSC expressed the same hope—that more arts organizations would be encouraged to follow in the RSC's footsteps.

The RSC's decision to reflect diversity in the summer 2019 season can be seen as a new model for arts organizations hoping to make their organizations inclusive. While there are some who are reluctant to accept diversity in classic plays, others welcome it with open arms. Although certain challenges remain, the RSC has earned its reputation as the face of progress.

記事のまとめ

資料などがついていないシンプルな長文問題だからといって，いきなり読み始めるのは厳禁！　先に必ず設問や選択肢をチェックして，探すべき情報をインプットしてから本文を読もう

- アメリカの**演劇部**に入った**交換留学生**という設定。
- 演劇部をよくするために，**芸術雑誌の記事**を読む。

STEP 2 設問と選択肢を読み解く

続いて設問や選択肢に目を通しましょう。**探すべき情報を押さえたうえで英文を読む**ことで，問題を解く時間を大幅に短縮できます。ここでは問1と問3に注目します。

問1　According to the article, the RSC ☐ 39 ☐ in the summer 2019 season.

> 2019年夏のシーズンに RSCがやったこと

　① gave job opportunities to famous actors

　② hired three differently-abled performers

　③ looked for plays that included 27 characters

　④ put on plays by Shakespeare and other authors

》 設問中の in the summer 2019 season という条件に注目。

》 この語句を本文から探せば，その付近に手がかりがあるはず。

問3　You are summarizing this article for other club members. Which of the following options best completes your summary?

[Summary] ◀ 記事全体の要約

The Royal Shakespeare Company (RSC) in the UK is making efforts to reflect the population of UK society in its productions. In order to achieve this, it has started to employ a balance of female and male actors and staff with a variety of backgrounds and abilities. It has also made changes to its plays. Consequently, the RSC has ☐ 41 ☐ .

　① attracted many talented actors from all over the world

　② completed the 2019 season without any objections

　③ contributed to matching social expectations with actions

　④ earned its reputation as a conservative theater company

》 記事の Summary「要約」が設問中に含まれていることに注目。

》 本文を読む前に要約に目を通すことで，時間短縮が図れそうだ。

162　第2日程 第6問A 攻略のプロセス

STEP 3 必要な情報を本文から探しながら小問を解く

問1 According to the article, the RSC ⬚39⬚ in the summer 2019 season.

① gave job opportunities to famous actors
② hired three differently-abled performers
③ looked for plays that included 27 characters
④ put on plays by Shakespeare and other authors

MOVIE 70

🔍 着眼点

» in the summer 2019 season「2019年夏のシーズン」のRSCの活動を探しながら本文を読む。

💡 解き方

» During the summer 2019 season「2019年夏のシーズンの間に」で始まる第3段落に注目。

> During the summer 2019 season, the RSC put on three of Shakespeare's comedies: *As You Like It, The Taming of the Shrew, and Measure for Measure.* Actors from all over the country were employed, forming a 27-member cast, reflecting the diverse ethnic, geographical, and cultural population of the UK today. To achieve gender balance for the entire season, half of all roles were given to male actors and half to female actors. The cast included three actors with disabilities (currently referred to as "differently-abled" actors)—one visually-impaired, one hearing-impaired, and one in a wheelchair.

» 第3段落では，2019年の夏にRSCが実施した様々な取り組みが詳しく紹介されている。

» 第4文の The cast included three actors with disabilities (currently referred to as "differently-abled" actors)—one visually-impaired, one hearing-impaired, and one in a wheelchair. 「キャストには障がいのある3人の役者（現在は「異なる能力のある」役者と呼ばれる）も含まれていた——1人は目が不自由な役者，1人は耳が不自由な役者，そして1人は車椅子の役者であった」という内容を，同じ "differently-abled" を用いて簡潔にまとめた②が正解。

163

問2 The author of this article most likely mentions Amy Trigg because she ⎡40⎦.

① performed well in one of the plays presented by the RSC
② struggled to be selected as a member of the RSC
③ was a good example of the RSC's efforts to be inclusive
④ was a role model for the members of the RSC

MOVIE 71

着眼点

» エイミー・トリッグについて言及されている箇所を特定し，前後の文脈を押さえる。
» 設問に含まれる most likely「最もありそうだ」という語句から，本文に答えが直接書かれているわけではなく，本文の内容から推測して最も適切な選択肢を選ぶ問題だとわかる。

解き方

» エイミー・トリッグの名前は第4段落に登場する。

> Changes went beyond the hiring policy. The RSC actually rewrote parts of the plays to encourage the audience to reflect on male/female power relationships. For example, female and male roles were reversed. In *The Taming of the Shrew*, the role of "the daughter" in the original was transformed into "the son" and played by a male actor. In the same play, a male servant character was rewritten as a female servant. That role was played by Amy Trigg, a female actor who uses a wheelchair. Trigg said that she was excited to play the role and believed that the RSC's changes would have a large impact on other performing arts organizations. Excited by all the diversity, other members of the RSC expressed the same hope—that more arts organizations would be encouraged to follow in the RSC's footsteps.

» 第4段落では，第3段落で取り上げた雇用方針の他の変化について述べられている。
» 第5文で本来は男性の役だった従者が女性役として書き換えられた事例を紹介し，第6文でこの役を演じたのが女性で車椅子を使うエイミー・トリッ

グだと説明されている。
- 第7文で「その役を演じることにワクワクしており，RSC の変化は他の舞台芸術団体に大きな影響を与えるだろうと信じている」という彼女の発言が紹介され，第8文では「より多くの芸術団体が RSC の足跡に続くよう促されるだろう」と RSC の他のメンバーも賛同している。
- つまりこの段落で筆者は一貫して，演劇に多様性を持ち込んだ RSC の活動を称賛していると判断できる。
- 以上からエイミー・トリッグは RSC の多様性を表す人物の1人だと考えられるので，空所には was a good example of the RSC's efforts to be inclusive「包括的であろうとする RSC の取り組みのよい例だった」が入る。
- よって正解は③。

- inclusive は「包括的な，すべてを含むような」という意味。
- 意味を知らなかった場合でも，第5段落・第1文に The RSC's decision to reflect diversity in the summer 2019 season can be seen as a new model for arts organizations hoping to make their organizations inclusive. 「2019 年夏シーズンの RSC の多様性を反映する決定は，自分たちの組織を包括的にしたいと望む芸術団体にとって，新しいモデルと見なされ得る」とあることから，RSC の活動が inclusive を目指していることを確認できる。

知らない単語が出てきても焦らないこと！
どこかにヒントが隠されている場合があるよ

- エイミーの演技が上手だったかどうかは本文に書かれていないので，①は不適切。
- エイミーが RSC の一員になるために奮闘したというような話はどこにもないので，②は不適切。
- ④に含まれる role model「ロールモデル」はカタカナの日本語としても使われる語句で，「他の人が模範とすべき人物」を意味する。エイミー・トリッグが RSC の他のメンバーにとって模範となるべき存在であるというような記述はないので，④は不適切だと判断できる。

問3 You are summarizing this article for other club members. Which of the following options best completes your summary?

[Summary]
The Royal Shakespeare Company (RSC) in the UK is making efforts to reflect the population of UK society in its productions. In order to achieve this, it has started to employ a balance of female and male actors and staff with a variety of backgrounds and abilities. It has also made changes to its plays. Consequently, the RSC has ⬚41⬚ .

① attracted many talented actors from all over the world
② completed the 2019 season without any objections
③ contributed to matching social expectations with actions
④ earned its reputation as a conservative theater company

MOVIE 72

着眼点
» 演劇部の部員のために，この記事を要約するという設定。
» Summary に目を通して概要を確認し，結果として RSC が何を行ったかを探しながら本文を読む。

解き方
» イギリス社会の人口比を作品に反映するために，様々な背景や能力をもつ女性と男性の俳優やスタッフを雇用するなど，Summary には RSC の取り組みがまとめられている。
» 空所を含む文が Consequently「その結果」で始まっているので，これらの取り組みの結果として正しい選択肢を選べばよい。

» ①は「世界中から多くの才能ある役者を引きつけた」という内容だが，取り組みの結果，才能ある俳優が世界中から集まったというような話は記事に書かれてないので，①は不適切。

» ②は「2019 年のシーズンを何の反論もなく終えた」という強い言い方になっているが，第 5 段落の第 2 文 there are some who are reluctant to accept diversity in classic plays「古典演劇に多様性を受け入れることに乗り気でない人々がいる」から反対意見があることがわかるので，②は不適切。

» ③は「社会的な期待を行動と一致させることに貢献した」という内容。「社会的な期待」については，第1段落で言及されていた。

Recent Changes at the Royal Shakespeare Company

By John Smith

Feb. 20, 2020

We are all different. While most people recognize that the world is made up of a wide variety of people, diversity—showing and accepting our differences—is often not reflected in performing arts organizations. For this reason, there is an increasing demand for movies and plays to better represent people from various backgrounds as well as those with disabilities. Arts Council England, in response to this demand, is encouraging all publicly funded arts organizations to make improvements in this area. One theater company responding positively is the Royal Shakespeare Company (RSC), which is one of the most influential theater companies in the world.

» 第 3 文 there is an increasing demand for movies and plays to better represent people from various backgrounds as well as the disabilities. 「映画や演劇が，障がいのある人々や様々な背景のある人々をより適切に描く需要が高まっている」で言及されていたような，多様性を反映した演劇に対する社会の期待を指すと考えられる。

» このような社会の期待を受けて RSC が行ってきた様々な取り組みが第2段落以降で詳しく説明されていることから，③は内容的に正しいと判断できる。

» ④は「保守的な劇団として評判を得た」という内容。第5段落・最終文 Although certain challenges remain, the RSC has earned its reputation as the face of progress. 「ある程度の課題は残っているが，RSC は進歩の顔だという評判を得たのである」からも，RSC の取り組みは conservative「保守的」とは真逆の革新的なものだと判断できる。

» よって正解は③。

問4 <u>Your drama club agrees with the RSC's ideas. Based on these ideas, your drama club might</u> 42 .

① perform plays written by new international authors
② present classic plays with the original story
③ raise funds to buy wheelchairs for local people
④ remove gender stereotypes from its performances

MOVIE 73

🔭 着眼点

» RSC's ideas「RSC の考え」に賛同する場合，自分が所属する演劇部にもたらされるであろう変化を問う問題。
» 設問文に might「〜かもしれない」という推量の助動詞が含まれることから，<u>本文の内容から推測</u>して最も適切な選択肢を選ぶ。

💡 解き方

» 記事の概要をざっくりまとめると，「演劇に多様性を持ち込む」というのが RSC の考えであった。

» ①は「新しい国際的な作家によって書かれた演劇を上演する」という内容だが，RSC が新しい国際的な劇作家の作品を演じたとはどこにも書かれていない。

» ②は「古典演劇を原作どおり上演する」という内容だが，RSC は劇に登場する男女の役を入れ換えるなどして多様性を反映させようとしていた。古典劇を元どおり上演するのであれば多様性を持ち込んだことにならないので，②は不適切。

» ③は「地域の人々のために車椅子を買う資金を集める」という内容だが，RSC が募金を行ったというような話はないし，多様性を認めるための「演劇部の活動」としては疑問が残る。

» ④は「性別に関する固定観念を公演から除外する」という内容。性別に関しては，第 4 段落で言及されていた。

> Changes went beyond the hiring policy. **The RSC actually rewrote parts of the plays to encourage the audience to reflect on male/female power relationships. For example, female and male roles were reversed.** In *The Taming of the Shrew*, the role of "the daughter" in the original was transformed into "the son" and played by a male actor. In the same play, a male servant character was rewritten as a female servant. That role was played by Amy Trigg, a female actor who uses a wheelchair. Trigg said that she was excited to play the role and believed that the RSC's changes would have a large impact on other performing arts organizations. Excited by all the diversity, other members of the RSC expressed the same hope—that more arts organizations would be encouraged to follow in the RSC's footsteps.

≫ 第2文には The RSC actually **rewrote parts of the plays to encourage the audience to reflect on male/female power relationship**.「実際，RSC は観客が男性／女性の力関係を深く考えるように，劇の数箇所を書き直した」とあり，続く第3文には **For example, female and male roles were reversed**.「たとえば，女性と男性の役が入れ替えられた」と具体的な変更内容が述べられている。

≫ RSC は演劇を通じて性別の固定観念を取り除こうとしていることがわかるので，RSC の考えに賛同する場合の演劇部の活動として最適な ④ が正解だと判断できる。

正解以外の選択肢は，本文に登場した単語を組み合わせたもの。
まぎらわしいけど騙されないように！

令和3年度 大学入学共通テスト 第2日程
第6問 B 攻略のプロセス

 まずは大問の全体像をつかむ

あらかじめリード文に目を通したうえで，**本文のどこに何が書いてあるかを****ざっくり把握**しましょう。

> B　You are one of a group of students making a poster presentation for a wellness fair at City Hall. Your group's title is *Promoting Better Oral Health in the Community*. You have been using the following passage to create the poster.
>
> 【口腔衛生に関するプレゼン用ポスターを作成する】
>
> 「口腔衛生：鏡をのぞき込む」
>
> Oral Health: Looking into the Mirror
>
> 　In recent years, governments around the world have been working to raise awareness about oral health. While many people have heard that brushing their teeth multiple times per day is a good habit, they most likely have not considered all the reasons why this is crucial. Simply stated, teeth are important. Teeth are required to pronounce words accurately. In fact, poor oral health can actually make it difficult to speak. An even more basic necessity is being able to chew well. Chewing breaks food down and makes it easier for the body to digest it. Proper chewing is also linked to the enjoyment of food. The average person has experienced the frustration of not being able to chew on one side after a dental procedure. A person with weak teeth may experience this disappointment all the time. In other words, oral health impacts people's quality of life.
>
> 　While the basic functions of teeth are clear, many people do not realize that the mouth provides a mirror for the body. Research shows that good oral health is a clear sign of good general health. People with poor oral health are more likely to develop serious physical diseases. Ignoring recommended daily oral health routines can have negative effects on those already suffering from diseases. Conversely, practicing good oral health may even prevent disease. A strong, healthy body is often a reflection of a clean, well-maintained mouth.
>
> 　Maintaining good oral health is a lifelong mission. The Finnish and US governments recommend that parents take their infants to the dentist before the baby turns one year old. Finland actually sends parents notices. New Zealand offers free dental treatment to everyone up to age 18. The Japanese government promotes an 8020 (Eighty-Twenty) Campaign. As people age, they can lose teeth for various reasons. The goal of the campaign is still to have at least 20 teeth in the mouth on one's 80th birthday.
>
> 　Taking a closer look at Japan, the Ministry of Health, Labour and Welfare has been analyzing survey data on the number of remaining teeth in seniors for many years. One researcher divided the oldest participants into four age groups: A (70-74), B (75-79), C (80-84), D (85+). In each survey, with

the exception of 1993, the percentages of people with at least 20 teeth were in A-B-C-D order from high to low. Between 1993 and 1999, however, Group A improved only about six percentage points, while the increase for B was slightly higher. In 1993, 25.5% in Group A had at least 20 teeth, but by 2016 the Group D percentage was actually 0.2 percentage points higher than Group A's initial figure. Group B increased steadily at first, but went up dramatically between 2005 and 2011. Thanks to better awareness, every group has improved significantly over the years.

Dentists have long recommended brushing after meals. People actively seeking excellent oral health may brush several times per day. Most brush their teeth before they go to sleep and then again at some time the following morning. Dentists also believe it is important to floss daily, using a special type of string to remove

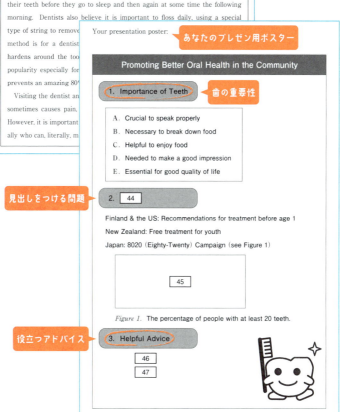

Your presentation poster: あなたのプレゼン用ポスター

Promoting Better Oral Health in the Community

1. Importance of Teeth　　歯の重要性

　A. Crucial to speak properly
　B. Necessary to break down food
　C. Helpful to enjoy food
　D. Needed to make a good impression
　E. Essential for good quality of life

見出しをつける問題　　2. ⎡44⎦

Finland & the US: Recommendations for treatment before age 1
New Zealand: Free treatment for youth
Japan: 8020 (Eighty-Twenty) Campaign (see Figure 1)

⎡45⎦

Figure 1. The percentage of people with at least 20 teeth.

役立つアドバイス　　3. Helpful Advice

⎡46⎦
⎡47⎦

- 健康フェアのために**ポスタープレゼン**の準備をしているという設定。
- 長めの英文に続いて，プレゼン用の**ポスター**がついている。
- 複数の資料を照らし合わせながら，英文を読む。

STEP 2 設問と選択肢を読み解く

続いて設問や選択肢に目を通しましょう。探すべき情報を押さえたうえで英文を読むことで、問題を解く時間を大幅に短縮できます。ここでは問3に注目します。

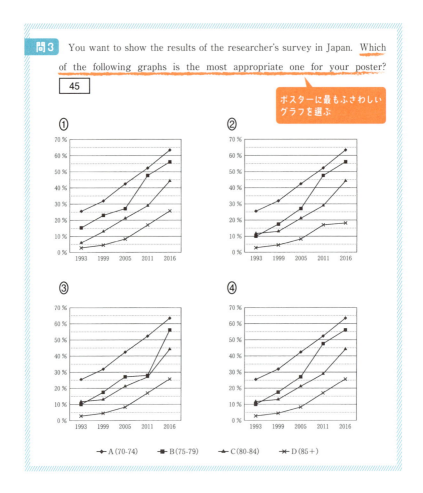

問3 You want to show the results of the researcher's survey in Japan. Which of the following graphs is the most appropriate one for your poster? 45

ポスターに最もふさわしいグラフを選ぶ

≫ 本文の内容に合致する線グラフを選ぶ問題。
≫ 縦軸が何かの割合を、横軸が年度を表しているようだ。
≫ A～Dが何を表すかは現時点では不明だが、本文中に必ず説明があるはず。
≫ ポスターの空所の下にある The percentage of people with at least 20 teeth.「少なくとも20本は歯がある人の割合」というタイトルにも目を通して、割合や年度、A～Dの説明を探しながら本文を読む。

STEP 3 必要な情報を本文から探しながら小問を解く

問1 Under the first poster heading, your group wants to express the importance of teeth as explained in the passage. Everyone agrees that one suggestion does not fit well. Which of the following should you not include?

43

① A
② B
③ C
④ D
⑤ E

MOVIE 74

Promoting Better Oral Health in the Community

1. Importance of Teeth

A. Crucial to speak properly
B. Necessary to break down food
C. Helpful to enjoy food
D. Needed to make a good impression
E. Essential for good quality of life

着眼点
» 設問から歯の重要性に関する項目として本文の内容にそぐわないものを選ぶ。
» ポスターの内容を確認してから本文中に登場する項目を消していき，**消去法**で正解を導こう。

解き方
» ①は「きちんと話すのにきわめて重要」という内容。
» ②は「食べ物を噛み砕くのに必要」という内容。
» ③は「食べ物を楽しむのに役立つ」という内容。
» ④は「よい印象を与えるのに必要」という内容。
» ⑤は「質のよい生活に欠かすことができない」という内容。

173

≫ これらを頭に入れた上で，歯の重要性を説明している箇所を本文から探す。
≫ 第1段落・第3文に Simply stated, teeth are important.「端的に言うと，歯は大切だ」とあるので，このあたりに手がかりがありそうだ。

Oral Health: Looking into the Mirror

In recent years, governments around the world have been working to raise awareness about oral health. While many people have heard that brushing their teeth multiple times per day is a good habit, they most likely have not considered all the reasons why this is crucial. Simply stated, teeth are important. Teeth are required to pronounce words accurately. In fact, poor oral health can actually make it difficult to speak. An even more basic necessity is being able to chew well. Chewing breaks food down and makes it easier for the body to digest it. Proper chewing is also linked to the enjoyment of food. The average person has experienced the frustration of not being able to chew on one side after a dental procedure. A person with weak teeth may experience this disappointment all the time. In other words, oral health impacts people's quality of life.

≫ 第4文の Teeth are required to pronounce words accurately.「歯は言葉を正確に発音するのに必要だ」は，ポスターでいうと A の Crucial to speak properly に該当する。
≫ 第6文の An even more basic necessity is being able to chew well.「さらに基本的で必要なのは，よく噛めるということだ」は，ポスターでいうと B の Necessary to break down food に該当。
≫ 第8文の Proper chewing is also linked to the enjoyment of food.「正しく噛むことはまた，食べ物を楽しむことにもつながる」は，ポスターでいうと C の Helpful to enjoy food に該当する。
≫ 最終文の In other words, oral health impacts people's quality of life.「言い換えれば，口腔衛生は人々の生活の質に影響を与えるのだ」は，ポスターでいうと E の Essential for good quality of life に該当する。
≫ 残った D の Needed to make a good impression「よい印象を与えるのに必要」は本文のどこにも記述がないので，ポスターから除外すべき項目は④だと判断できる。よって正解は④。

174　第2日程　第6問B 攻略のプロセス

問2　You have been asked to write the second heading for the poster. Which of the following is the most appropriate?　44

① National 8020 Programs Targeting Youth
② National Advertisements for Better Dental Treatment
③ National Efforts to Encourage Oral Care
④ National Systems Inviting Infants to the Dentist

MOVIE 75

2.　44

Finland & the US: Recommendations for treatment before age 1
New Zealand: Free treatment for youth
Japan: 8020 (Eighty-Twenty) Campaign (see Figure 1)

着眼点

» ポスターの2つめの見出しを書くように依頼されたという設定。
» 見出しの下に並ぶ，Finland や the US，New Zealand や Japan といった国々の様々な対策について説明している箇所を本文から探す。
» これらの国々のうち一部だけを取り上げた見出しではなく，全体をまとめた見出しを選ぶ必要がある。

解き方

» ①は「若者を対象とした国の 8020 プログラム」という内容だが，これはポスターを確認すると日本でのみ行われている部分的なものなので，全体の見出しとしては不適切。
» ②は「よりよい歯科治療のための国の宣伝」という内容。全体をまとめた言い方をしているので，ポスターを見る限りでは正解の可能性がある。
» ③は「口腔ケアを促す国の取り組み」という内容。全体をまとめた言い方をしているので，ポスターを見る限りでは正解の可能性がある。
» ④は「乳幼児を歯医者へ招待する国のシステム」という内容だが，これはポスターを確認するとフィンランドとアメリカでのみ行われている部分的なものだと考えられるので，全体の見出しとしては不適切。

» ②と③のどちらが適切かを確認するために，ポスターに登場する国々の名前を本文から探すと，第3段落にたどり着く。

> Maintaining good oral health is a lifelong mission. The Finnish and US governments recommend that parents take their infants to the dentist before the baby turns one year old. Finland actually sends parents notices. New

» 第1文が Maintaining good oral health is a lifelong mission.「よい口腔衛生を維持することは，生涯にわたる任務だ」と始まり，続いてよい口腔衛生を保つための各国における具体的な取り組みが紹介されている。

» よってこの段落の内容をまとめた見出しとして最適なのは，③の National Efforts to Encourage Oral Care だと判断できる。よって正解は③。

» 各国は宣伝ではなく具体的な対策を行っているので，②は不適切。

一部だけを取り上げた選択肢は，内容的に正しくても不正解になるんだったね

問3 You want to show the results of the researcher's survey in Japan. Which of the following graphs is the most appropriate one for your poster? $\boxed{45}$

① ②
③ ④

◆ A(70-74)　■ B(75-79)　▲ C(80-84)　✶ D(85+)

MOVIE 76

Figure 1. The percentage of people with at least 20 teeth.

🔍 着眼点

» 本文の内容に合致する線グラフを選ぶ問題。

» ポスターの空所を確認すると, すぐ下に Figure 1. The percentage of people with at least 20 teeth.「図1. 少なくとも20本は歯がある人の割合」というタイトルが付いている。

» 空所の上の Japan: 8020 (Eighty-Twenty) Campaign (see Figure 1)「8020 キャンペーン (図1を見る)」からも, 日本の8020運動に関する記述や, 少なくとも20本歯が残っている人の割合について書かれている箇所を本文から探せばよい。

» 選択肢に並ぶ線グラフを確認すると, 縦軸が割合, 横軸が年度になっているようだ。

💡 解き方

» 日本の8020運動については第3段落の後半で言及されている。

» Taking a closer look at Japan「より詳しく日本を見ると」という出だしから, より詳しい日本の調査結果は第4段落に書かれていると推測できる。

Taking a closer look at Japan, the Ministry of Health, Labour and Welfare has been analyzing survey data on the number of remaining teeth in seniors for many years. One researcher divided the oldest participants into four age groups: A (70-74), B (75-79), C (80-84), D (85+). In each survey, with the exception of 1993, the percentages of people with at least 20 teeth were in A-B-C-D order from high to low. Between 1993 and 1999, however, Group A improved only about six percentage points, while the increase for B was slightly higher. In 1993, 25.5% in Group A had at least 20 teeth, but by 2016 the Group D percentage was actually 0.2 percentage points higher than Group A's initial figure. Group B increased steadily at first, but went up dramatically between 2005 and 2011. Thanks to better awareness, every group has improved significantly over the years.

» 第2文 One researcher divided the oldest participants into four age groups: A (70−74), B (75−79), C (80−84), D (85＋),「ある研究員は, 最高齢の参加者をA (70−74歳), B (75−79歳), C (80−84歳), そしてD (85歳以上) の4つの年齢グループに分けた」から, 線グラフの下の4つのアルファベット横の数字は年齢を表していることがわかる。

» 続く第3文の In each survey, with the exception of 1993, the percentage of

178 第2日程 第6問B 攻略のプロセス

people with at least 20 teeth were in A-B-C-D order from high to low.「それぞれの調査で，1993年の例外はあるものの，少なくとも20本の歯がある人々の割合は高い方から低い方へA-B-C-Dの順番であった」から，1993年のみA-B-C-Dの順になっていないことがわかる。この時点で，どの年度でもA-B-C-Dの順になっている①は不適切。

» 第5文のIn 1993, 25.5% in Group A had at least 20 teeth, but by 2016 the Group D percentage was actually 0.2 percentage higher than Group A's initial figure.「1993年にはグループAの25.5%が少なくとも20本の歯を持っていたが，2016年の時点でグループDの割合はグループAの最初の数字を0.2%上回っていた」から，2016年のグループDの数値が1993年のグループAの数値を下回っている②は不適切。

» 第6文のGroup B increased steadily at first, but went up dramatically between 2005 and 2011.「グループBは最初じわじわと増加したが，2005年と2011年の間で劇的に上昇した」から，2005年から2011年の間でグループBの数値がほぼ横ばいになっている③は不適切。

» よって，これらの条件を唯一満たしている④が正解だと判断できる。

本文から条件を探す→条件に合わないグラフ消していく→最後に残ったグラフが正解！

問4 Under the last poster heading, you want to add specific advice based on the passage. Which two of the following statements should you use? (The order does not matter.) 46 ・ 47

① Brush your teeth before you eat breakfast.
② Check your teeth in the mirror every day.
③ Make at least one visit to the dentist a year.
④ Put plastic gel on your teeth frequently.
⑤ Use dental floss between your teeth daily.

MOVIE 77

3. Helpful Advice
46
47

着眼点
» ポスターの最後の見出し Helpful Advice「役立つアドバイス」に入る具体的なアドバイスを2つ選ぶ。
» 先に選択肢に目を通し，本文の内容と照らし合わせていく。

解き方
» ①は「朝食を食べる前に歯を磨く」という内容。
» ②は「毎日，鏡で歯を確認する」という内容。
» ③は「少なくとも1年に1回は歯医者を訪れる」という内容。
» ④は「プラスチックのジェルを頻繁に歯に塗る」という内容。
» ⑤は「毎日，歯の間にデンタルフロスを使う」という内容。

» 第1~4段落に目を通してきたがアドバイスは書かれていなかったので，まだ読んでいない残りの段落に手がかりがありそうだ。

> Dentists have long recommended brushing after meals. People actively seeking excellent oral health may brush several times per day. Most brush their teeth before they go to sleep and then again at some time the following morning. Dentists also believe it is important to floss daily, using a special type of string to remove substances from between teeth. Another prevention method is for a dentist to seal the teeth using a plastic gel (sealant) that hardens around the tooth surface and prevents damage. Sealant is gaining popularity especially for use with children. This only takes one coating and prevents an amazing 80% of common dental problems.
>
> Visiting the dentist annually or more frequently is key. As dental treatment sometimes causes pain, there are those who actively avoid seeing a dentist. However, it is important that people start viewing their dentist as an important ally who can, literally, make them smile throughout their lives.

» 第5段落では，冒頭から歯医者がすすめる様々な対策が紹介されている。

» 第1文 Dentists have long recommended brushing after meals.「歯医者は長い間，食後に歯を磨くことを推奨してきた」から，朝食前の歯みがきをすすめる①は不適切。

» 第4文の Dentists also believe it is important to floss daily, using a special type of string to remove substances from between teeth.「歯医者はまた，歯の間から物質を除去する特別な種類の糸を使って，**毎日フロスをすることが大切だと考えている**」に該当するのが，選択肢の⑤である。

» 第5文以降で説明されている plastic gel (sealant) は選択肢の④に登場するが，第7文に「これはわずか1回の塗布で，一般的な歯の問題の80%をも予防してくれる」とある。頻繁な使用は推奨されていないので，④は不適切だと判断できる。

» さらに，第6段落の第1文 Visiting the dentist annually or more frequent is key.「年に一度，あるいはより頻繁に歯医者を訪れることが重要だ」を言い換えたのが選択肢③だと考えられる。

» ②の「毎日，鏡で歯を確認する」というアドバイスは本文に登場しないので不適切。

» よって正解は③と⑤。

令和3年度 大学入学共通テスト
第1問A　全訳&語注

和訳

寮のルームメイトのジュリーが，あなたの携帯電話にお願いのテキストメッセージを送ってきました。

> 助けて！！！
> 昨日の夜，歴史の宿題をUSBメモリースティックに保存したの。今日の午後，大学の図書館で印刷するつもりだったんだけど，そのUSBを持ってくるのを忘れてしまって。今日の午後4時までに先生に1部渡さなきゃいけないのよ。図書館まで私のUSBを持ってきてくれない？　私の机の上の歴史の本の上にあると思う。本はいらなくて，USBだけでいいからね。

> ごめん，ジュリー，見つけられなかった。歴史の本はそこにあったけど，USBメモリースティックはなかったよ。机の下にいたるまで，あらゆる場所を探したんだけど。手元に持っていないのは確かなの？　念のため，君のノートパソコンを持って行くね。

> あなたの言うとおりだったわ！　確かに私が持ってた。私のカバンの底にあったの。本当にほっとした！とにかくありがとう。

問1 ジュリーのお願いは何か？ ☐ **1**
① 彼女の USB メモリースティックを持って行くこと
② 彼女の歴史の宿題を提出すること
③ 彼女に USB メモリースティックを貸すこと
④ 彼女の歴史の宿題をプリントアウトすること

問2 あなたはジュリーの 2 つめのテキストメッセージにどのように返信するか？ ☐ **2**
① 心配しないで。見つかるよ。
② それを聞いて本当に良かった。
③ もう一度カバンの中を見てみて。
④ きっとがっかりしているに違いない。

本文の語注

☐ dormitory	名 寮	☐ request	名 依頼，要望
☐ save	動 ～を保存する	☐ print	動 ～を印刷する
☐ copy	名 部，冊	☐ on top of ～	～の上に
☐ look for ～	～を探す	☐ even	副 ～でさえ
☐ sure	形 確信している	☐ laptop computer	ノートパソコン
☐ just in case	念のため	☐ bottom	名 底
☐ relief	名 安堵，安心		

設問・選択肢の語注

☐ hand in ～	～を提出する	☐ lend A B	A に B を貸す
☐ print out ～		☐ reply to ～	～に返信する，答える
～をプリントアウトする，打ち出す			
☐ worry	動 心配する	☐ glad	形 うれしく思う
☐ look in ～	～の中を見る	☐ disappointed	形 失望した，がっかりした

183

令和3年度 大学入学共通テスト
第1問 B　全訳＆語注

和訳

好きなミュージシャンが日本でコンサートツアーを行うので，あなたはファンクラブへの入会を検討しています。公式ファンクラブのウェブサイトを訪問します。

TYLER QUICK ファンクラブ

　TYLER QUICK（TQ）のファンクラブ会員になると，たくさんの楽しみがあります！　最新ニュースについていけますし，ワクワクするような数々のファンクラブ会員イベントに参加できます。新規会員の方は皆，新規会員パックが手に入ります。それには会員カードと無料のサイン入りポスター，そして TQ の3枚目のアルバム *Speeding Up* が含まれます。新規会員パックはご自宅に郵送され，ファンクラブ入会後，約1週間でお届けできる見込みです。

　TQ は世界中で愛されています。どの国からも入会でき，会員カードは1年間利用いただけます。TQ のファンクラブには，Pacer, Speeder, Zoomer という3種類の会員タイプがございます。

　　以下の会員の選択肢からお選びください。

手に入るもの（♬）	会員の選択肢		
	Pacer (20ドル)	Speeder (40ドル)	Zoomer (60ドル)
定期的な e メールとオンラインマガジンのパスワード	♬	♬	♬
コンサートツアー日程の早期情報	♬	♬	♬
TQ の週刊ビデオメッセージ	♬	♬	♬
毎月の絵はがき		♬	♬
TQ のファンクラブカレンダー		♬	♬
特別なサイン会への招待			♬
20%引きのコンサートチケット			♬

◇5月10日までに入会すると，会費が10ドル割引になります！
◇新規会員パックには4ドルの配送料がかかります。
◇初年度の終わりに，50パーセント割引で更新またはアップグレードできます。

PacerでもSpeederでもZoomerでも，TQのファンクラブの会員でいることに満足いただけるでしょう。さらなる情報あるいは入会するには，こちらをクリックしてください。

問1 新規会員パックは ☐3☐ 。
① TQのファーストアルバムを含む
② 5月10日に配達される
③ 10ドルの配送料が必要である
④ 到着まで約7日かかる

問2 新しくPacer会員になったら何が手に入るか？ ☐4☐
① コンサートチケットの割引とカレンダー
② 定期的なeメールとサイン会への招待
③ ツアー情報と毎月のポストカード
④ ビデオメッセージとオンラインマガジンへのアクセス権

問3 1年間ファンクラブの会員であった後，あなたは ☐5☐ 。
① 50ドルの料金でZoomerになれる
② 新規会員パックを4ドルでもらえる
③ 半額で会員資格を更新できる
④ 無料で会員資格をアップグレードできる

▎本文の語注

- ☐ join 動 〜に加入する
- ☐ official 形 公式の
- ☐ member 名 会員
- ☐ latest 形 最新の
- ☐ take part in 〜 〜に参加する
- ☐ event 名 イベント
- ☐ contain 動 〜を含む
- ☐ free 形 無料の
- ☐ deliver 動 〜を配達する
- ☐ choose from 〜 〜から選ぶ
- ☐ below 副 下記の
- ☐ online 形 オンラインの
- ☐ date 名 日程，日取り
- ☐ monthly 形 毎月の，月に1回の
- ☐ invitation 名 招待
- ☐ fee 名 料金
- ☐ renew 動 〜を更新する
- ☐ click 動 クリックする，押す

- ☐ visit 動 〜を訪問する
- ☐ website 名 ウェブサイト
- ☐ keep up with 〜 〜に遅れないでついて行く
- ☐ news 名 情報，知らせ
- ☐ exciting 形 刺激的な
- ☐ receive 動 〜を受け取る
- ☐ membership 名 会員資格
- ☐ signed 形 サイン入りの
- ☐ arrive 動 到着する
- ☐ option 名 選択肢
- ☐ regular 形 定期的な
- ☐ magazine 名 雑誌
- ☐ weekly 形 毎週の，週に1回の
- ☐ picture postcard 絵はがき
- ☐ discount 名 割引
- ☐ either A or B AかBのどちらか
- ☐ upgrade 動 アップグレードする

▎設問・選択肢の語注

- ☐ include 動 〜を含む
- ☐ access to 〜 〜の利用の権利

- ☐ require 動 〜を必要とする
- ☐ at half price 半額で

186 第1日程 全訳&語注

令和3年度 大学入学共通テスト
第2問A　全訳＆語注

和訳

あなたはイギリスの学園祭のバンドコンテストを担当する学生として、順位を理解し説明するために、3人の審査員の点数とコメントをすべて精査しています。

審査員による最終得点の平均					
バンド名＼資質	演奏 (5.0)	歌唱 (5.0)	曲のオリジナリティー (5.0)	合計 (15.0)
グリーン・フォレスト	3.9	4.6	5.0	13.5
サイレント・ヒル	4.9	4.4	4.2	13.5
マウンテン・ペア	3.9	4.9	4.7	13.5
サウザンド・アンツ	(演奏せず)			

審査員による個別コメント	
ホッブズ氏	サイレント・ヒルの演奏は優れていて、実に聴衆との一体感が生まれているように感じられた。マウンテン・ペアの歌唱は素晴らしかった。グリーン・フォレストのオリジナル曲がとても気に入った。素晴らしかった！
リー氏	サイレント・ヒルは見事な演奏をした。聴衆が彼らの音楽に反応する様子は信じられないほどだった。サイレント・ヒルはきっと人気が出ると思う！　マウンテン・ペアは素敵な声をしているが、舞台上ではワクワクさせてくれなかった。グリーン・フォレストは素晴らしい新曲を演奏してくれたが、もっと練習する必要があるだろう。
ウェルズ氏	グリーン・フォレストには新曲がある。とても気に入った！大ヒットになるかもしれない！

審査員による共同評価（ホッブズ氏による要約）
各バンドの総得点は同じだが、それぞれのバンドは実に異なっている。リー氏と私は、演奏がバンドの最も重要な資質だという意見で一致した。ウェルズ氏もまた同意した。よって、1位は簡単に決定される。 　2位と3位を決めるために、ウェルズ氏は曲のオリジナリティーのほうが歌唱の上手さよりも重要であるべきだと提案した。リー氏と私はこの意見に賛成した。

問1 審査員による最終得点の平均にもとづくと，最も上手に歌ったのはどのバンドか？ 6
① グリーン・フォレスト
② マウンテン・ペア
③ サイレント・ヒル
④ サウザンド・アンツ

問2 肯定と否定の両方のコメントを出したのはどの審査員か？ 7
① ホッブズ氏
② リー氏
③ ウェルズ氏
④ 該当なし

問3 審査員による個別コメントからわかる1つの<u>事実</u>は，8 ということである。
① 全審査員がグリーン・フォレストの歌を称賛した
② グリーン・フォレストはもっと練習する必要がある
③ マウンテン・ペアはとても上手に歌える
④ サイレント・ヒルは将来有望だ

問4 審査員のコメントと共同評価からわかる1つの<u>意見</u>は，9 ということである。
① 評価されたそれぞれのバンドが同じ総得点を獲得した
② ウェルズ氏のオリジナリティーについての提案は同意された
③ サイレント・ヒルは実に聴衆と一体感があった
④ 審査員のコメントが順位を決定した

問5 審査員の共同評価にもとづくと，最終順位となるのは次のうちどれか？
10

	1位	2位	3位
①	グリーン・フォレスト	マウンテン・ペア	サイレント・ヒル
②	グリーン・フォレスト	サイレント・ヒル	マウンテン・ペア
③	マウンテン・ペア	グリーン・フォレスト	サイレント・ヒル
④	マウンテン・ペア	サイレント・ヒル	グリーン・フォレスト
⑤	サイレント・ヒル	グリーン・フォレスト	マウンテン・ペア
⑥	サイレント・ヒル	マウンテン・ペア	グリーン・フォレスト

■本文の語注

□ in charge of ～	～を担当して	□ school festival	学園祭
□ band	名 バンド，楽団	□ competition	名 コンテスト，競技会
□ examine	動 ～を吟味する，調査する	□ score	名 スコア，得点
□ comment	名 コメント	□ judge	名 審査員
□ ranking	名 ランキング，順位		

【スコア表】

□ average	形 平均の	□ quality	名 資質
□ performance	名 演奏	□ originality	名 オリジナリティー，独創性
□ total	名 総計		

【コメント表】

□ individual	形 個別の，個人の	□ seem	動 ～のように見える
□ audience	名 聴衆	□ original	形 オリジナルの，独自の
□ amazing	形 素晴らしい，見事な	□ incredible	形 信じられない
□ respond to ～	～に反応する	□ fantastic	形 素晴らしい
□ shared	形 共有の，共通の	□ therefore	副 それゆえに，したがって
□ evaluation	名 評価	□ summarise	動 ～を要約する
□ easily	副 容易に，楽に	□ determine	動 ～を決定する
□ agree on ～	～に意見がまとまる		

■設問・選択肢の語注

□ based on ～	～に基づいて	□ positive	形 肯定的な
□ critical	形 批判的な	□ praise	動 ～を称賛する，ほめる
□ promising	形 前途有望な		

令和３年度 大学入学共通テスト
第２問 B 全訳＆語注

和訳

交換留学生として現在勉強しているイギリスの学校の方針の変更についてあなたは耳にしました。オンライン掲示板でその方針についての議論を読んでいます。

新しい学校の方針＜2020年9月21日投稿＞
宛先：P.E. バーガー
差出人：K. ロバーツ

バーガー博士
　すべての生徒を代表し，聖マークス校へ歓迎いたします。ビジネスの経歴をもつ初めての校長だと聞きましたので，あなたの経験が私たちの学校をよくしてくれると期待しています。
　放課後の活動スケジュールについてあなたが提案なさっている変更に関して，懸念を表明したいと思います。エネルギーを節約することは重要で，これから日が暮れるのが早くなっていくことはわかっています。これが，スケジュールを1時間半短くされた理由でしょうか？聖マークス校の生徒は学業と放課後の活動の両方にとても真剣に取り組んでいます。多くの生徒が私に，これまでいつもしてきたように午後6時まで学校に残りたいと言ってきました。したがって，この唐突な方針の変更について考え直していただきたく思います。

よろしくお願いいたします。
ケン・ロバーツ
生徒代表

件名：Re：学校の新しい方針＜ 2020 年 9 月 22 日投稿＞
宛先：K. ロバーツ
差出人：P.E. バーガー

ケン君
　思いやりある投稿に感謝します。あなたは重要な懸念をいくつか，特にエネルギー費用と学内の活動に関する生徒の意見について述べてくれました。
　新しい方針はエネルギーの節約とは何の関係もありません。この決定は 2019 年の警察の報告書にもとづいてなされました。報告書によると，重大犯罪が 5 パーセント増えたことにより，私たちの市は以前より安全ではなくなってきているということです。私は生徒を守りたいので，暗くなる前に帰宅してもらいたいのです。

よろしくお願いします。
P.E. バーガー博士
校長

問1 ケンは新しい方針は ┃ 11 ┃ と思っている。
① 生徒にもっと勉強させることができる
② 学校の安全性を高めるかもしれない
③ 直ちに導入されるべきだ
④ 放課後の活動時間を減らすことになる

問2 ケンの掲示板の投稿で述べられている 1 つの<u>事実</u>は，┃ 12 ┃ ということである。
① 方針についてもっと議論が必要だ
② 校長の経験が学校をよくしている
③ 学校は生徒の活動について考えるべきだ
④ 新しい方針を歓迎していない生徒がいる

問3 方針の目的がエネルギーを節約することだと考えているのは誰か？
13
① バーガー博士
② ケン
③ 市
④ 警察

問4 バーガー博士は新しい方針の根拠を **14** という**事実**に置いている。
① 早く帰宅することは大切だ
② 市の安全性が低下した
③ 学校は電力を節約しなくてはならない
④ 生徒は保護を必要としている

問5 ケンが新しい方針に反対することを手助けするとしたら，あなたは何を調べるか？ **15**
① 犯罪率とその地域との関連性
② 学校のエネルギー予算と電力コスト
③ 予算に対する学校の活動時間の長さ
④ 放課後の活動を行う生徒の勉強時間

本文の語注

□ policy	名 方針	□ exchange student	交換留学生
□ forum	名 掲示板，公開討論の場	□ on behalf of 〜	〜の代表として
□ background	名 経歴	□ express	動 〜を表明する
□ concern	名 懸念	□ propose	動 〜を提案する
□ after-school	形 放課後の	□ schedule	名 予定，計画
□ save	動 〜を節約する	□ seriously	副 真剣に，まじめに
□ a number of 〜	多くの〜	□ therefore	副 したがって
□ sudden	形 突然の	□ have nothing to *do* with 〜 〜と何の関係もない	
□ decision	名 決定	□ based on 〜	〜に基づいて
□ report	名 報告書	□ due to 〜	〜のため
□ serious	形 重大な，深刻な	□ crime	名 犯罪
□ protect	動 〜を守る，保護する	□ return	動 戻る，帰る

設問・選択肢の語注

□ improve	動 〜を向上させる	□ safety	名 安全性
□ introduce	動 〜を導入する	□ immediately	副 すぐに
□ state	動 〜を述べる	□ welcome	動 〜を喜んで受け入れる，歓迎する
□ aim	名 目的	□ base A on B	B に A の基礎を置く
□ electricity	名 電力	□ protection	名 保護
□ oppose	動 〜に反対する	□ rate	名 率，割合
□ relation	名 関連	□ local	形 地元の
□ budget	名 予算	□ length	名 長さ
□ versus	前 〜に対して		

令和3年度 大学入学共通テスト
第3問 A 全訳&語注

和訳

あなたはイギリスのホテルに滞在する予定です。旅行のアドバイスサイトのQ&Aコーナーで,役に立つ情報を見つけました。

2021年3月にキャッスルトンのホーリーツリーホテルに滞在することを検討しています。このホテルをおすすめしますか,そしてバクストン空港から行くのは簡単ですか？　　　　　　　　（リズ）

回答
はい,ホーリーツリーを強くおすすめします。私は2度,泊まったことがあります。高くないですし,サービスは立派です！　無料の素晴らしい朝食もあります。（アクセス情報は<u>ここ</u>をクリック）

そこへ行った自分の経験を伝えさせてください。

最初の訪問時は地下鉄を利用しましたが,これは安くて便利です。電車は5分ごとに運行しています。空港から,レッド線を利用してモスフィールドまで行きました。ヴィクトリア行きのオレンジ線に乗り換えるには通常7分ほどかかるはずですが,道案内がはっきりしておらず,5分余計にかかりました。ヴィクトリアからは,ホテルまでバスに乗って10分でした。

2回目はヴィクトリアまで高速バスに乗ったので,乗り換えを心配する必要はありませんでした。ヴィクトリアで,2021年の夏まで道路工事をしているという掲示を見つけました。現在,市バスでホテルまで行くのに普段の3倍の時間がかかりますが,バスは10分ごとに運行しています。歩くこともできますが,天気が悪かったので私はバスに乗りました。

楽しいご滞在を！　　　　　　　　　　　　　　　　　（アレックス）

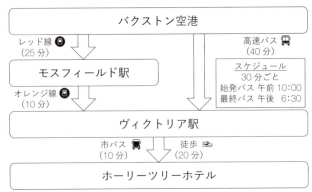

問1 アレックスの回答から、アレックスが [16] ことがわかる。
① ホテルの便利な立地を評価している
② キャッスルトンへの最初の訪問時、ヴィクトリア駅で迷った
③ ホテルは値段の割に価値があると考えている
④ 2回とも空港から同じルートを利用した

問2 あなたは2021年3月15日の午後2時に空港から公共交通機関で出発しようとしている。ホテルへ行くのに最も早い方法は何か？ [17]
① 高速バスと市バス
② 高速バスと徒歩
③ 地下鉄と市バス
④ 地下鉄と徒歩

本文の語注

☐ section	名 欄	☐ advice	名 助言, アドバイス
☐ consider	動 ～を検討する	☐ recommend	動 ～をすすめる
☐ strongly	副 強く	☐ twice	副 2度, 2回
☐ inexpensive	形 安い	☐ brilliant	形 素晴らしい
☐ underground	名 地下鉄	☐ convenient	形 便利な
☐ transfer	動 乗り換える	☐ normally	副 標準的に, 普通は
☐ direction	名 道順	☐ extra	形 余分の
☐ express	形 高速の, 直通の	☐ notice	名 掲示
☐ roadworks	名 道路工事	☐ although	接 ～だが
☐ on foot	徒歩で		

設問・選択肢の語注

☐ appreciate	動 ～を評価する	☐ location	名 立地
☐ get lost	道に迷う	☐ value	名 価値
☐ route	名 ルート	☐ depart	動 出発する
☐ public transport	公共交通		

令和3年度 大学入学共通テスト
第3問 B　全訳&語注

和訳

学校のニュースレターに掲載されている,イギリスからの交換留学生が書いた次のメッセージを,クラスメイトがあなたに見せてくれました。

ボランティア募集！

こんにちは,みなさん。私はロンドンからきた交換留学生のセーラ・キングです。今日は大切なことを皆さんと共有したいと思います。

サクラ国際センターについて聞いたことがあるかもしれません。センターは日本人と在留外国人がお互いを知る貴重な機会を提供しています。料理教室やカラオケ大会などの人気イベントが毎月開催されています。しかし,深刻な問題があります。建物が老朽化しつつあり,高額な修理が必要なのです。センターを維持する資金集めの手助けをするために,多くのボランティアが必要です。

私は数か月前にこの問題について知りました。町で買い物をしているときに,募金活動に参加している人たちを見かけたのです。活動のリーダーであるケイティに話しかけると,状況を説明してくれました。私がいくらかお金を寄付すると,感謝してくれました。彼らは町長に経済的支援を求めたものの,その要請は却下されたと私に話してくれました。彼らは資金集めを始める以外に選択肢はなかったのです。

先月,私はセンターで行われたアートについての講義に参加しました。再び,資金を集めようとしている人たちを見かけ,私は手助けすることに決めました。通行人に募金を求めるのに私が加わると,彼らは喜んでいました。私たちは一生懸命頑張りましたが,たくさんお金を集めるには人数が少なすぎました。ケイティは泣きそうな顔で私に,建物はもうそれほど長く使えないだろうと言いました。私は,もっと何かをしなければと感じました。それから,他の生徒も喜んで手助けをしてくれるかもしれない,という考えを思いつきました。ケイティはこれを聞いて喜んでいました。

そこで,サクラ国際センターを助けるための募金活動で私に加わってくれませんか。今日,

195

私にメールを送ってください！交換留学生として，私が日本にいられる時間は限られていますが，私はその時間を最大限活用したいと思っています。力を合わせることで，私たちは実際に変化をもたらすことができるのです。

3年A組
セーラ・キング
(sarahk@sakura-h.ed.jp)

問1 次の出来事（①～④）を起こった順番に並べなさい。

　　| 18 | → | 19 | → | 20 | → | 21 |

① セーラはセンターのイベントに参加した。
② セーラはセンターにお金を寄付した。
③ セーラはケイティに提案をした。
④ 活動参加者が町長に助けを求めた。

問2 セーラのメッセージによると，サクラ国際センターは | 22 | ことがわかる。

① 外国人の住民に経済的支援を与える
② 親交を深めるための機会を提供する
③ 地域社会向けのニュースレターを発行する
④ イギリスに交換留学生を送っている

問3 セーラのメッセージを読んだ後，あなたは活動を手伝うことに決めた。あなたはまず何をすべきか？ | 23 |

① センターでのイベントを宣伝する。
② さらなる情報を求めてセーラに連絡する。
③ 学校でボランティア活動を組織する。
④ 新しく募金活動を始める。

本文の語注

☐ following	形 次の	☐ newsletter	名 ニュースレター，会報
☐ exchange student	交換留学生	☐ volunteer	名 ボランティア
☐ provide A for B	B に A を提供する	☐ valuable	形 貴重な
☐ resident	名 居住者	☐ get to do	～するようになる
☐ each other	お互いに	☐ serious	形 深刻な
☐ require	動 ～を必要とする	☐ expensive	形 高価な
☐ repair	名 修理	☐ raise	動 （お金など）を集める
☐ fund	名 資金	☐ maintain	動 ～を維持する
☐ take part in ～	～に参加する	☐ fund-raising	形 資金集めの
☐ situation	名 状況	☐ donate	動 ～を寄付する
☐ mayor	名 町長，市長	☐ financial	形 財政上の
☐ assistance	名 支援	☐ request	名 要請
☐ reject	動 ～を断る	☐ choice	名 選択
☐ attend	動 ～に参加する，出席する	☐ lecture	名 講義
☐ join	動 ～に加わる	☐ passer-by	名 通行人
☐ donation	名 寄付	☐ collect	動 ～を集める
☐ tearful	形 涙でいっぱいの	☐ be willing to do	快く～する
☐ delighted	形 喜んで	☐ limited	形 限られた
☐ make the most of ～	～を最大限に活かす		

設問・選択肢の語注

☐ order	名 順番	☐ suggestion	名 提案
☐ campaigner	名 運動家	☐ aid	名 援助
☐ develop	動 ～を発展させる	☐ friendship	名 親睦，友情
☐ publish	動 ～を発行する	☐ advertise	動 ～を宣伝する
☐ contact	動 ～に連絡する	☐ further	形 さらなる
☐ organise	動 ～を組織する		

令和3年度 大学入学共通テスト
第4問 全訳&語注

和訳

英語の先生であるエマが，あなたとクラスメイトのナツキに，姉妹校からの生徒を迎える日のスケジュールを立てる手伝いをするように依頼しました。スケジュール案をつくるために，ナツキとエマの間で交わされたEメールを読んでいます。

こんにちは，エマ先生

来月の12人の来校客との校外活動のスケジュールについてアイデアと質問があります。お話しいただいたように，両校の生徒は午前10時から私たちの講堂でプレゼンテーションをすることになっています。そこで，添付された予定表に目を通しています。彼らはアズマ駅に午前9時39分に到着して，それから学校までタクシーに乗るのでしょうか？

私たちは午後の活動についても話し合っています。科学に関するものを見学するのはどうでしょうか？ 2つのアイデアがありますが，もし3つめが必要でしたら教えてください。

ウエストサイド水族館で来月開催される特別展についてお聞きになりましたか？ 海洋プランクトンから作られた新しい栄養補助食品に関するものです。私たちはそれがいい選択になるのではないかと考えています。人気なので，いちばん混雑していない時間に訪れるのがよいでしょう。水族館のホームページで見つけたグラフを添付します。

イーストサイド植物園は，私たちの地元の大学と共同で，植物から電気を生み出す興味深い方法を開発しています。運のいいことに，責任者である教授がそれについて当日の午後の早い時間に短い講演をするそうです！ 私たちも行ってみませんか？

皆，お土産を買いたがるのではないでしょうか？ ヒバリ駅の横のウエストモールが最適だと思うのですが，一日中お土産を持ち歩きたくはありません。

最後に，アズマを訪れる人は皆，町のシンボルである，学校の隣のアズマ記念公園にある像を見るべきですが，うまくスケジュールを組めません。それから，昼食の予定がどうなっているのか教えていただけますか？

よろしくお願いいたします。
ナツキ

こんにちは，ナツキ

メールをありがとう。頑張ってくれていますね。質問の答えですが，彼らは駅に午前9時20分に到着し，それからスクールバスに乗ります。

午後の主な訪問先の2つである水族館と植物園は，両校とも科学教育に力を入れており，このプログラムの目的は生徒の科学知識を向上させることなので，よいアイデアですね。しかし，念のため3つめの提案を用意しておくのが賢明でしょう。

お土産はその日の最後に買うことにしましょう。バスに乗ってモールまで行けば，午後5時に到着できます。こうすることで買い物に1時間近く使えますし，ホテルはカエデ駅から徒歩でわずか数分のところにあるので，来校客は午後6時30分の夕食までに戻る余裕があります。

昼食については，学校の食堂が昼食のお弁当を提供します。あなたが話に出していた像の下で食べられます。もし雨が降ったら，屋内で食べましょう。

提案の数々，本当にありがとう。2人でスケジュール案を作ってもらえますか？

よろしくお願いします。
エマ

添付された時刻表：

電車の時刻表
カエデ ― ヒバリ ― アズマ

駅	電車番号			
	108	109	110	111
カエデ	8:28	8:43	9:02	9:16
ヒバリ	8:50	9:05	9:24	9:38
アズマ	9:05	9:20	9:39	9:53

駅	電車番号			
	238	239	240	241
アズマ	17:25	17:45	18:00	18:15
ヒバリ	17:40	18:00	18:15	18:30
カエデ	18:02	18:22	18:37	18:52

添付されたグラフ：

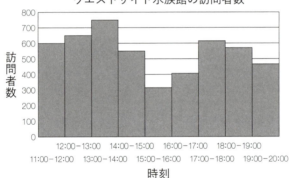

問1 姉妹校からの来校客は　24　番の電車で到着し，　25　番の電車でホテルに戻る。
① 109　② 110　③ 111
④ 238　⑤ 239　⑥ 240

問2 スケジュール案を最も適切に完成させるのはどれか？ **26**
A：水族館　B：植物園　C：モール　D：学校

姉妹校からの訪問スケジュール案

9:30 → 13:30 → 15:30 → 17:00

① D → A → B → C
② D → B → A → C
③ D → B → C → A
④ D → C → A → B

問3 もし雨が降らなければ，来校客は昼食を **27** で食べる。
① 植物園
② 学校の隣の公園
③ 駅の隣の公園
④ 学校の庭園

問4 来校客は当日，**28** は移動しない。
① バスで
② タクシーで
③ 電車で
④ 徒歩で

問5 3つめの選択肢として，あなたのプログラムに最もふさわしいものはどれか？ **29**
① ヒバリ遊園地
② ヒバリ美術館
③ ヒバリ城
④ ヒバリ宇宙センター

201

本文の語注

☐ host	動 ～をもてなす	☐ exchange	名 やり取り
☐ so that ～	～できるように	☐ draft	動 ～の下書きをする
【1つめのEメール】			
☐ be supposed to *do*	～することになっている	☐ assembly hall	名 講堂, 集会場
☐ attached	形 添付の	☐ timetable	名 時刻表
☐ related to ～	～に関係のある	☐ special exhibition	特別展
☐ supplement	名 栄養補助食品	☐ plankton	名 プランクトン
☐ least	副 最も～でなく	☐ attach	動 ～を添付する
☐ botanical	形 植物の	☐ local	形 地元の
☐ produce	動 ～を生み出す	☐ electricity	名 電気
☐ plant	名 植物	☐ luckily	副 幸運にも
☐ professor	名 教授	☐ in charge	責任者で, 担当して
☐ souvenir	名 お土産	☐ carry ～ around	～を持ち歩く
☐ symbol	名 シンボル, 象徴	☐ statue	名 像
☐ work out ～	～を作り出す		
【2つめのEメール】			
☐ in answer to ～	～に答えて	☐ catch	動 ～に乗る
☐ location	名 場所	☐ emphasis	名 強調, 重要視
☐ wise	形 賢明な	☐ just in case	念のため
☐ allow A for B	AをBに充てる	☐ provide	動 ～を提供する
☐ boxed lunch	お弁当		

設問・選択肢の語注

☐ complete	動 ～を完成させる	☐ unless	接 ～しない限り
☐ get around	動き回る	☐ on foot	徒歩で
☐ suitable	形 適した, ふさわしい		

令和3年度 大学入学共通テスト
第5問 全訳&語注

和訳

国際的なニュース記事を使って、あなたは英語の口頭プレゼンテーション大会に参加する予定です。プレゼンテーションに備えて、次のフランスのニュース記事を読みなさい。

　5年前、サビーヌ・ルアスは馬を亡くした。その馬が老衰で死ぬまで、彼女は20年間をともに過ごしていた。当時、別の馬を飼えるとは到底思っていなかった。さみしさから、彼女は近くの酪農場で何時間も乳牛を眺めて過ごした。そしてある日、農場主に乳牛の世話を手伝わせてもらえないかと尋ねた。

　農場主は同意し、サビーヌは働き始めた。すぐに乳牛のうちの1頭と友情を築いた。その乳牛は妊娠していたので、他の乳牛とよりも多くの時間を一緒に過ごした。生まれた後、乳牛の赤ちゃんはサビーヌの後をついて回るようになった。残念なことに、農場主は酪農場で雄牛－オスの乳牛－を飼うことには関心が無かった。農場主は、スリー・オー・ナイン（309）と呼んでいたその雄牛の赤ちゃんを食肉市場に売ろうと計画していた。そんなことは起こさせないとサビーヌは心に決めたので、赤ちゃんと母牛を買い取ることはできないかと農場主に尋ねた。農場主は同意し、サビーヌはその2頭を買い取った。サビーヌはそれから309を町へ散歩に連れて行くようになった。およそ9か月後、サビーヌはついにその牛たちを連れて行ってもよいという許可を得たので、牛たちはサビーヌの農場へ引っ越した。

　その後すぐ、サビーヌは子馬を譲ろうかと提案された。はじめこそ彼女は子馬を飼いたいかどうか迷っていたが、もはや自分の馬の思い出はつらいものではなくなっていたので、その子馬を受け入れてレオンと名付けた。それからかつての自分の趣味を再開することに決め、見せ物のジャンプのために子馬を訓練しはじめた。スリー・オー・ナインはサビーヌによってアストンと改名され、大抵の時間をレオンと過ごし、2頭は親友になった。しかし、レオンとの習慣的な訓練にアストンが注意を払うとはサビーヌは思っておらず、またアストンがいくつか芸を身につけるとも思っていなかった。たちまちこの若い雄牛は命令に応じて、歩行、襲歩、停止、後退、そして周回することを身につけた。ちょうど馬のようにサビーヌの声に反応したのだ。そして

体重が 1,300 キログラムあるにもかかわらず，サビーヌを背中に乗せたまま，1 メートルの馬用の障害物の飛び越え方を習得するのにわずか 18 か月しかかからなかった。アストンはレオンを観察することなしに，そういった芸を身につけることは決してなかったかもしれない。さらにアストンは距離を理解し，ジャンプの前に歩幅を調整することができた。また自分の間違いに気づき，サビーヌからの手助けもなしに修正した。これはオリンピックに出場するような最上級の馬だけができることだ。

現在，サビーヌとアストンはヨーロッパ各地の週末市や馬の展示会に出向き，芸を披露している。サビーヌは語る，「私たちは良い反応を得ています。ほとんどの場合，人々はとても驚いて，最初こそ少し怖いと感じることがあります，というのもアストンは大きくて—馬よりもずっと大きいので。たいていの人は角を持つ雄牛にあまり近づきたがりません。でも，ひとたびアストンの本当の性格がわかり，彼が演じている姿を見ると，『まぁ，実に美しいじゃないか』とよく言うんですよ」と。

「見てください！」サビーヌはスマートフォンのアストンの写真を見せる。そして続けて語る，「アストンがとても幼かったとき，人間に慣れさせるために，リードをつけて犬のように散歩に連れて行ったものです。それで人を気にしなくなったのでしょう。とても穏やかなので，特に子どもは彼を眺めるのが好きで，近づくチャンスを得ようとしますよ」と。

この数年間で，ジャンプ芸をする巨大な雄牛のニュースは急速に広まり，アストンは現在ますます数多くのオンラインのフォロワーの大きな関心を集めている。アストンとサビーヌは時に自宅から 200 〜 300 キロメートルも離れて移動する必要があり，これは宿泊しなくてはならないことを意味する。アストンは馬用の運搬車で寝なくてはならないが，彼にとって十分な大きさではない。

「彼は嫌がっていますね。私が運搬車の中で一緒に寝なくてはならないんです」とサビーヌは言う。「でもほら，目覚めて体勢を変えるとき，彼は私を押しつぶさないようにとても注意してくれるんです。本当に優しいんですよ。彼はさみしくなることがあり，レオンと長い間離れているのは嫌いですが，それを除けばとても幸せにしています」

あなたのプレゼンテーションのスライド

30

セントラル高校
英語プレゼンテーション大会

『誰が誰か？』

主役
☐ , ☐ , ☐ ⎫
                  ⎬ 31
脇役   ⎭
☐ , ☐

有名になる前の物語の展開

サビーヌの馬が死ぬ。
↓
| 32 |
| 33 |
| 34 |
| 35 |

アストンとサビーヌがショーに出始める。

アストンの能力

アストンができること：
・レオンのトレーニングを観察するだけで学べる。
・サビーヌが命じたときに，歩き，駆け，止まることができる。
・距離を理解し歩幅を調整できる。
・ 36
・ 37

アストンの現在

今日のアストンは：
・見せ物のためのジャンプをする雄牛である。
・サビーヌと一緒に市場やイベントに行く。
・ 38

問1 あなたのプレゼンテーションに最も適切なタイトルはどれか？ 　30

① 動物を愛する人が子馬の命を救う

② アストンの夏のジャンプ芸ツアー

③ 馬のように振る舞う雄牛のアストンに会おう

④ ある農場主と乳牛の関係

問2 『誰が誰？』のスライドに最も適切な組み合わせはどれか？ 　31

	主役	脇役
①	309，アストン，農場主	サビーヌ，子馬
②	アストン，アストンの母，サビーヌ	309，農場主
③	アストン，レオン，農場主	アストンの母，サビーヌ
④	アストン，サビーヌ，子馬	アストンの母，農場主

問3 『有名になる前の物語の展開』のスライドを埋めるために，4つの出来事を起こった順に選びなさい。 　32 ～ 　35

① アストンがジャンプできるようになる。

② サビーヌとアストンが何百キロも一緒に旅する。

③ サビーヌが309と母親を買う。

④ サビーヌが近所の農場の仕事に行く。

⑤ サビーヌが309を散歩に連れて行く。

問4 『アストンの能力』のスライドに最も適切な項目を2つ選びなさい。（順序は問わない。） 　36 ・ 　37

① 自分の間違いを自分で修正する

② 子馬の横に並んでジャンプする

③ 背中に騎手を乗せてジャンプする

④ 馬よりも速く芸を身につける

⑤ 写真のためにポーズをとる

問5 『アストンの現在』のスライドを最も適切な項目で完成させなさい。 　38

① ファンの数がますます増えている

② サビーヌを非常に裕福にした

③ 非常に有名なのでもう人々を怖がらせることはない

④ 馬の運搬車の中で1年の大半の夜を過ごしている

本文の語注

☐ take part in ～	～に参加する	☐ oral	形 口頭の
☐ following	形 次の	☐ in preparation for ～	～に備えて

【第 1 段落】

☐ loneliness	名 さみしさ	☐ nearby	形 近くの
☐ look after ～	～の世話をする		

【第 2 段落】

☐ friendship	名 友情	☐ pregnant	形 妊娠している
☐ follow ～ around	～について回る	☐ unfortunately	副 残念なことに
☐ bull	名 雄牛	☐ at last	ついに, やっと
☐ permission	名 許可		

【第 3 段落】

☐ no longer	もはや～ない	☐ painful	形 つらい, 苦しい
☐ accept	動 ～を受け入れる	☐ return to ～	～に戻る
☐ train	動 ～を訓練する	☐ rename	動 ～に新しい名前をつける
☐ expect A to do	Aが～すると思う	☐ pay attention to ～	～に注意を払う
☐ pick up ～	～を身に付ける	☐ trick	名 芸当
☐ gallop	動 ギャロップで駆ける	☐ backwards	副 後ろへ
☐ turn around	回転する	☐ on command	命令に応じて, 命令すると
☐ respond to ～	～に反応する	☐ despite	前 ～にもかかわらず
☐ weigh	動 重さが～である	☐ leap over ～	～を飛び越える
☐ on one's back	背負って	☐ moreover	副 さらに
☐ distance	名 距離	☐ adjust	動 ～を調整する
☐ fault	名 間違い, 誤り		

【第 4 段落】

☐ show off	見せびらかす	☐ scared	形 こわがった, おびえた
☐ horn	名 角	☐ once	接 ひとたび～すると
☐ nature	名 性質	☐ perform	動 芸をする

【第 5 段落】

☐ lead	名 リード, ひも	☐ get used to ～	～に慣れる
☐ mind	動 ～を気にする	☐ calm	形 穏やかな
☐ in particular	特に		

【第 6 段落】

☐ massive	形 巨大な	☐ spread	動 広がる
☐ rapidly	副 急速に	☐ major	形 主要な
☐ attraction	名 引き付けるもの, 呼び物	☐ stay overnight	一泊する
☐ enough	形 十分な		

【第 7 段落】

☐ crush	動 ～を押しつぶす	☐ gentle	形 優しい
☐ lonely	形 さみしく思う		

【スライド】

☐ figure	名 登場人物	☐ minor	形 比較的重要でない
☐ storyline	名 (話の) 筋, 構想	☐ simply	副 ただ, 単に

設問・選択肢の語注

☐ save	動 ～を救う	☐ behave	動 振る舞う
☐ relationship	名 関係	☐ combination	名 組み合わせ
☐ order	名 順番, 順序	☐ complete	動 ～を完成させる
☐ matter	動 重要である	☐ side-by-side	(横に) 並んで
☐ appropriate	形 適当な, 適切な	☐ wealthy	形 裕福な
☐ frighten	動 ～を怖がらせる	☐ trailer	名 運搬車, 被牽引車

207

令和3年度 大学入学共通テスト
第6問 A　全訳&語注

和訳

あなたはスポーツの安全性に関する授業プロジェクトに取り組んでおり，次の記事を見つけました。調べたことをクラスメイトに発表するために，記事を読んでポスターを作っています。

アイスホッケーをもっと安全に

　アイスホッケーは世界中で様々な人々に楽しまれているチームスポーツだ。このスポーツの目的は「パック」と呼ばれる硬いゴム製の円盤をホッケースティックで相手チームのネットに入れることだ。それぞれに6人の選手がいる2つのチームが，硬くてつるつる滑る氷のリンクの上で，この展開の速いスポーツに参加する。選手のスピードは時速30キロメートルに達することもあり，パックは宙を舞う。このような速度では，選手もパックも重大なけがの原因となりうる。

　このスポーツのスピードと氷のリンクのつるつる滑る表面によって選手は転倒したり互いに衝突したりしやすくなり，様々なけがにつながっている。選手を守ろうと，ヘルメットやグローブ，そして肩や肘や足用のパッドなどの装備品が長年にわたって導入されてきた。これらの努力にもかかわらず，アイスホッケーでは脳震とうの割合が高い。

　脳震とうは脳に対する損傷で，脳の機能の仕方に影響を与えるが，頭や顔，首あるいは別の場所への直接的または間接的な衝撃により引き起こされ，時には一時的な意識の喪失をもたらす。それほど深刻ではない短期間の症例では，選手はまっすぐ歩けなかったり，はっきり見えなくなったり，または耳鳴りを経験する可能性がある。軽い頭痛がしているだけだと思って，脳を傷つけてしまったことに気づかない選手もいる。

　この損傷の深刻さを理解しないのにくわえて，選手は監督がどう思うかを気にかけがちだ。かつて監督は，痛みにもかかわらずプレイする屈強な選手を好んだものだ。つまり，負傷した選手が負傷後にプレイを止めるのは合理的に思われるにもかかわらず，多くの選手はそうしなかったということだ。しかし最近では，脳震とうは生涯にわたって続く深刻な影響を及ぼしうることがわかってきた。脳震とう歴のある人々は集中や睡眠に障がいを抱える可能性があるのだ。さらに，脳

震とう歴のある人々は，鬱や気分のむらなどの精神的な問題に苦しむ可能性がある。場合によっては，選手は嗅覚と味覚の障がいを発症する可能性がある。

　ナショナルホッケーリーグ（NHL）はカナダとアメリカ合衆国のチームからなり，脳震とうに対処するために，より厳しいルールとガイドラインを定めてきた。たとえば 2001 年に NHL はバイザー，すなわちヘルメットに取りつけて顔を守る透明なプラスチックの装着を導入した。当初は任意だったので，多くの選手は着用しないことを選んだ。しかし 2013 年以降は必須となった。さらに 2004 年，NHL は故意に他の選手の頭を打った選手に対して，出場停止や罰金などのより厳しい罰則を与えるようになった。

　NHL はまた 2015 年に脳震とう監視員制度を導入した。この制度では，NHL の職員が生中継とビデオのリプレイを利用して，各試合中の目に見える脳震とうの兆候を監視する。最初は，医療トレーニングを受けていない 2 人の脳震とう監視員が，アリーナで試合を監視した。翌年，医療トレーニングを受けた 1 人から 4 人の脳震とう監視員が加わった。監視員はニューヨークにあるリーグの本部オフィスから各試合を監視した。選手が脳震とうを起こしていると監視員が思えば，その選手は試合から外されて医師の検査を受けるために「静かな部屋」に運ばれる。医師が許可を出すまで，選手は試合に戻ることが許されない。

　NHL はアイスホッケーをより安全なスポーツにすることに関して大きな進歩を遂げてきた。脳震とうの原因と影響についてさらに多くのことがわかるにつれ，NHL は選手の安全を確保するためにさらなる対策を講じるに違いないだろう。安全性が高まれば，アイスホッケーの選手とファンの数の増加につながるかもしれない。

アイスホッケーをもっと安全に

アイスホッケーとは何か？
・選手は相手チームのネットに「パック」を入れることで得点する
・各チームに6人の選手
・氷の上で高速で行われるスポーツ

主な問題：高い脳震とう率

脳震とうの定義
脳の機能の仕方に影響を与える脳への損傷

影響

短期間	長期間
・意識の喪失	・集中力の障がい
・まっすぐ歩くことの困難	・ 40
・ 39	・精神的な障がい
・耳鳴り	・嗅覚と味覚の障がい

解決策

ナショナルホッケーリーグ（NHL）
・バイザーつきのヘルメットを義務づける
・危険な選手に厳しい罰を与える
・ 41 ために脳震とう監視員を導入した

まとめ
アイスホッケー選手は脳震とうを起こすリスクが高い。
したがってNHLは 42 。

問1 ポスターの 39 に最もふさわしい選択肢を選べ。
① 攻撃的な行動
② 思考の困難
③ 人格の変化
④ 不明瞭な視界

問2 ポスターの 40 に最もふさわしい選択肢を選べ。
① 視力の低下
② 記憶障がい
③ 睡眠障がい
④ 不安定な歩行

問3 ポスターの 41 に最もふさわしい選択肢を選べ。
① 選手が試合に戻ることを許す
② 脳震とうを起こしている選手を検査する
③ 脳震とうの原因となった選手に罰金を課す
④ 脳震とうの兆候を示している選手を特定する

問4 ポスターの 42 に最もふさわしい選択肢を選べ。
① 選手がもっと強くなることを期待してきた
② 新しいルールとガイドラインを実施してきた
③ 監督に医療トレーニングを施してきた
④ バイザーの着用を任意にしてきた

■ 本文の語注

□ safety	名 安全性	□ article	名 記事
□ present	動 ～を発表する		
【第1段落】			
□ a variety of ～	様々な～	□ wide	形 広い，広範囲にわたる
□ object	名 目的	□ rubber disk	ゴム製の円盤
□ engage in ～	～に従事する，参加する	□ fast-paced	形 ペースの速い
□ slippery	形 つるつる滑る	□ per hour	毎時，時速
□ cause	名 原因	□ serious	形 重大な
【第2段落】			
□ surface	名 表面	□ fall down	転倒する
□ bump into ～	動 ～に衝突する	□ result in ～	～という結果になる
□ injury	名 けが	□ in an attempt to *do*	～しようとして
□ protect	動 ～を守る	□ equipment	名 装備
□ introduce	動 ～を導入する	□ despite	前 ～にもかかわらず
□ effort	名 努力，取り組み	□ rate	名 割合
□ concussion	名 脳震とう		
【第3段落】			
□ affect	動 ～に影響を与える	□ function	動 機能する
□ either A or B	AかBのどちらか	□ impact	名 衝撃
□ elsewhere	副 別の場所に	□ temporary	形 一時的な
□ loss	名 喪失	□ consciousness	名 意識
□ case	名 症例	□ be unable to *do*	～することができない
□ slight	形 わずかな，軽い		

【第 4 段落】
- ☐ in addition to ~ ～に加えて
- ☐ tend to *do* 形 ～しがちである
- ☐ tough 形 屈強な
- ☐ in other words 言い換えれば
- ☐ last 動 続く
- ☐ concentrate 動 集中する
- ☐ suffer from ~ ～に苦しむ
- ☐ depression 名 うつ
- ☐ seriousness 名 深刻さ
- ☐ prefer 動 ～を好む
- ☐ in spite of ~ ～にもかかわらず
- ☐ logical 形 理にかなっている
- ☐ lifetime 名 生涯
- ☐ moreover 副 さらに
- ☐ psychological 形 精神的な
- ☐ disorder 名 障がい

【第 5 段落】
- ☐ consist of ~ ～からなる
- ☐ deal with ~ ～に対処する
- ☐ required 形 必須の
- ☐ severe 形 厳しい
- ☐ suspension 名 出場停止
- ☐ deliberately 副 故意に
- ☐ strict 形 厳しい
- ☐ optional 形 任意の
- ☐ in addition さらに，その上
- ☐ penalty 名 罰則
- ☐ fine 名 罰金

【第 6 段落】
- ☐ spotter 名 監督者，見張り
- ☐ access to ~ ～の利用の権利
- ☐ indication 名 兆候
- ☐ monitor 動 ～を監視する
- ☐ remove 動 ～を外す，取り除く
- ☐ allow A to *do* Aが～することを許す，許可する
- ☐ permission 名 許可
- ☐ official 名 職員
- ☐ visible 形 目に見える
- ☐ medical 形 医療の
- ☐ add 動 ～を加える
- ☐ examination 名 検査
- ☐ return to ~ ～に戻る

【第 7 段落】
- ☐ progress 名 進歩
- ☐ surely 副 きっと
- ☐ further 形 さらなる
- ☐ lead to ~ ～につながる
- ☐ effect 名 影響
- ☐ take ~ measures ～な対策を講じる
- ☐ ensure 動 ～を確保する

【ポスター】
- ☐ score 動 得点する
- ☐ difficulty 名 困難
- ☐ solution 名 解決策
- ☐ therefore 副 したがって
- ☐ definition 名 定義
- ☐ concentration 名 集中力
- ☐ summary 名 まとめ，要約

設問・選択肢の語注

- ☐ aggressive 形 攻撃的な
- ☐ personality 名 人格
- ☐ unsteady 形 不安定な
- ☐ identify 動 ～をつきとめる
- ☐ implement 動 ～を実施する
- ☐ behavior 名 行動，振る舞い
- ☐ eyesight 名 視界
- ☐ fine 動 ～に罰金を課す
- ☐ expect A to *do* Aが～することを期待する

令和3年度 大学入学共通テスト
第6問B　全訳&語注

和訳

あなたは保健の授業で栄養について学んでいます。様々な甘味料についてもっと学ぶために，教科書にある次の文章を読もうとしています。

　ケーキ，キャンディ，ソフトドリンク―ほとんどの人は甘いものが大好きです。実際，若者は英語で「スイート！」と言って，何かが「よい」ことを意味します。甘さについて考えるとき，私たちはサトウキビやテンサイから作られる普通の白砂糖を思い浮かべます。しかし，科学的な発見が甘味料の世界を変えました。いまや私たちは他の多くの植物から砂糖を抽出できるようになったのです。最も顕著な例はトウモロコシです。トウモロコシは豊富にあり，安く，簡単に処理できます。高フルクトースコーンシロップ（HFCS）は通常の砂糖の約1.2倍甘いのですが，かなり高カロリーです。科学をもう一歩進めて，科学者たちはこの70年間で様々な人工甘味料を開発してきました。

　最近のアメリカの国民健康栄養調査は，平均的なアメリカ人のエネルギー摂取のうち14.6パーセントが，自然食品に由来していない砂糖を指す「添加糖類」からだと結論づけました。たとえばバナナは自然食品ですが，クッキーは添加糖類を含みます。添加糖類の半分以上が甘味飲料とデザートからのものです。多量の添加糖類は，過度の体重増加や他の健康問題など，体に悪影響を及ぼす可能性があります。このため，多くの人は飲み物やお菓子，デザートにカロリーの低い代用品を選びます。

　白砂糖の天然代用品には黒砂糖やハチミツ，メープルシロップがありますが，これらもカロリーが高い傾向にあります。その結果，大半は人工的で化学的な化合物である「低カロリー甘味料」（LCS）が別の選択肢として人気になってきました。現在，最も一般的なLCSはアスパルテーム，アセスルファムK，ステビア，そしてスクラロースです。すべてのLCSが人工的というわけではなく，ステビアは植物の葉に由来します。

　代用甘味料には加熱できないものもあり，大半が白砂糖よりはるかに甘いので，料理では使いづらいことがあります。アスパルテームとアセスルファムKは砂糖の200倍の甘さがあります。ステビアは300倍甘く，スクラロースはステビアの2倍の甘さです。新しい甘

味料の中にはさらに一層強烈なものがあります。最近，ある日本の企業が開発した「アドバンテーム」は砂糖の 20,000 倍甘いのです。何かを甘くするには，この物質のほんのわずかな量しか必要になりません。

　甘味料を選ぶときは，健康問題を考慮するのが重要です。たとえば，たくさんの白砂糖を使ってデザートを作ると，体重増加につながりかねない高カロリーの料理になってしまいます。まさにこの理由でLCS を好む人たちがいます。しかしカロリーを別にすれば，人工的なLCS を摂取することと他の様々な健康問題に関連があるとする研究もあります。LCS の中にはガンを引き起こす疑いのある強い化学物質を含むものがある一方で，記憶や脳の発達に影響を与えることが示されているものもあるため，特に若い子どもや妊娠中の女性，高齢者にとって危険になりえます。カロリーが低いキシリトールやソルビトールのような比較的自然に近い代用甘味料がいくつかあります。残念なことに，これらは極めてゆっくりと体内を移動するため，大量に摂取すると腹痛を起こす可能性があります。

　何か甘いものが欲しいとき，こういった情報があったとしても，砂糖のようになじみのある高カロリーの甘味料にこだわるか，LCS を使うかを決めるのは難しいものです。今日では様々な種類のガムやキャンディが１つ以上の人工甘味料を含んでいますが，それにもかかわらず，人工甘味料を温かい飲み物に入れようとしない人々の中に，それでもこのような製品を買う人がいるかもしれないのです。一人ひとりがこれらの選択肢を比較検討し，それから自分たちの必要性と状況に最適な甘味料を選ぶ必要があるのです。

問1 現代の科学が甘味料の世界を　**43**　によって変えたことがわかる。
① 新しくてもっと甘い白砂糖の種類を発見すること
② アメリカ人のエネルギー摂取量を計測すること
③ 様々な種類の新しい選択肢を提供すること
④ 自然環境から新しく開発された多くの植物を利用すること

問2 あなたは学んだばかりの情報をまとめている。どのように表を完成させるべきか？ 44

甘さ	甘味料
高い	アドバンテーム
	(A)
	(B)
	(C)
低い	(D)

① (A) ステビア　　　　　　　　　　　　(B) スクラロース
　 (C) アセスルファム K とアスパルテーム　 (D) HFCS
② (A) ステビア　　　　　　(B) スクラロース
　 (C) HFCS　　　　　　　 (D) アセスルファム K とアスパルテーム
③ (A) スクラロース　　　　　　　　　　(B) ステビア
　 (C) アセスルファム K とアスパルテーム　 (D) HFCS
④ (A) スクラロース　　　(B) ステビア
　 (C) HFCS　　　　　　 (D) アセスルファム K とアスパルテーム

問3 あなたが読んだ記事によると，次のうち正しいものはどれか？（選択肢を2つ選びなさい。順序は問わない。）45 ・ 46
① 代用甘味料は体重増加を引き起こすことが証明されてきた。
② アメリカ人はエネルギーの 14.6％を代用甘味料から摂取している。
③ 植物から代用甘味料を得ることは可能だ。
④ 大抵の人工甘味料は料理しやすい。
⑤ キシリトールやソルビトールのような甘味料は，ただちには消化されない。

問4 著者の立場を描写するのに，最も適切なものは次のうちどれか？
47
① 著者は，飲み物とデザートに人工甘味料を使うことに反対している。
② 著者は，人工甘味料は伝統的な甘味料にうまく取って代わったと思っている。
③ 著者は，将来の利用のためにもっと甘い製品を開発することが重要だと述べている。
④ 著者は，人々は自分にふさわしい甘味料を選ぶことに重点を置くべきだと提案している。

215

■ 本文の語注

☐ nutrition	名 栄養	☐ passage	名 文章，一節
☐ various	形 様々な	☐ sweetener	名 甘味料

【第1段落】

☐ in fact	実際	☐ sweetness	名 甘み
☐ imagine	動 ～を想像する	☐ ordinary	形 普通の
☐ sugar cane	サトウキビ	☐ sugar beet	テンサイ
☐ discovery	名 発見	☐ extract	動 ～を抽出する
☐ obvious	形 明らかな	☐ abundant	形 豊富な
☐ inexpensive	形 安い	☐ process	動 ～を処理する
☐ regular	形 通常の	☐ further	副 さらにまた
☐ a variety of ～	様々な	☐ wide	形 広い，広範囲の
☐ artificial	形 人工の		

【第2段落】

☐ examination	名 検査	☐ survey	名 調査
☐ conclude	動 ～と結論づける	☐ average	形 平均の
☐ intake	名 摂取	☐ refer to ～	～を指す
☐ be derived from ～	～から由来する	☐ whole	形 未加工の
☐ contain	動 ～を含む	☐ negative	形 悪い
☐ effect	名 影響	☐ including	前 ～を含めて
☐ excessive	形 過度の	☐ weight	名 体重
☐ gain	名 増加	☐ substitute	名 代用品

【第3段落】

☐ alternative	名 代用品，代替物	☐ tend to be	～な傾向がある
☐ consequently	副 その結果	☐ chemical	形 化学の
☐ combination	名 化合物	☐ common	形 一般的な

【第4段落】

☐ heat	動 ～を熱する	☐ intense	形 強烈な
☐ tiny	形 ごくわずかの	☐ substance	名 物質
☐ sweeten	動 ～を甘くする		

【第5段落】

☐ consider	動 ～を考慮する	☐ issue	名 問題
☐ lead to ～	～につながる	☐ prefer	動 ～を好む
☐ very	形 まさに	☐ apart from ～	～は別として
☐ link	動 ～を関連づける	☐ consume	動 ～を摂取する，消費する
☐ concern	名 問題，懸案事項	☐ suspect A of B	AにBの疑いをかける
☐ cancer	名 ガン	☐ affect	動 ～に影響を与える
☐ pregnant	形 妊娠している	☐ elderly	形 年配の人たち
☐ relatively	副 比較的	☐ extremely	副 極めて

【第6段落】

☐ whether A or B	AかBか	☐ stick to ～	～にこだわる，執着する
☐ nonetheless	副 それにもかかわらず	☐ individual	名 個人
☐ weigh	動 ～を比較考慮する	☐ suit	動 ～に適している
☐ circumstance	名 状況		

■ 設問・選択肢の語注

☐ measure	動 ～を測る	☐ newly-developed	形 新しく開発された
☐ summarize	動 ～をまとめる，要約する	☐ order	名 順序
☐ matter	動 重要である	☐ prove	動 ～を証明する
☐ digest	動 ～を消化する	☐ describe	動 ～を描写する
☐ author	名 筆者	☐ appropriate	形 適切な
☐ argue against ～	～に反対する	☐ successfully	副 うまく
☐ replace	動 ～に取って代わる	☐ traditional	形 伝統的な
☐ state	動 ～と述べる	☐ invent	動 ～を開発する，創り出す
☐ product	名 製品	☐ focus on ～	～に重点を置く
☐ make sense	意味をなす，有意義である		

令和3年度 大学入学共通テスト
第1問 A 全訳&語注

和訳

あなたは友だちのシェリーを、家族で1泊するキャンプ旅行に加わるよう招待しました。彼女があなたの携帯電話にテキストメッセージを送っていくつか質問しています。

> ねぇ！　明日に向けてバッグに荷物を詰めているところなんだけど、確認したいことがあるの。夜、テントの中は冷える？　毛布を持って行く必要があるかしら？　先週、伝えてくれてたと思うんだけど、念のため、どこで何時に会うことになってるんだっけ？

> シェリー、私が全員分の暖かい寝袋を持って行くけど、もしかしたら自分のダウンジャケットを持って来るべきかも。次の日はカナヤマ山を歩いて登るから、履きやすい靴を持ってきてね。朝6時に家の外にあなたを迎えに行くわ。もしあなたが外にいなかったら、電話するわ。朝に会いましょう！

> ありがとう！　待ちきれないわ！　ジャケットとハイキング用のブーツを持って行くね。準備しておくわ！

問1 シェリーは 　1　 を持って行く必要があるか，あなたに尋ねている。

① 毛布

② ジャケット

③ 寝袋

④ ウォーキング用の靴

問2 明日の朝，あなたはシェリーに 　2　 ことを望んでいる。

① 準備ができたらすぐにあなたに電話する

② キャンプ場であなたに会いに来る

③ あなたの家の前であなたを車に乗せてくれる

④ 彼女の家の外であなたを待っている

▌本文の語注

☐ invite A to *do*	～するよう A を誘う	☐ overnight	形 一泊の
☐ camping	名 キャンプすること	☐ mobile phone	携帯電話
【テキストメッセージ】			
☐ pack	動 ～にものを詰める	☐ check	動 ～を確認する
☐ bring	動 ～を持ってくる	☐ just to be sure	念のために
☐ warm	形 暖かい	☐ sleeping bag	寝袋
☐ maybe	副 もしかすると，たぶん	☐ comfortable	形 快適な
☐ footwear	名 履き物	☐ walk up	歩いて上がる，登る
☐ pick A up	A を迎えに行く	☐ outside	前 ～の外で
☐ hiking	名 ハイキング		

▌設問・選択肢の語注

☐ expect A to *do*	A が～するだろうと思う	☐ as soon as ～	～するとすぐに
☐ campsite	名 キャンプ場	☐ in front of ～	～の前で

令和3年度 大学入学共通テスト
第1問 B 全訳&語注

和訳

あなたは英語のスピーチ大会のチラシを先生から受け取り，応募したいと思っています。

第7回 青年リーダースピーチ大会

青年リーダー協会は，年に1度のスピーチ大会を開催します。私たちの目標は，日本の若者たちがコミュニケーションとリーダーシップのスキルを伸ばす手助けをすることです。

今年の大会には3つのステージがあります。審査員が各ステージの勝者を選びます。決勝戦に参加するには，3つのステージをすべて突破しなければなりません。

決勝戦

場所：センテニアルホール
日付：2022年1月8日
トピック：今日の若者，明日のリーダー

豪華賞品
優勝者は2022年3月にニュージーランドのウェリントンで行われる，リーダーシップワークショップに参加することができます。

大会情報：

ステージ	アップロードするもの	詳細	2021年の締め切りと日付
ステージ1	簡潔な概要	語数：150－200	8月12日の午後5時までにアップロード
ステージ2	あなたがスピーチをしている動画	時間：7－8分	9月19日の午後5時までにアップロード
ステージ3		各地域の大会：勝者が発表されて，決勝戦に進みます。	11月21日開催

決勝戦の評価に関する情報

内容	ジェスチャーと パフォーマンス	声とアイ コンタクト	スライド	審査員からの 質問に対する回答
50%	5%	5%	10%	30%

▷資料はオンラインでアップロードしなければなりません。すべての
　日付と時間は日本標準時（JST）です。
▷ステージ１と２の結果は，それぞれのステージの締め切りの５日
　後からウェブサイトで確認できます。

さらなる詳細と応募フォームは，<u>こちら</u>をクリックしてください。

問1 最初のステージに参加するためには，　3　をアップロードしなけれ
ばならない。
① 完成されたスピーチ原稿
② スピーチ用のスライド一式
③ スピーチの要約
④ あなた自身が話をしている動画

問2 ２つめのステージの結果は何日から確認できるか？　4
① ９月 14 日
② ９月 19 日
③ ９月 24 日
④ ９月 29 日

問3 決勝戦で高得点を獲得するためには，内容と　5　に最も注意を払う
べきだ。
① 表現とジェスチャー
② 審査員への応答
③ 視覚的な資料
④ 声の調整

本文の語注

☐ flyer	名 チラシ	☐ contest	名 コンテスト
☐ apply	動 応募する，申し込む		

【チラシ】

☐ youth	名 青少年	☐ society	名 クラブ，団体
☐ hold	動 ～を開催する	☐ annual	形 年1度の，毎年の
☐ develop	動 ～を伸ばす，発達させる	☐ leadership	名 リーダーシップ
☐ skill	名 スキル	☐ competition	名 コンテスト，協議会
☐ judge	名 審査員	☐ select	動 ～を選ぶ
☐ winner	名 勝者	☐ each	形 それぞれの
☐ take part in ～	～に参加する	☐ grand final	決勝戦
☐ successfully	副 うまく，首尾よく	☐ pass	動 ～を合格する，通過する
☐ grand	形 豪華な	☐ prize	名 賞品
☐ attend	動 ～に参加する	☐ workshop	名 ワークショップ，研修会
☐ upload	動 ～をアップロードする	☐ detail	名 詳細
☐ deadline	名 締め切り	☐ brief	形 簡潔な
☐ outline	名 概要	☐ local	形 地域の
☐ announce	動 ～を発表する	☐ grade	動 ～に成績をつける
☐ gesture	名 ジェスチャー	☐ slide	名 スライド
☐ online	副 オンラインで	☐ standard	形 標準の
☐ result	名 結果	☐ application	名 応募，申し込み
☐ form	名 フォーム，申込み用紙		

設問・選択肢の語注

☐ completed	形 完成した	☐ script	名 原稿
☐ set	名 セット，ひとまとまり	☐ summary	名 要約
☐ pay attention to ～	～に注意を払う	☐ expression	名 表現
☐ visual	形 視覚の		

221

令和３年度 大学入学共通テスト
第２問 A 全訳＆語注

和訳

あなたはイギリスの環境保護キャンペーンの一環として、クラスメイトが回答した使い捨てボトルと再利用ボトルに関する調査の結果に目を通しています。

質問１：１週間に使い捨てボトルの飲み物を何本購入しますか？

ボトルの本数	生徒の人数	週の小計
0	2	0
1	2	2
2	2	4
3	3	9
4	4	16
5	9	45
6	0	0
7	7	49
合計	29	125

質問２：自分の再利用可能なボトルを持っていますか？

回答の概要	生徒の人数	生徒の割合
はい，持っています。	3	10.3
はい，しかし使っていません。	14	48.3
いいえ，持っていません。	12	41.4
合計	29	100.0

質問３：再利用可能なボトルを使用していない場合，理由は何ですか？

回答の概要	生徒の人数
再利用ボトルを洗うのに時間がかかりすぎる。	24
使い捨てボトルの方が便利だと思う。	17
様々な味つきの飲み物が使い捨てボトルで販売されている。	14
使い捨てボトルを購入するのにそれほど費用がかからない。	10
学校の自動販売機で飲み物を購入できる。	7
再利用ボトルは重すぎると感じる。	4
家に多数の使い捨てボトルがある。	3
使い捨てボトルの水は長期間未開封で保管できる。	2
（その他の理由）	4

問1 質問1の結果は，　6　　ということを示している。

① それぞれの生徒は平均して週に4本より少ない使い捨てボトルを購入している

② 多くの生徒は週に2本より少ないボトルを購入している

③ 半分以上の生徒は週に少なくとも5本のボトルを購入している

④ 生徒たちは週に125本より多いボトルを購入している

問2 質問2の結果は，半分より多くの生徒が　7　　ということを示している。

① 自分の再利用ボトルを持っていない

② 自分の再利用ボトルを持っている

③ 自分の再利用ボトルを持っているが，使っていない

④ 自分の再利用ボトルを使っている

問3 質問3でクラスメイトによって述べられている1つの<u>意見</u>は，　8　　ということである。

① 何人かの生徒は自宅に使い捨てボトルのストックがある

② 学校に飲み物を買うための自動販売機がある

③ 再利用ボトルを洗うのはとても時間がかかる

④ 未開封の使い捨てボトルに入った水は長期間持つ

問4 質問3でクラスメイトによって述べられている1つの<u>事実</u>は，使い捨てボトルは　9　　ということである。

① 学校で購入可能である

② 使うのに便利である

③ 持ち運ぶのに十分軽い

④ 購入するのに高すぎない

問5 クラスメイトが再利用ボトルを使わない理由として最もありそうなものは何か？　10

① 自宅に保管されている使い捨てボトルの飲み物がたくさんある。

② 購入できる飲み物の種類がより少ない。

③ クラスメイトにとって高い。

④ 取り扱うのがやっかいだ。

■ 本文の語注

☐ result	名 結果	☐ survey	名 調査
☐ single-use	形 使い捨ての	☐ reusable	形 再利用できる
☐ as	前 ～として	☐ part of ～	～の一環，一部
☐ environmental	形 環境保護の	☐ campaign	名 キャンペーン
【質問1】			
☐ purchase	動 ～を購入する	☐ per	前 ～につき
☐ weekly	形 1週間の	☐ subtotal	名 小計
【質問2】			
☐ own	形 自分自身の	☐ summary	名 概要
☐ response	名 回答	☐ percent	名 パーセント，割合
【質問3】			
☐ wash	動 ～を洗う	☐ convenient	形 便利な
☐ flavoured	形 味をつけた	☐ available	形 購入できる
☐ cost	動 （費用）がかかる	☐ vending machine	自動販売機
☐ heavy	形 重い	☐ dozens of ～	多数の～
☐ store	動 ～を保管する	☐ unopened	形 開いていない，未開封の
☐ other	形 他の		

■ 設問・選択肢の語注

☐ show	動 ～を示す	☐ few	形 少数の
☐ on average	平均して	☐ half	形 半分の
☐ at least	少なくとも，最低	☐ opinion	名 意見
☐ express	動 ～を述べる	☐ stock	名 ストック
☐ last	動 持ちこたえる，続く	☐ fact	名 事実
☐ state	動 ～をはっきり述べる	☐ light	形 軽い
☐ enough to do	～するのに十分	☐ carry around	持ち運ぶ
☐ expensive	形 高価な，値段が高い	☐ likely	形 ありそうな
☐ variety	名 種類	☐ troublesome	形 やっかいな
☐ deal with ～	～を取り扱う		

令和３年度 大学入学共通テスト
第２問Ｂ　全訳＆語注

和訳

イギリスでのサマープログラムで何の授業を受講するか決める必要があるため，講座情報とその講座に対する以前の学生のコメントを読んでいます。

コミュニケーションと異文化研究

クリストファー・ベネット博士
bennet.christopher@ire-u.ac.uk
電話番号：020-9876-1234
相談受付時間：要予約

2021年8月3日～31日
火曜日と金曜日
午後1時から午後2時半
9回の授業 ― 1単位

講座説明：異文化を研究し，異文化出身の人々とコミュニケーションをとる方法を学びます。本講座では，学生は異文化間で起こる問題に対処するための自分の考えを発表する必要があります。

目標：本講座受講後にできるようになっていること：
― 異文化間の人間関係を理解する
― 異文化間で起こる様々な問題の解決策を提示する
― 議論やプレゼンテーションを通じて自分の意見を述べる

教科書：スミス, S.（2019）.『異文化研究』ニューヨーク：DNC社

評価：合格するには全体の60％が必要
― プレゼンテーション2回：90％（各45％）
― 参加：10％

講座受講者による評価（87人の評価者）★★★★★（平均：4.89）

コメント
☺この授業を受講してください！　クリスは素晴らしい先生です。彼はとても頭がよくて優しいです。講座は少しだけ難しくやりがいがありますが，十分合格できます。文化の違いをたくさん学ぶことになり

ます。助言するとしたら，すべての授業に参加するということでしょう。よいプレゼンテーションをするのにとても役立ちました。

問1 この講座であなたは何をするか？ **11**
① 文化に関する様々なトピックについて話し合う
② 様々な国をいくつも訪問する
③ 人間関係に関する映画を見る
④ 文化に関する最終レポートを書く

問2 この授業は **12** 生徒を対象にしている。
① 異文化間で起こる問題に興味がある
② よいプレゼンテーションができる
③ イギリスで観光することが好きである
④ 英語を話せるようになる必要がある

問3 ベネット博士に関する1つの<u>事実</u>は **13** ということである。
① 教える技術が高い
② よい教師である
③ この講座の担当である
④ 講座を難しくやりがいのあるものにしている

問4 授業に関して述べられている1つの<u>意見</u>は **14** ということである。
① 単位を取るのはそれほど難しくない
② ほとんどの生徒は講座に満足している
③ 参加が最終成績の一部である
④ 生徒は週に2回授業がある

問5 この講座に合格するためには何をする必要があるか？ **15**
① すべての授業に出席して議論に参加する
② 異文化間で起こる問題を発見して解決策を話し合う
③ 異文化間で起こる問題についてよいプレゼンテーションを行う
④ ベネット博士と面会の予約をする

226 第2日程 全訳&語注

■ 本文の語注

□ take	動 ～を受講する	□ programme	名 プログラム
□ information	名 情報	□ former	形 前の
【資料】			
□ intercultural	形 異文化間の	□ Dr [doctor]	名 博士
□ office hour	営業時間, 応接時間	□ appointment	名 予約
□ description	名 説明	□ different	形 異なる
□ how to do	～する方法	□ present	動 ～を発表する
□ deal with ～	～に対処する	□ issue	名 問題
□ be able to do	～することができる	□ human	形 人間の
□ relation	名 関係	□ among	前 ～の間で
□ solution	名 解決策	□ problem	名 問題
□ express	動 ～を述べる	□ through	前 ～を通して
□ discussion	名 議論	□ evaluation	名 評価
□ overall	副 全体で	□ require	動 ～を必要とする
□ pass	動 合格する	□ participation	名 参加, 関与
□ average	名 平均	□ a little	少し, わずかに
□ challenging		□ enough to do	～するのに十分
	形 挑戦的な, 難しいがやりがいのある		
□ advice	名 アドバイス		

■ 設問・選択肢の語注

□ various	形 様々な	□ film	名 映画
□ final	形 最後の	□ aim A at ～	Aを～に向ける
□ fact	名 事実	□ skill	名 技術
□ instructor	名 教師	□ in charge of ～	～の担当で
□ credit	名 単位	□ be satisfied with ～	～に満足して
□ grade	名 成績	□ join	動 ～に参加する

227

令和3年度 大学入学共通テスト
第3問A 全訳＆語注

和訳

イギリス人の友だちであるジャンが新しい遊園地を訪れて、自分の体験についてブログを投稿しました。

サニーマウンテンパーク：素晴らしい訪問先
ジャンの投稿　2020年9月15日　午後9時37分

　サニーマウンテンパークが先月ついに開園しました！　巨大なジェットコースターを含む、ワクワクするようなアトラクションがたくさんある大きな遊園地です（地図を見てください）。先週、私はそこで友だちと素晴らしい時間を過ごしました。

　私たちはジェットコースターに乗ってみるのが待ちきれなかったのですが、全体像を理解するために、まずパーク内を周遊する電車に乗りました。電車からはピクニックゾーンが見えて、昼食を取るのにいい場所だろうと思いました。しかし、そこはすでにとても混んでいたので、私たちは代わりにフードコートへ行くことに決めました。昼食の前に、私たちはディスカバリーゾーンに行きました。そこでの科学的なアトラクションの体験は、十分待つ価値がありました。午後、私たちはマウンテンステーションの近くでいくつかの乗り物を楽しみました。もちろんジェットコースターに乗ってみましたが、がっかりすることはありませんでした。もっと多くのアトラクションを楽しむためにディスカバリーゾーンへ戻る途中、私たちは休憩所で短い休息を取りました。そこで、私たちは湖越しに美しい城を眺めました。私たちは最後にショッピングゾーンに行き着き、そこで友だちや家族にお土産を買いました。

　サニーマウンテンパークは素晴らしいです！　私たちの最初の訪問はきっと、最後のものにはならないでしょう。

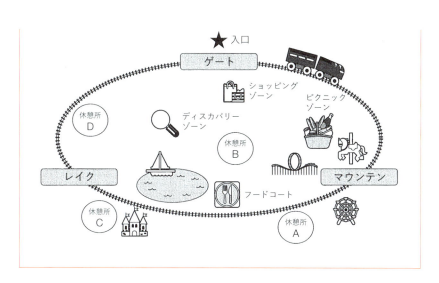

問1 ジャンの投稿から，[16] ということがわかる。
① ジャンはお土産のためにショッピングゾーンに行くのを省いた
② ジャンは科学的なアトラクションを楽しむためにしばらく待った
③ フードコートはピクニックゾーンよりも混んでいた
④ ジェットコースターはジャンの期待に見合わなかった

問2 午後，ジャンと友だちはどの休憩所で休息を取ったか？ [17]
① 休憩所 A
② 休憩所 B
③ 休憩所 C
④ 休憩所 D

本文の語注

□ amusement park	遊園地	□ post	動 ～を投稿する
【ブログ】		□ attraction	名 アトラクション
□ finally	副 ついに	□ huge	形 巨大な
□ include	動 ～を含む	□ fantastic	形 素晴らしい
□ roller coaster	ジェットコースター	□ already	副 すでに
□ layout	名 配置	□ worth	形 ～に値する
□ crowded	形 混みあった	□ several	形 いくつかの
□ scientific	形 科学の	□ take a break	休憩を取る
□ disappointed	形 失望した，がっかりした	□ lovely	形 美しい
□ rest stop	休憩所	□ over	前 ～じゅうの
□ view	名 眺め	□ souvenir	名 お土産
□ end up ～	最終的に～になる	□ certainly	副 きっと
□ amazing	形 素晴らしい	□ entrance	名 入口
□ last	名 最後，終わり		
□ gate	名 門		

設問・選択肢の語注

□ skip	動 ～を省く	□ for a while	しばらくの間
□ meet	動 ～を満たす	□ expectation	名 期待

令和3年度 大学入学共通テスト
第3問B 全訳&語注

> **和訳**
> イギリスにいるあなたの友だちが，好きなミュージシャンを紹介してくれました。もっと知りたいと思い，あなたは音楽雑誌で次の記事を発見しました。

デイヴ・スター，生ける伝説

　かつてブラック・スワンはイギリス最大のロックバンドであり，彼らの精力的なリーダーであるデイヴ・スターはその功績において大きな役割を演じた。いまだにソロの歌手として活動しながら，デイヴの並外れた才能は若いミュージシャン世代に刺激を与えている。

　幼い少年の頃，デイヴはいつも歌い，おもちゃの楽器で遊んでばかりいた。彼はおもちゃのドラムを演奏しているとき以上に幸せを感じることはなかった。7歳で彼は最初の本物のドラムセットを与えられ，10歳になる頃には上手に演奏することができた。14歳になるまでに，彼はギターも習得した。まだ高校生だったとき，彼はザ・ブルーバーズのメンバーになり，リズムギターを弾いた。経験を得るために，ザ・ブルーバーズは学校行事やコミュニティセンターで無料で演奏した。バンドは熱心なファンの小さな輪を築き上げた。

　18歳の誕生日にブラック・スワンのドラマーになるように頼まれたとき，デイヴの大きなチャンスがやって来た。わずか2年で，大きなコンサートホールで行われたバンドのライブは完売していた。だからこそ，リードボーカルがもっと多くの時間を家族と過ごすために辞めたときは衝撃的だった。しかし，デイヴはリードシンガーを引き継ぐチャンスに飛びついたが，それは彼がもはやお気に入りの楽器を演奏できないことを意味していた。

　それから数年でブラック・スワンはますます成功をおさめ，音楽チャートのトップに載り，さらに多くのファンを獲得した。デイヴは第一線の作曲家になり，バンドへの貢献を誇りに感じていた。しかし，キーボード奏者の加入とともに，バンドの音楽は徐々に方向性を変えた。デイヴは不満を抱き，彼とリードギタリストは脱退して新しいグ

ループを始めることに決めた。残念ながら，デイヴの新しいバンドは
ブラック・スワンほどの成功に達することはできず，結成されていた
のはわずか 18 か月であった。

問1 次の出来事（①〜④）を起こった順番に並べ替えなさい。
$$\boxed{18} \to \boxed{19} \to \boxed{20} \to \boxed{21}$$
① デイヴはソロのアーティストになった。
② デイヴはドラムの演奏をあきらめた。
③ デイヴはギタリストとしてバンドに加入した。
④ デイヴはキャリアの頂点に達した。

問2 $\boxed{22}$ ので，デイヴはブラック・スワンのリードシンガーになった。
① ドラムを演奏することよりも歌うことが好きだった
② バンドの音楽の方向性を変えたいと思っていた
③ 他のバンドメンバーがさらなる成功を望んでいた
④ 以前の歌手が個人的な理由で脱退した

問3 この話から，$\boxed{23}$ ということがわかる。
① ブラック・スワンはロックミュージックの方向性を変えることに貢
  献した
② ブラック・スワンのグッズはコンサートホールでとてもよく売れた
③ デイヴは幼い頃から音楽の才能を発揮した
④ デイヴはリードギタリストに不満を抱いたのでソロになった

本文の語注

☐ introduce	動 ～を紹介する	☐ favourite	形 お気に入りの
☐ following	形 次の	☐ article	名 記事
☐ magazine	名 雑誌	☐ legend	名 伝説

【第 1 段落】

☐ at one time	かつて	☐ dynamic	形 活動的な
☐ play a part in ～	～で役割を果たす	☐ achievement	名 功績
☐ still	副 まだ，今もなお	☐ perform	動 演奏する
☐ solo	形 ソロの，単独の	☐ incredible	形 並外れた，信じられない
☐ talent	名 才能	☐ inspire	動 ～に活気を与える
☐ generation	名 世代		

【第 2 段落】

☐ little	形 年少の	☐ toy	形 おもちゃの
☐ instrument	名 楽器	☐ never	副 決して～ない
☐ drum	名 ドラム	☐ real	形 本物の
☐ master	動 ～を習得する	☐ rhythm	名 リズム
☐ for free	無料で	☐ centre	名 センター
☐ build up ～	～を築き上げる	☐ circle	名 団体，仲間
☐ passionate	形 情熱的な	☐ fan	名 ファン

【第 3 段落】

☐ break	名 好機	☐ sell out	売り切れる
☐ hall	名 ホール	☐ shock	名 衝撃的な出来事
☐ therefore	副 それゆえに	☐ lead	名 リード，先導
☐ vocalist	名 歌手，ボーカリスト	☐ quit	動 仕事をやめる
☐ spend	動 ～を過ごす	☐ jump at ～	～に飛びつく
☐ take over	引き継ぐ	☐ even though	～だとしても
☐ mean	動 ～を意味する	☐ no longer	もはや～ない

【第 4 段落】

☐ increasingly	副 ますます	☐ successful	形 成功した
☐ top	動 ～のトップに載る	☐ chart	名 チャート
☐ gain	動 ～を獲得する	☐ principal	形 主要な
☐ contribution	名 貢献	☐ addition	名 追加，加入
☐ keyboard	名 キーボード	☐ gradually	副 徐々に
☐ direction	名 方向	☐ frustrated	形 失望した，不満を抱いた
☐ leave	動 仕事をやめる	☐ unfortunately	副 残念ながら
☐ fail to *do*	～できない	☐ reach	動 ～に達する

設問・選択肢の語注

☐ order	名 順番	☐ peak	名 ピーク，頂点
☐ career	名 キャリア	☐ prefer A to B	B より A の方を好む
☐ other	形 他の	☐ previous	形 以前の
☐ personal	形 個人的な	☐ contribute	動 貢献する
☐ display	動 ～を発揮する		

233

令和3年度 大学入学共通テスト
第4問　全訳&語注

和訳

あなたは日本の観光業に関するプレゼンテーションの準備をしています。クラスメイトのハンナとリックに，2018年の訪日客に関するデータをEメールで送りました。彼らの返答をもとに，プレゼンテーションの概要を下書きします。

データ：

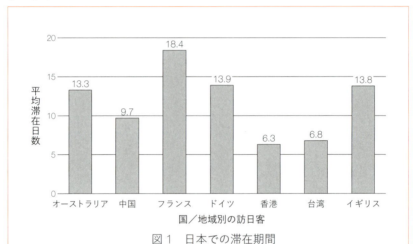

図1　日本での滞在期間

表1

訪日中に使った平均金額

訪日客の国／地域	食べ物	娯楽	買い物
オーストラリア	58,878	16,171	32,688
中国	39,984	7,998	112,104
フランス	56,933	7,358	32,472
ドイツ	47,536	5,974	25,250
香港	36,887	5,063	50,287
台湾	28,190	5,059	45,441
イギリス	56,050	8,341	22,641

（1人あたりの円）

あなたのＥメールへの返答：

こんにちは，

Ｅメールをありがとう！ 興味深いデータね。海外からの訪日客数が過去に増えていたのは知っているけど，滞在期間に注意を向けたことはなかったわ。アジアからの訪日客は簡単に行き来できるから，より短い滞在期間で来日しているんじゃないかしら。

ヨーロッパやオーストラリアからの訪日客と比べて，アジアからの訪日客は全体として，より買い物にお金を費やす傾向があることも，その表は示しているわね。これはたぶん，アジアの文化では贈り物がとても重要で，友だちや家族にお土産を買いたいと思っているからじゃないかしら。たとえば銀座や原宿，秋葉原周辺で買い物をしている大勢のアジア人観光客を見かけたことがあるわ。もしかしたら彼らはそれほど多くのお金を宿泊施設にかける必要がないから，買い物にもっとお金を費やせるのかもしれない。私はこれについて話したいと思っているの。

でもアジアからの訪日客は今，買い物の代わりに何か他のことをするのに興味を持ち始めていると聞いたわ。近い将来，この種のデータに変化が見られるかもしれないわね！

よろしく
ハンナ
追伸　このメッセージはリックにも送られます。

やあ，

データを送ってくれてありがとう！ 僕たちがプレゼンテーションの準備をする助けになるよ！

データから，オーストラリア人はいちばん娯楽にお金を費やしていることに気づいたんだ。僕はこれについて発表するよ。

それに先日，日本のテレビで，北海道でウィンタースポーツを楽しんでいるオーストラリア人に関する番組を見たんだ。彼らはいくらお金

を使うのかな。もっと情報を探してみるよ。もし何か見つけたら，僕に知らせて。これは将来のプロジェクトにふさわしいかもね。

それから，訪日客の出身国や地域によって，滞在期間に大きな差があるらしいという点では，ハンナと同じ考えだよ。

君はどうする？　お金の使い道に関してハンナが発見したことを話したいかい？　僕はとても面白いと思うよ。

よろしく
リック
追伸　このメッセージはハンナにも送られます。

プレゼンテーションの下書き：

プレゼンテーションのタイトル：_____ 24 _____

発表者　　　　トピック

ハンナ：_____ 25 _____

リック：_____ 26 _____

私：　　　滞在期間との関係
　　　　　　比較の例：
　　　　　 27 　から来た人々は， 28 　から来た人々と比べると半分よりわずかに長い期間だけ日本に滞在するが，娯楽に少しだけ多くお金を使っている。

将来の調査テーマ：_____ 29 _____

問1 　24 　に最もふさわしいのはどれか？
① 北海道での冬季休暇に使われるお金
② 東京における海外からの観光客の買い物にかける予算
③ 海外からの訪日客の消費傾向
④ 日本における娯楽への支出の増加

236　第2日程　全訳＆語注

問2 　25　 に最もふさわしいのはどれか？
① オーストラリアからの訪日客の活動
② アジアからの訪日客の食費
③ ヨーロッパの文化における贈り物の習慣
④ アジアからの訪日客の支出パターン

問3 　26　 に最もふさわしいのはどれか？
① オーストラリアからの観光客の娯楽への関心
② 東京における中国人のお金の使い道
③ 北海道に関するオーストラリアのテレビ番組
④ アジアの人々が楽しめる日本での様々な経験

問4 あなたはリックの提案に同意してデータを見る。　27　 と 　28　 に最もふさわしいものを選べ。
① オーストラリア
② 中国
③ フランス
④ 台湾

問5 　29　 に最もふさわしい組み合わせはどれか？
Ａ：オーストラリアの人々が日本でのウィンタースポーツにかける予算
Ｂ：東京への海外からの訪日客数の将来的な変化
Ｃ：海外から北海道への訪日客に人気の食べ物
Ｄ：アジアからの訪日客が将来お金を使うであろうもの

237

■本文の語注

☐ tourism	名 観光事業	☐ data	名 データ
☐ based on ～	～に基づいて	☐ response	名 返答
☐ draft	動 ～の下書きを書く	☐ outline	名 概要

【データ】

☐ average	形 平均の	☐ Germany	名 ドイツ
☐ Hong Kong	名 香港	☐ region	名 地域
☐ figure	名 図	☐ length	名 期間
☐ table	名 表	☐ amount	名 額
☐ spend	動 （お金）を使う	☐ per	前 ～につき

【ハンナのメール】

☐ international	形 国際的な	☐ increase	動 増える
☐ previously	副 以前に，もともと	☐ pay attention to ～	～に注意を向ける
☐ assume	動 ～だと思う	☐ go back and forth	行ったり来たりする，往復する
☐ easily	副 簡単に	☐ overall	副 全体で
☐ tend to do	動 ～する傾向がある	☐ compared to ～	～に比べて
☐ probably	副 おそらく	☐ gift-giving	贈り物
☐ perhaps	副 もしかすると	☐ accommodation	名 宿泊施設
☐ instead of ～	～の代わりに		

【リックのメール】

☐ help A do	Aが～するのを手伝う	☐ notice	動 ～だと気づく
☐ entertainment	名 娯楽	☐ present	動 ～を発表する
☐ the other day	先日，このあいだ	☐ program	名 番組
☐ wonder	動 ～かなと思う	☐ in addition	さらに，加えて
☐ seem	動 ～のように見える	☐ depend on ～	～によって，～次第で
☐ in relation to ～	～に関して	☐ habit	名 癖，習慣

【プレゼンテーションの下書き】

☐ presenter	名 発表者	☐ comparison	名 比較
☐ half	名 半分	☐ slightly	副 わずかに
☐ theme	名 テーマ		

■設問・選択肢の語注

☐ budget	名 予算	☐ activity	名 活動
☐ pattern	名 パターン	☐ various	形 様々な
☐ combination	名 組み合わせ		

令和3年度 大学入学共通テスト
第5問 全訳＆語注

和訳

あなたは，まだ存命であればインタビューをしたい人物について話をする予定です。選んだ人物に関する次の文章を読んで，メモを完成させなさい。

ヴィヴィアン・マイヤー

　これは，亡くなるまで写真を撮ることへの情熱を秘密にし続けた，アメリカ人のストリートフォトグラファーの物語だ。彼女は介護士として人生を送り，もしオークション会場で所持品が売りに出されていなかったら，彼女の素晴らしい作品が発見されることは決してなかったかもしれない。

　2007年のこと。シカゴのあるオークション会場で，ヴィヴィアン・マイヤーという名前の年配の女性の所持品が売りに出されていた。彼女が倉庫料の支払いをやめたので，会社は彼女の物を売ることに決めた。彼女の所持品—主に古い写真やネガ—は，マルーフ，スラッタリー，そしてプラウという3人の買い手に売られた。

　スラッタリーはヴィヴィアンの作品を面白いと思い，2008年7月に写真共有ウェブサイトで彼女の写真を公表した。写真はほとんど注目されなかった。それから10月に，マルーフがブログに自分で選んだヴィヴィアンの写真へのリンクを貼りつけるとすぐ，数千人が閲覧した。マルーフは写真に添えられたヴィヴィアン・マイヤーの名前を見つけてはいたが，彼女に関する情報は何も見つけられなかった。その後，インターネットでの検索によって，彼は彼女の死を報じる2009年の新聞記事にたどり着いた。ヴィヴィアンの人生についてもっと知るためにマルーフはこの情報を利用したが，皆の注目を集めたのは，ヴィヴィアンの謎に満ちた人生の物語と写真の結びつきだった。

　ヴィヴィアンの人生に関する情報は，2つの理由で限定されている。まず，彼女が生きている間に誰もインタビューをしたことがなかったので，なぜ彼女がそれほど多くの写真を撮ったのか誰も知らなかった。2つめに，彼女が仕えていた一家とのインタビューから，ヴィヴィアンはほとんど人前に出たがらない人物であったことは明らかである。彼女はほとんど友だちがいなかった。さらに彼女は自分の趣味を秘密にしていた。

　1926年，ヴィヴィアンはアメリカでオーストリア人の父とフランス人の母のもとに生まれた。結婚生活は幸せなものではなく，彼女の母親と父親は数年間別々に暮らしたようだ。子ども時代，ときにはフランスに住み，ときにはアメリカに住みながら，ヴィヴィアンは頻繁にアメリカとフランスを移動した。

「ネガフィルム」

「プリントされた写真」

　しばらくの間，ヴィヴィアンと彼女の母親は，ジャンヌ・ベルトランという成功した写真家と一緒にニューヨークで暮らした。ヴィヴィアンは成人初期に写真撮影に興味をもつようになったと考えられているが，というのも彼女の初期の写真は非常にシンプルなカメラを使って1940年代後半にフランスで撮られていたからだ。彼女は1951年にニューヨークに戻り，1956年にギンズバーグ一家の介護士として働くためにシカゴへ引っ越した。この仕事は彼女に，写真を撮るためのもっとたくさんの自由時間を与えた。
　1952年，26歳で彼女は最初の6×6判カメラを購入したが，シカゴの街の暮らしの写真の大半を撮影したのはこのカメラであった。30年以上の間，彼女は子どもやお年寄り，お金持ちや貧しい人々の写真を撮った。自分の写真が撮られていることに気づきさえしなかった人もいた。彼女はまた，数多くの自画像を撮影した。店のウインドウに映った彼女自身の姿の写真もあった。彼女自身の影を写したものもあった。ヴィヴィアンは1970年代前半までシカゴの生活を記録し続け，それから新しい写真撮影のスタイルに移行した。
　国際的な賞を受賞した『ヴィヴィアン・マイヤーを探して』というドキュメンタリー映画は，より多くの観客に彼女の作品への興味をもたらした。その映画はヨーロッパとアメリカでの展覧会につながった。彼女のスタイルを最もよく表す写真を選ぶために，展覧会の責任者たちは「ヴィヴィアン・マイヤーなら，何を現像しただろうか？」という問いに答えようとしている。この問いに答えるために，彼らは彼女のメモや彼女が実際に現像した写真，そしてギンズバーグ家が報告した彼女の好みに関する情報を利用した。ヴィヴィアンは成果物というよりもむしろ，瞬間を捕らえることに関心があった。だからこそヴィヴィアンの作品の背後にある謎は，大部分が"未解明"のままであると言えそうだ。

プレゼンテーションの下書き：

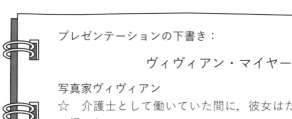

写真家ヴィヴィアン
☆ 介護士として働いていた間に，彼女はたくさんの写真を撮った。
☆ 彼女が生きている間に誰もインタビューしなかったので，私たちは彼女についてあまり知らない。
☆ 　30　

ヴィヴィアンの作品
☆ 彼女の写真が主に対象としているのは：
・若者や老人，お金持ちや貧しい人々
・　31　
・　32　

彼女の作品はどのように認知されたか
☆ ヴィヴィアンの倉庫料が支払われなかった。
☆ 　33　
☆ 　34　
☆ 　35　
☆ 　36　
☆ 彼女の人生と作品に関する情報の結びつきが人々の興味を増大させた。

彼女の作品はどのように世界的に知られたのか
☆ 彼女の人生と作品に関する，賞を受賞したドキュメンタリー映画が，新たな観客を魅了するのに役立った。
☆ 　37　

「大きな」未解答の問い：　38

問1 30 に入る最もふさわしい記述を選びなさい。
① オークションで販売されるまで彼女の作品は未発見のままだった。
② 彼女は 30 代で写真に魅了されたと考えられている。
③ 彼女はどこへ行くにもカメラを持って行き，写真を他の人に見せた。
④ 彼女の写真の大半がニューヨークで撮影された。

問2 31 と 32 に入る最もふさわしい 2 つの選択肢を選びなさい。（順番は問わない。）
① ドキュメンタリー風の写真
② 工業的な風景
③ 自然の風景
④ 彼女自身の写真
⑤ 店のウインドウ

問3 次の出来事を起こった順番に並べなさい。 33 ～ 36
① ある買い手がブログに彼女の写真の一部へのリンクを貼った。
② ヴィヴィアンの死に関する記事が新聞で公表された。
③ あるオークション会社が彼女の古い写真とネガを販売し始めた。
④ 彼女の作品がインターネットで公表された。

問4 37 に入る最もふさわしい記述を選びなさい。
① 彼女の作品の展覧会が，世界の様々な場所で開催された。
② 路上の風景を特集した彼女の写真集が賞を受賞した。
③ 彼女は自分の写真の取り扱い方法について詳細な指示を残した。
④ ヴィヴィアンの雇用主の子どもたちは彼らの写真を提供した。

問5 38 に入る最もふさわしい質問を選びなさい。
①「写真を撮るのにどんな種類のカメラを使ったのか？」
②「ネガや写真のすべてをどこに保管していたのか？」
③「なぜ介護士になるためにニューヨークを離れたのか？」
④「なぜ誰にも見せることなくそれほど多くの写真を撮ったのか？」

本文の語注

☐ give a talk on 〜	〜について発表する	☐ interview	動	〜にインタビューする
☐ alive	形 生きて	☐ following	形	次の
☐ passage	名 (文章の) 一節	☐ choose	動	〜を選ぶ
☐ complete	動 〜を完成させる			

【第1段落】

☐ street	名 (形容詞的に) 通りで活動する	☐ photographer	名	写真家
☐ keep A B	AをBにしておく	☐ passion for 〜		〜に対する情熱
☐ secret	形 秘密の	☐ until	前	〜まで
☐ death	名 死	☐ caregiver	名	介護士
☐ sale	名 競売, せり売り	☐ belonging	名	所持品, 私物
☐ auction	名 オークション	☐ incredible	形	素晴らしい
☐ work	名 作品	☐ discover	動	〜を発見する

【第2段落】

☐ sell off	〜を売り払う	☐ pay	動	〜を支払う
☐ storage fee	保管料	☐ mainly	副	主に
☐ negative	名 ネガ, 陰画	☐ buyer	名	買い手

【第3段落】

☐ publish	動 〜を公表する	☐ photo-sharing	形	写真共有の
☐ receive	動 〜を受ける	☐ little	形	ほとんどない
☐ attention	名 注目	☐ link A to B		AをBにつなぐ
☐ blog	名 ブログ	☐ selection	名	選集, 選抜
☐ right away	すぐに	☐ thousands of 〜		何千もの〜
☐ view	動 〜を見る	☐ print	名	印画
☐ be unable to *do*	〜することができない	☐ search	名	調査
☐ lead A to B	AをBに導く	☐ newspaper article		新聞記事
☐ combination of A and B	AとBの組み合わせ	☐ mysterious	形	不思議な, 謎めいた
☐ grab one's attention	〜の注目を集める			

【第4段落】

☐ detail	名 詳細	☐ limit	動	〜を制限する
☐ no one	だれも〜ない	☐ it is clear that 〜		〜だということは明らかだ
☐ private	形 内気な, 人と交わらない	☐ few	形	ほとんどない
☐ besides	副 加えて			

【第5段落】

☐ be born	生まれる	☐ marriage	名	結婚生活
☐ it seems (that) 〜	〜のようだ	☐ apart	副	別々に
☐ several years	数年	☐ during	前	〜の間
☐ childhood	名 子供時代	☐ frequently	副	頻繁に, しばしば
☐ between A and B	AとBの間	☐ for a while		しばらくの間
☐ successful	形 成功した	☐ become interested in 〜		〜に興味を持つようになる
☐ photography	名 写真撮影	☐ young adult		若年成人
☐ late	形 後期の	☐ simple	形	簡単な, シンプルな
☐ return	動 戻る, 帰る	☐ free time	名	自由時間

【第6段落】

☐ at the age of 〜	〜歳で	☐ purchase	動	〜を購入する
☐ most of 〜	ほとんどの〜	☐ the elderly		年配の人々
☐ the rich	お金持ちの人々	☐ the poor		貧しい人々
☐ be aware that 〜	〜だと気づいている	☐ even	副	〜さえ
☐ a number of 〜	多数の〜	☐ self-portrait		自画像
☐ reflection	名 反射, 反映	☐ other	代	ほかのもの
☐ shadow	名 影	☐ continue	動	〜を続ける
☐ document	動 〜を記録する	☐ early	形	初期の

243

【第7段落】

☐ international	形 国際的な	☐ award-winning	形 受賞歴のある
☐ documentary film	ドキュメンタリー映画	☐ wide	形 広い
☐ audience	名 観客	☐ exhibition	名 展覧会
☐ represent	動 ～を表す，象徴する	☐ those	代 人々
☐ in charge of ～	～の担当の	☐ in order to *do*	～するために
☐ actually	副 実際に	☐ preference	名 好み
☐ report	動 ～を報告する	☐ capture	動 ～を捕らえる
☐ moment	名 瞬間	☐ rather than	～よりもむしろ
☐ outcome	名 結果	☐ mystery	名 秘密，謎
☐ behind	前 ～の後ろに	☐ remain A	A のままである
☐ largely	副 大部分は	☐ undeveloped	形 未発達の，未解明の

【メモ】

☐ nobody	代 だれも～ない	☐ concentrate on ～	～に集中する
☐ gain recognition	認知度を高める	☐ combine	動 結合する
☐ known	形 有名な，知られている	☐ worldwide	副 世界中で
☐ unanswered	形 答えのない		

▌設問・選択肢の語注

☐ statement	名 記述	☐ undiscovered	形 未発見の
☐ in one's thirties	～の 30 代で	☐ wherever	接 どこへ～しようとも
☐ majority	名 大部分	☐ order	名 順番
☐ industrial	形 産業の	☐ landscape	名 風景
☐ natural	形 自然の	☐ report	名 記事
☐ hold	動 ～を開催する	☐ feature	動 ～を特集する
☐ leave	動 ～を残す	☐ detailed	形 詳細な
☐ instruction on ～	～に関する指示	☐ treat	動 ～を扱う
☐ employer	名 雇用主	☐ without	前 ～なしで

令和３年度 大学入学共通テスト
第６問 A 全訳＆語注

和訳

あなたはアメリカにいる交換留学生で、学校の演劇部に所属しています。クラブをよくする助けとなるアイデアを得るために、アメリカのオンライン美術雑誌の記事を読みます。

ロイヤル・シェイクスピア・カンパニーの最近の変化

ジョン・スミス
2020年2月20日

　私たちは皆、違っている。ほとんどの人々が世界は多様な人々で構成されていると認識している一方で、多様性─私たちの違いを示したり受け入れたりすること─は舞台芸術団体にしばしば反映されていない。このため映画や演劇が、障がいのある人々や様々な背景のある人々をより適切に描く需要が高まっている。英国芸術評議会はこの需要に応じ、公的資金を受けた芸術団体が、この分野に改善をもたらすことを奨励している。前向きな反応を示している劇団の１つがロイヤル・シェイクスピア・カンパニー（RCS）で、世界で最も影響力のある劇団の１つだ。

　RSCはイギリスのストラトフォード＝アポン＝エイヴォンに拠点を置き、ウィリアム・シェイクスピアや他の多くの有名な劇作家による演劇を上演している。最近ではイギリス社会のすべてを正確に描写しようとして、多様性に焦点を当てている。雇用時に、役者とスタッフ両方の民族や社会的背景、性別や身体能力の均衡がとれるように、RSCは熱心に取り組んでいる。

　2019年夏のシーズンの間に、RSCは『お気に召すまま』『じゃじゃ馬ならし』『尺には尺を』というシェイクスピアの３つの喜劇を上演した。国中の俳優が雇用され、27名のキャスト陣を形成し、今日のイギリスの多様な民族的、地理的、文化的人口を反映した。シーズン全体を通して性別の均衡を達成するために、すべての役の半分が男性の役者に、半分が女性の役者に与えられた。キャストには障がいのある３人の役者（現在は「異なる能力のある」役者と呼ばれる）も含まれていた─１人は目が不自由な役者、１人は耳が不自由な役者、そ

して 1 人は車椅子の役者であった。

　変化は雇用方針だけに留まらなかった。実際，RSC は観客が男性
／女性の力関係を深く考えるように，劇の数か所を書き直した。たと
えば，女性と男性の役が入れ替えられた。『じゃじゃ馬ならし』では，
原作の「娘」の役が「息子」に変更され，男性の役者によって演じら
れた。同じ劇で，男性の従者役が女性の従者として書き直された。そ
の役は車椅子を使う女性の役者であるエイミー・トリッグによって演
じられた。トリッグはその役を演じることにワクワクしており，RSC
の変化は他の舞台芸術団体に大きな影響を与えるだろうと信じている
と語った。すべての多様性にワクワクしながら，RSC の他のメンバー
も同様の希望を述べた—より多くの芸術団体が RSC の足跡に続くよ
う促されるだろうと。

　2019 年夏シーズンの RSC の多様性を反映する決定は，自分たち
の組織を包括的にしたいと望む芸術団体にとって，新しいモデルと見
なされ得る。古典演劇に多様性を受け入れることに乗り気でない人々
がいる一方で，両手を広げて歓迎する人々もいる。ある程度の課題は
残っているが，RSC は進歩の顔だという評判を得たのである。

問 1　記事によると，RSC は 2019 年夏のシーズンに　**39**　。
① 有名な俳優たちに仕事の機会を与えた
② 3 人の異なる能力のある役者を雇った
③ 27 人の登場人物を含む演劇を探した
④ シェイクスピアや他の作家による演劇を上演した

問 2　この記事の筆者はおそらく，エイミー・トリッグが　**40**　ので，彼女
に言及している。
① RSC によって上演された劇の 1 つで好演した
② RSC のメンバーとして選ばれようと奮闘していた
③ 包括的であろうとする RSC の取り組みのよい例だった
④ RSC のメンバーにとっての模範になる人物であった

問3 あなたは他の部員のためにこの記事を要約している。次の選択肢のうち，要約を最も適切に完成させるのはどれか？

【要約】
イギリスのロイヤル・シェイクスピア・カンパニー（RSC）は，イギリス社会の人口を公演内に反映しようと取り組んでいる。これを達成するために，様々な背景や能力をもつ女性と男性の役者やスタッフをバランスよく雇用し始めた。また，演劇に変更を加えた。その結果，RSCは　**41**　。

① 世界中から多くの才能ある役者を引きつけた
② 2019年のシーズンを何の反論もなく終えた
③ 社会的な期待を行動と一致させることに貢献した
④ 保守的な劇団として評判を得た

問4 あなたの演劇部は RSC の考えに賛同している。これらの考えにもとづけば，演劇部は　**42**　かもしれない。
① 新しい国際的な作家によって書かれた演劇を上演する
② 古典演劇を原作どおり上演する
③ 地域の人々のために車椅子を買う資金を集める
④ 性別に関する固定観念を公演から取り除く

本文の語注

☐ exchange student	交換留学生	☐ drama club	演劇クラブ
☐ online	形 オンラインの	☐ magazine	名 雑誌
☐ improve	動 ～を改善する		
【第1段落】			
☐ while	接 ～だが一方	☐ recognize	動 ～を認識する
☐ be made up of ～	～でできている，成り立つ	☐ a variety of ～	様々な～
☐ wide	形 広い，多岐に及ぶ	☐ diversity	名 多様性
☐ accept	動 ～を受け入れる	☐ reflect	動 ～を反映する
☐ performing arts organization		☐ for this reason	このような理由で
	舞台芸術団体		
☐ increasing	形 ますます増加する	☐ demand	名 需要
☐ play	名 劇	☐ represent	動 ～を表現する，描写する
☐ various	形 様々な	☐ background	名 背景
☐ as well as A	Aだけでなく	☐ those with ～	～がある人
☐ disability	名 障がい	☐ council	名 評議会
☐ in response to ～	～に応じて	☐ encourage A to do	～するよう A を奨励する
☐ publicly	副 公的に	☐ fund	動 ～に資金を提供する
☐ improvement	名 改善	☐ theater company	劇団
☐ positively	副 前向きに	☐ influential	形 影響力のある

【第 2 段落】

□ be based in ～	～を拠点とする	□ produce	動 ～を上演する，制作する
□ a number of ～	多くの～	□ author	名 作家
□ these days	最近	□ focus A on B	A を B に集中させる
□ attempt to *do*	～しようとする試み	□ society	名 社会
□ accurately	副 正確に	□ balance A and B	A と B の均衡をとる
□ ethic	名 民族	□ gender	名 性別
□ physical ability	身体能力	□ both A and B	A と B どちらも
□ hire	動 ～を雇う		

【第 3 段落】

□ during	前 ～の間に	□ put on ～	～を上演する
□ comedy	名 コメディー	□ tame	動 ～を飼いならす
□ shrew	名 口うるさい女	□ measure	名 尺度，基準
□ actor	名 俳優	□ employ	動 ～を雇う
□ form	動 ～を形成する	□ cast	名 キャスト
□ diverse	形 多様な	□ geographical	形 地理的な
□ cultural	形 文化的な	□ population	名 人々
□ achieve	動 ～を達成する	□ entire	形 全体の
□ half	名 半分	□ role	名 役
□ male	形 男性の	□ female	形 女性の
□ include	動 ～を含む	□ currently	副 現在は
□ refer to A as B	A を B と呼ぶ	□ differently-abled	形 身体に障がいのある
□ visually-impaired	形 視覚に障がいのある	□ hearing-impaired	形 聴覚に障がいのある
□ wheelchair	名 車椅子		

【第 4 段落】

□ beyond	前 ～を越えて	□ policy	名 方針
□ rewrite	動 ～を書き直す	□ audience	名 観客
□ reflect on ～	～をよく考える	□ relationship	名 関係
□ reverse	動 ～を入れ替える	□ original	名 原作
□ transform A into ～	A を～に変える	□ servant	名 使用人，給仕係
□ impact	名 衝撃	□ follow in one's footsteps ～の足跡をたどる	

【第 5 段落】

□ decision to *do*	～しようとする決定	□ model	名 モデル
□ make A B	A を B にする	□ inclusive	形 包括的な
□ be reluctant to *do*	～することに乗り気でない	□ classic	形 伝統的な
□ welcome A with open arms A を大歓迎する		□ although	接 ～だが
□ certain	形 ある程度の	□ earn	動 ～を得る
□ reputation	名 評判	□ progress	名 進歩

▌設問・選択肢の語注

□ according to ～	～によると	□ opportunity	名 機会
□ look for ～	～を探す	□ mention	動 ～に言及する
□ one of ～	～のうちの 1 つ	□ present	動 ～を上演する
□ struggle to *do*	～しようともがく	□ example	名 例
□ effort	名 努力	□ summarize	動 ～を要約する
□ complete	動 ～を完成させる	□ production	名 上演，作品
□ in order to *do*	～するために	□ consequently	副 結果として，その結果
□ attract	動 ～を引きつける	□ talented	形 才能のある
□ all over the world	世界中	□ without	前 ～なしで
□ objection	名 反対，異議	□ contribute to *doing*	～することに貢献する
□ match A with B	A を B と一致させる	□ expectation	名 期待
□ action	名 行動	□ conservative	形 保守的な
□ based on ～	～に基づいて	□ international	形 国際的な
□ raise	動 ～を集める	□ remove	動 ～を取り除く
□ stereotype	名 固定観念		

令和3年度 大学入学共通テスト
第6問 B 全訳&語注

> **和訳**
>
> あなたは市役所で開催される健康フェアの発表用ポスターを作っている生徒グループの1人です。あなたのグループのタイトルは「地域におけるよりよい口腔衛生の促進」です。ポスターを作るために,次の文章を使っています。

口腔衛生：鏡をのぞき込む

　近年,世界中の政府が口腔衛生の意識を高めるために働きかけている。一日に複数回歯を磨くことはよい習慣だと多くの人々が耳にする一方で,なぜこれが重要なのか,すべての理由を考えてみたことはおそらくないだろう。端的に言うと,歯は大切だ。歯は言葉を正確に発音するのに必要だ。実際,口腔衛生がよくないと本当に話すことが困難になり得る。さらに基本的で必要なのは,よく噛めるということだ。噛むことで食べ物を分解し,体が消化しやすくなる。正しく噛むことはまた,食べ物を楽しむことにもつながる。普通の人なら歯の治療のあと,片側で噛むことができない苛立ちを経験している。歯が弱い人は常にこの失望を経験しているのかもしれない。言い換えれば,口腔衛生は人々の生活の質に影響を与えるのだ。

　歯の基本的な機能は明確だが,多くの人々は口が体を映す鏡を与えてくれていることに気づいていない。調査によると,優れた口腔衛生は優れた全身の健康状態の明確な印である。口腔衛生がよくない人は深刻な身体の病気によりなりやすい。推奨される毎日の口腔衛生の日課を怠ることは,すでに病気に苦しんでいる人々に悪影響を与える可能性がある。反対に,よい口腔衛生を実践することは,病気を予防しさえするかもしれない。強くて健康な肉体は,清潔でよく手入れされた口の現れであることが多い。

　よい口腔衛生を維持することは,生涯にわたる任務だ。フィンランドとアメリカの政府は,乳児が1歳になる前に両親が歯医者へ連れて行くことを推奨している。フィンランドは実際,両親に通知を送っている。ニュージーランドは18歳までのすべての人に無料の歯科治療を提供している。日本政府は8020キャンペーンを促進している。人々は年をとるにつれ,様々な理由で歯を失う可能性がある。キャンペーンの目標は,80歳の誕生日に口の中に少なくとも20本の歯が

まだ残っていることだ。

　より詳しく日本を見ると，厚生労働省は高齢者の残っている歯の本数に関する調査データを何年もの間分析している。ある研究員は，最高齢の参加者を A（70-74 歳），B（75-79 歳），C（80-84 歳），そして D(85 歳以上)の 4 つの年齢グループに分けた。それぞれの調査で，1993 年の例外はあるものの，少なくとも 20 本の歯がある人の割合は高い方から低い方へ A-B-C-D の順番であった。しかし 1993 年と 1999 年の間に，グループ A はわずか約 6％しか向上せず，B の増加率がわずかに上回った。1993 年にはグループ A の 25.5％ が少なくとも 20 本の歯を持っていたが，2016 年の時点でグループ D の割合はグループ A の最初の数字を 0.2％ 上回っていた。グループ B は最初じわじわと増加したが，2005 年と 2011 年の間で劇的に上昇した。意識が向上したおかげで，すべてのグループが長い年月をかけて著しく改善した。

　歯医者は長い間，食後に歯を磨くことを推奨してきた。素晴らしい口腔衛生を積極的に求める人々は，一日に数回歯を磨くだろう。ほとんどの人は寝る前と，翌朝のどこかでもう一度歯を磨く。歯医者はまた，歯の間から物質を除去する特別な種類の糸を使って，毎日フロスをすることが大切だと考えている。別の予防法は，歯の表面付近を固めてダメージを防ぐプラスチックのジェル（シーラント）を使って，歯医者に歯を密封してもらうことだ。シーラントは特に子どもたちへの使用で人気を得ている。これはわずか 1 回の塗布で，一般的な歯の問題の 80％をも予防してくれる。

　年に一度，あるいはより頻繁に歯医者を訪れることが重要だ。歯科治療はときどき痛みを引き起こすので，歯医者に通うことをなんとか避けようとする人々がいる。しかし，生涯を通じて文字どおり笑顔にしてくれる大切な味方として歯医者を考え始めることが重要である。

あなたのプレゼンテーション用ポスター：

地域におけるよりよい口腔衛生の促進

1. 歯の重要性

A．きちんと話すのにきわめて重要
B．食べ物を噛み砕くのに必要
C．食べ物を楽しむのに役立つ
D．よい印象を与えるのに必要
E．質のよい生活に欠かすことができない

2. 44

フィンランドとアメリカ：1歳になる前の治療の推奨
ニュージーランド：若い世代への無料治療
日本：8020 キャンペーン（図1を見ること）

45

図1．少なくとも 20 本は歯がある人の割合

3. 役立つアドバイス

46
47

問1 ポスターの最初の見出しの下に，文章で説明されているように歯の重要性を表したいとあなたのグループは考えている。提案の1つがあまりふさわしくないということで全員の意見が一致している。次のうち含めるべきではないのはどれか？ 43
① A
② B
③ C
④ D
⑤ E

問2 あなたはポスターの2つめの見出しを書くよう頼まれた。次のうちどれが最もふさわしいか？ 44
① 若者を対象とした国の8020プログラム
② よりよい歯科治療のための国の宣伝
③ 口腔ケアを促すための国の取り組み
④ 乳幼児を歯医者へ招待する国のシステム

問3 あなたは日本の研究員の調査結果を示したいと思っている。次のグラフのうち，ポスターに最もふさわしいのはどれか？ 45

①
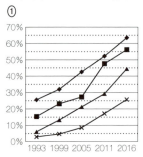

②
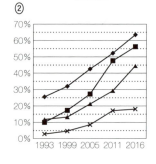

③
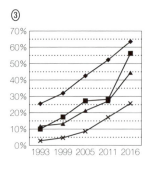

④
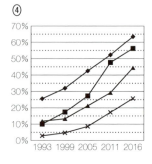

◆ A(70-74)   ■ B(75-79)   ▲ C(80-84)   ✕ D(85＋)

問4 ポスターの最後の見出しの下に，あなたは文章にもとづいて具体的なアドバイスを加えたいと思っている。次の記述のうち，どの２つを使うべきか？（順番は問わない。） 46 ・ 47

① 朝食を食べる前に歯を磨く。
② 毎日，鏡で歯を確認する。
③ 少なくとも１年に１回は歯医者を訪れる。
④ プラスチックのジェルを頻繁に歯に塗る。
⑤ 毎日，歯の間にデンタルフロスを使う。

本文の語注

□ one of ～	～のうちの１つ，１人	□ group of ～	～のグループ
□ poster	名 ポスター	□ wellness	名 健康
□ fair	名 フェア	□ promote	動 ～を促進する
□ oral	形 口の，口腔の	□ community	名 地域社会
□ following	形 次の	□ create	動 ～を創造する
□ look into ～	～をのぞき込む	□ mirror	名 鏡

【第１段落】

□ recent	形 最近の	□ raise	動 ～を高める，上げる
□ awareness	名 意識	□ brush	動 ～を磨く
□ teeth	名 歯	□ multiple	形 多数の
□ per	前 ～につき	□ consider	動 ～をよく考える
□ crucial	形 重大な，重要な	□ simply stated	端的に言うと
□ be required to *do*	～することを必要とする	□ pronounce	動 ～を発音する
□ accurately	副 正確に	□ poor	形 （健康状態が）悪い
□ actually	副 本当に	□ make A B	A を B にする
□ even	副 いっそう	□ basic	形 基本的な
□ necessity	名 必要性	□ be able to *do*	～することができる
□ chew	動 噛む	□ break down ～	～を分解する
□ digest	動 ～を消化する	□ proper	形 正しい
□ link A to B	A を B につなげる	□ enjoyment	名 楽しみ
□ average	形 平均の，普通の	□ frustration	名 落胆，苛立ち
□ one side	片側	□ dental	形 歯の，歯科の
□ procedure	名 処置	□ weak	形 弱い
□ disappointment	名 失望	□ all the time	いつも，常に
□ in other words	言い換えると	□ impact	動 ～に影響を与える
□ quality	名 質		

【第２段落】

□ function	名 機能	□ clear	形 明確な，はっきりした
□ realize	動 ～だと気づく	□ provide	動 ～を提供する
□ research	名 調査	□ sign	名 サイン，表れ
□ general	形 全体的な	□ develop	動 （病気に）なる
□ serious	形 深刻な	□ physical	形 身体の
□ ignore	動 ～を無視する	□ recommended	形 推奨される
□ daily	形 毎日の	□ routine	名 いつもの手順
□ negative	形 良くない，マイナスの	□ effect	名 影響
□ those	代 （～する）人たち	□ suffer from ～	～に苦しむ
□ conversely	副 反対に	□ prevent	動 ～を防ぐ
□ reflection	名 反映	□ well-maintained	形 よく管理された

253

【第3段落】

☐ maintain	動 ～を維持する	☐ lifelong	形 生涯続く
☐ mission	名 任務，使命	☐ Finnish	形 フィンランドの
☐ recommend	動 ～を推奨する	☐ infant	名 幼児，乳児
☐ dentist	名 歯科医	☐ turn	動 (ある年齢) に達する
☐ send A B	A に B を送る	☐ notice	名 知らせ
☐ offer	動 ～を提供する	☐ treatment	名 治療
☐ up to ～	～まで	☐ campaign	名 キャンペーン
☐ as	接 ～するにつれて	☐ age	動 年をとる
☐ lose	動 ～を失う	☐ various	形 様々な
☐ at least	少なくとも，最低		

【第4段落】

☐ take a look at ～	～を見る	☐ close	形 近い
☐ the Ministry of Health, Labour and Welfare 厚生労働省		☐ analyze	動 ～を分析する
☐ survey	名 調査	☐ data	名 データ
☐ number of ～	～の数	☐ remaining	形 残っている
☐ senior	名 高齢者	☐ researcher	名 研究者
☐ divide A into B	A を B に分ける	☐ participant	名 参加者
☐ exception	名 例外	☐ percentage	名 割合
☐ from A to B	A から B へ	☐ improve	動 向上する，上がる
☐ increase	名 増加	☐ slightly	副 わずかに
☐ initial	形 最初の	☐ figure	名 数字
☐ steadily	副 着々と，だんだんと	☐ go up	上がる，上昇する
☐ dramatically	副 劇的に	☐ thanks to ～	～のおかげで
☐ over	前 ～にわたって		

【第5段落】

☐ meal	名 食事	☐ actively	副 積極的に
☐ seek	動 ～を探し求める	☐ excellent	形 素晴らしい
☐ several times	数回	☐ most	名 多くの人々，大多数
☐ at some time	ある時間に	☐ floss	動 デンタルフロスで掃除する
☐ type	名 種類，タイプ	☐ string	名 糸
☐ substance	名 物質	☐ prevention	名 予防
☐ method	名 方法	☐ seal	動 ～を密閉する，ふさぐ
☐ gel	名 ジェル，ゲル	☐ sealant	名 シーラント
☐ harden	動 固くなる，固まる	☐ surface	名 表面
☐ damage	名 損害，ダメージ	☐ gain	動 ～を得る
☐ especially	副 特に	☐ use	名 使用
☐ coating	名 コーティング	☐ amazing	形 びっくりするような，驚くほどよい
☐ common	形 一般的な		

【第6段落】

☐ annually	副 年に1度	☐ frequently	副 頻繁に
☐ cause	動 ～を引き起こす	☐ pain	名 痛み
☐ avoid	動 ～を避ける	☐ view A as B	A を B とみなす
☐ ally	名 助け，支え	☐ literally	副 文字通り
☐ throughout	前 ～を通じて，～の間じゅう		

【プレゼンテーションのポスター】

☐ importance	名 重要性	☐ properly	副 きちんと
☐ necessary	形 必要な	☐ helpful	形 役に立つ
☐ impression	名 印象	☐ essential	形 不可欠の
☐ recommendation	名 推奨，提案	☐ youth	名 若い人たち，青年

設問・選択肢の語注

☐ heading	名 見出し	☐ express	動 ～を表現する
☐ explain	動 ～を説明する	☐ suggestion	名 提案，提言
☐ fit	動 合う	☐ include	動 ～を含む
☐ appropriate	形 適切な，ふさわしい	☐ national	形 国家の
☐ target	動 ～を対象にする	☐ advertisement	名 宣伝
☐ encourage	動 ～を促進する	☐ add	動 ～を加える
☐ specific	名 具体的な	☐ based on ～	～に基づいて
☐ statement	名 声明，記述	☐ order	名 順番
☐ check	動 ～調べる，確認する	☐ put A on B	A を B に乗せる

255

武藤一也

東進ハイスクール・東進衛星予備校講師。英語の音読量を記録するアプリ「音読メーター」開発。入試問題・英文を作成する「英語問題作成所」代表。英語専門塾セプトアドバイザー。Cambridge CELTA Pass A（合格者の上位5％）。英検1級。TOEIC 990 点満点。TOEIC S／W 各 200 点満点。著書に『イチから鍛える英語長文』シリーズ、『イチから鍛える英語リスニング』シリーズ、『イチから鍛える英文法』シリーズ、『高校英文読解をひとつひとつわかりやすく』、『キリトリ式でペラっとスタディ！ 中学英語の総復習ドリル』（学研）など多数。本書では監修ならびに動画の総合演出を担当。

高山のぞみ

河合塾講師。「英語問題作成所」ディレクター。高校での指導経験のほか、米国でインターンとしての指導経験を持つ。河合塾では文法からリスニングまでの幅広いジャンル、基礎から難関までの幅広いレベルの講座や映像授業を担当し、同時に教材の執筆も手掛けている。TOEIC990 点満点。著書に『キリトリ式でペラっとスタディ！ 中学英語の総復習ドリル』（学研）。本書では解説ならびに動画出演を担当。

［過去問］×［解説］×［実況動画］
やさしくひもとく 共通テスト
英語 リーディング

ブックデザイン	株式会社 dig
動画デザイン	株式会社 dig
イラスト	間芝勇輔
編集協力	株式会社 メディアビーコン，渡辺泰葉
DTP	株式会社 四国写研
動画編集	株式会社 四国写研
印刷所	株式会社 リーブルテック

読者アンケートご協力のお願い　※アンケートは予告なく終了する場合がございます。

この度は弊社商品をお買い上げいただき、誠にありがとうございます。本書に関するアンケートにご協力ください。右の QR コードから、アンケートフォームにアクセスすることができます。ご協力いただいた方のなかから抽選でギフト券（500 円分）をプレゼントさせていただきます。

アンケート番号：　305309